D1587950

GLASGOW CALEDONIAN UNIVERSITY

GLASGOW CALEDONIAN UNIVERSITY

Its Origins and Evolution

Carole McCallum and Willie Thompson

TUCKWELL PRESS

First Published in 1998 by

Tuckwell Press Ltd
The Mill House
Phantassie
East Linton EH40 3DG
Scotland

Text copyright © Glasgow Caledonian University

All rights reserved

ISBN 1 86232 026 8 (hardback)

British Library Cataloguing-in-Publication Data:
A catalogue record for this book is available
on request from the British Library

Typeset by Trinity Typesetting, Edinburgh
Printed and bound by The Bath Press, Glasgow

Dedication

This volume is dedicated to the memory of

Jean Haining,
Student at Glasgow and West of Scotland College of Domestic Science,
died in Auschwitz, 1944

and

Lewis Brodie,
Academic Registrar of Glasgow College of Technology from 1973 until
his death in 1985

Acknowledgements

We would like to express our gratitude to the individuals and bodies who have enabled this project to be brought to completion. They include in the first place the management of Glasgow Caledonian University, who took the decision that it should go ahead and provided resources to enable both authors to pursue the research and writing required to undertake it. The University Court has since made available the additional resources needed to ensure its appearance in book form. We have to express our gratitude to the past and present members of staff of both predecessor institutions, who courteously responded to our invitation to be interviewed for their recollections and patiently answered the queries put to them, as well as supplying photographs, and also to library and administrative staff who assisted us with the documentary records. We would like particularly to thank the publisher of this volume, Dr John Tuckwell, for his unfailing helpfulness and understanding.

All assessments and opinions expressed in this history are those of the authors and do not necessarily reflect the views of the University.

Willie Thompson
Carole McCallum

Contents

Preface

With the exception of the Papacy and the Japanese monarchy, universities are the oldest institutions in the world possessing a continuous history. In less than a thousand years they have multiplied prodigiously, expanded from their original centres to cover the entire globe and become intrinsic to the functioning of modern societies.

The word 'university' when it was coined in twelfth century Europe had roughly the same significance as 'union' does in the present, but the inflection that it has come to have nowadays derives more from the purpose embodied in the other medieval term used for these institutions, *studium generale*, namely the production and dissemination of advanced knowledge across all major disciplines. In medieval Europe their concern was with the advanced communicative systems — hence logic and rhetoric — and the ideological fabric of the existing society — hence theology; as well as in some instances with practicalities in the shape of medicine and law.

In the era which followed their medieval glories the universities declined greatly in overall importance, and some, such as the two English foundations, though wealthy and privileged, were intellectually moribund by the eve of the industrial revolution. Only in Scotland and Germany did universities make any significant contribution to the eighteenth century Enlightenment or the technological advances which followed it. The universities' function nevertheless was an indispensable one, and the nineteenth century's response to the failure of existing establishments was not to abolish them but to enforce reform and reorganisation, as well as to create new ones to undertake the kinds of study and produce the educated personnel in which their older counterparts were deficient.

Universities are designated as the summit of the educational pyramid. Their full-time academic personnel are the prime creators and purveyors of new knowledge; the initial degree which they award to students who have successfully completed their studies and become competent in the foundational stage of advanced learning constitutes the basic, universally recognised academic or scientific qualification. In Britain the attempt of the

'60s, for what at the time appeared to be good reasons, to create an officially designated two-tier system of higher education institutions and degrees was abandoned a quarter of a century later, with the result that the country now possesses around 100 universities (and more if the London University colleges are counted separately).

Indeed, since the early ninteenth century the British university system has grown relentlessly, although if one calculates the university-per-population ratio the expansion is not quite so dramatic. Very roughly the proportion is one university per 500,000 people, and in the Scottish case that is about the same as it was 300 years ago — though in other than crude terms the comparison is meaningless, since the potential reservoir of university entrants was then much smaller, as was the size of the universities.

Throughout the entire modern period the universities' growth, though propelled by the demand for post-school education, has never been able to keep pace with it — quite apart from the fact that universities have regarded certain forms and disciplines of post-school education as beneath their dignity. In consequence, alternative institutions catering to that market (not least to supply teachers to a developing state school system) came into being, grew and flourished. While many have been absorbed into the university structure, others continue in Britain to supply a major sector of tertiary education, distinguished by the appellation 'further education' in contrast to 'higher'. In addition these institutions have a narrower focus of disciplines, their main qualifications not being degrees. They are expected to concentrate on their teaching function and not primarily on the generation of new knowledge, termed 'research'. In the words of Eric Robinson, the prophet of the polytechnic system:

> After the war the most spectacular development in English education — the phenomenal expansion of the technical colleges — was the result not of political decision but of steady pressure from progressive employers and their employees; the employers wanted better workers and the workers wanted better jobs.[1]

---

[1] Eric Robinson, *The New Polytechnics*, Penguin, 1968.

Although a number of completely new universities, such as Sussex or
Stirling, were created in the British expansion of the '60s following the
Robbins Report, the majority which then came into existence were
institutions of further education which had outgrown their original remit
— in England, these were called colleges of advanced technology; in
Scotland, there were equivalent establishments such as Strathclyde or
Heriot Watt University. In the great extension of the '90s when the binary
line was abolished (at least in principle) all the new entrants were, with at
most three partial exceptions, former centres of further education which
had taken on a higher education role under the polytechnic regime.

One of these partial exceptions is the institution with which this
volume is concerned. One half of its ancestry, Queen's College, exactly
fits the pattern that has been sketched above, but the other is anomalous.
Glasgow College of Technology ('GCT') was established deliberately as
an equivalent to the English polytechnics, but while all the polytechnics
were based upon pre-existing tertiary establishments, GCT was founded
ab initio[2] by decision of the then Glasgow municipality, to stand as the
city's own polytechnic[3] beside its two universities. The motivation for this
course of action will be examined in the context both of the position of
Glasgow as a city still dominated in the '60s by its traditional industries
and the revolution occurring in British tertiary education during the same
decade.

The origins of Queen's College, nearly a century older, were a good deal
more modest. They lay in the philanthropic endeavour so central to the self-
image of the middle classes of high Victorian Britain, Scotland as much as
England. Queen's College began institutional life as two schools of cookery
intended to tackle one aspect of the social problems which were the
underside of the city's then prosperity. They aimed to assist working-class
women (and, to be fair, middle-class ones as well) to improve their families'
nutritional standards. They commenced upon a shoestring and their long-
term survival was problematic, but they did have the blessing and financial

---

[2]It drew staff and courses from pre-existing institutions, but these colleges were not
integrated into the new one.

[3]It did not for many years use the term 'polytechnic', for reasons which are indicated
below. Had adjacent Paisley been part of Glasgow rather than a separate municipality, GCT
would almost certainly never have been proposed, as an equivalent college (now Paisley
University) existed in Paisley, which would have satisfied civic aspirations.

support — albeit modest — of the city's bourgeoisie, particularly the then powerful temperance lobby which viewed well-prepared food and beverages as one way of diminishing the prevalent attraction to hard liquor.

The schools survived, developed, amalgamated, received the royal accolade and as Queen's College expanded into educational areas far beyond the original purpose, though retaining nutrition as a central element. Under the Council for National Academic Awards, the linchpin of the polytechnic system, the College commenced to grant degrees and in the reorganisations of the '90s, which also saw Jordanhill College of Education absorbed into Strathclyde University, it emerged as a potential (though by no means inevitable) partner for GCT, now at last calling itself Glasgow Polytechnic, in the move towards university status.

The amalgamation and redesignation was accomplished in 1993. This history is intended to interpret the development of the two institutions within the context of the city's evolution and the changing character of tertiary education over more than a century. It therefore aims to avoid the character of an institutional chronicle but instead to present the history of the University's predecessors as part of the social history of Glasgow and the west of Scotland as well as a reflection of the course of tertiary educational development in Scotland and Britain as a whole. Within this framework, the treatment is largely though not wholly chronological. The opening chapter deals with the emergence and development of the cookery schools through to their amalgamation as the Glasgow and West of Scotland School of Domestic Science and the outbreak of the First World War. The subsequent two chapters follow the development of the institution up to its emergence as Queen's College in 1975. Attention is then shifted to the origins in the '60s of Glasgow College of Technology, before returning in Chapter 5 to the remainder of Queen's College's independent career up to the eve of the amalgamation. Three subsequent chapters interpret the somewhat troubled history of the College of Technology (from 1991, Glasgow Polytechnic) during its years as a separate institution; a final chapter deals with the amalgamation and comments briefly upon events between 1993 and 1997. The text attempts to do justice both to the circumstances which formed Caledonian University and the individuals whose decisions and choices determined the eventual outcome.

Chapter One

The Glasgow and West of Scotland College of Domestic Science, 1875–1915

The fact of Glasgow Caledonian University's creation in 1993 makes it naturally tempting to treat the two institutions which went into its formation as though they were in some sense destined to arrive at that outcome. Any such perspective is of course wholly misleading: what began respectively as a school of domestic science and Glasgow College of Technology were established, almost a century apart, with their own specific purposes and remits and in response to pressures and challenges all of which were very different from those of the early '90s which resulted in their amalgamation and elevation to university status.

The origins of the two components were entirely different in conception and separated in time by an era of extreme historical trauma on a world scale and of volcanic social and cultural changes at a national and local level. There are nevertheless parallels of a sort in their foundation. The first came into being at the time of Glasgow's heyday as an industrial and imperial centre and was viewed by its founders as one form of partial answer to the social disasters and problems which were the obverse of Glasgow's civic prosperity. The second emerged out of the dilemmas associated with the city's industrial decline and consequent search by the then city fathers for alternative forms of municipal progress and restoration of a satisfactory civic identity at a time when higher education was viewed as the key to solving national economic problems.

The Glasgow of the late nineteenth century was a remarkable entity. Its leaders and publicists liked to refer to it as the 'Second City of the Empire', and there was some substance in the boast.[1] A relative backwater during the medieval and early modern period, undistinguished except for its episcopal seat and university, its rise to importance began with the Atlantic trade of the eighteenth century (though the river had to be artificially modified to make it consistently navigable). The tobacco trade brought the first great injection of wealth and the university was a major contributor to the Scottish Enlightenment, Adam Smith being only the most renowned of its luminaries. At the end of that century and the beginning of the nineteenth the city was substantially involved in the initial phase of industrial revolution as a centre of textile manufacture, the single most significant individual involved in that process, James Watt, having received his initial training within the university.

A particularly favourable combination of natural endowments was the foundation for Glasgow's spectacular industrial rise in the second part of the nineteenth century. To its situation as an Atlantic port was added the ready local availability of coal and iron ore in apparently limitless quantities alongside prodigious inputs of cheap labour from Ireland and the Scottish highlands. The era of the iron-, then steel-, hulled steam-driven ship had arrived, as had that of the global railway network. The region's entrepreneurs established their firms to exploit the possibilities. Glasgow and the surrounding area became the concentrated expression, the biggest in the kingdom, of an interlocked economy of metal manufacture, heavy engineering, shipbuilding and locomotive manufacture with their numberless ancillary trades and industries.[2] Firms of major importance to the expanding imperial economy were centred in Glasgow or had their beginnings there.

As this was occurring the city remained a centre of intellectual accomplishment, if in different spheres from those of the previous century. The university grew and flourished, transferring in the 1870s from its cramped and decaying quarters in the city centre to the salubrious environs of Gilmorehill in the west. It boasted among its professoriat the most renowned physicist of the time, William Thomson, later Lord Kelvin. Antiseptics first emerged from its medical faculty. Beside it there

---

[1]For the most comprehensive examination of Glasgow at this period see W Hamish Fraser and Irene Maver (eds), *Glasgow Volume II: 1830 to 1912*, Manchester University Press, Manchester, 1996.

[2]For a succinct and expressive account see S G Checkland, *The Upas Tree: Glasgow 1875–1975*, University of Glasgow Press, Glasgow, 1976.

existed from 1887 the Glasgow and West of Scotland Technical College, whose core institution, going back to 1796,[3] had only reluctantly surrendered its claim to a university title and was itself a major provider of higher education and research centre. In the fine arts too Glasgow was producing painters, designers and architects who would attain world renown.

The business leaders, as was characteristic of the times, controlled local government as well as their enterprises. Glasgow Corporation was an enormously self-confident collective, only too conscious of the economic and intellectual accomplishments of the city which it governed, dominated by individuals filled with the sense of their personal and municipal importance. A London legal journal in the 1880s was to complain that they regarded the imperial parliament as no more than a mechanism for ratifying and registering their own decrees. With energy and dynamism they addressed the issues of public health, public parks, building control, urban blight, sanitation, lighting, elementary education, poor relief, alcoholism — being both inherited from the earlier phase of industrial growth and generated on an expanding scale by the current one. The only competitor in this kind of endeavour among late Victorian British cities was Joseph Chamberlain's Birmingham. Considered overall, Glasgow is probably unique among provincial cities anywhere in the world in its combination of industrial and cultural significance.

The story of course was not one of unshadowed triumph. If the achievements taking place in and around its boundaries were monumental, so correspondingly were the deprivation and squalor which accompanied them. It was for a start, except in showpiece localities, a gloomy and cavernous city, its universal high sandstone buildings soon rendered soot-black by the smoke pall which perpetually hung above them. Nor was that the worst, atmospherically speaking. A legacy from the textile era of industrialisation, the St Rollox chemical works, spewed over the city around the clock its cocktail of filth and noxious pollutants from its landmark chimney stalk.

Socially Glasgow was also the victim of its geography. Crammed between the sides of a narrow valley, its growth created unprecedented and unequalled

[3]See John Butt, *John Anderson's Legacy: The University of Strathclyde and its Antecedents 1797–1996*, Tuckwell Press, 1996.

population densities. A population roughly equivalent to that of Birmingham was squeezed into an area no bigger than Sheffield. To accommodate such numbers the city built upwards, the universal form of housing—for all except the topmost elite, who usually moved to more spacious satellite towns — consisting of the three- or four- storey tenement dwelling with communal street entrance (and, at the lower end of the market, communal stairhead lavatory). The flats within these buildings in middle-class areas of occupation could be extremely spacious and elegant; in the working-class districts they consisted more often than not of single-room or one room and kitchen dwellings, very frequently in a desperate state of overcrowding and dereliction.

What a later era would refer to as multiple deprivation did not spring only from overcrowding and poorly constructed housing. It sprang primarily from an employment and wages structure (the labour aristocracy of skilled and highly paid workmen comprised about 15 per cent of employees) which ensured that between a quarter and a third of the male workforce,[4] most significantly its unskilled component whose lot was not merely minimal wages but irregular and constantly interrupted employment, earned less than what was regarded as the minimum viable family income, £1 per week. The social consequences were predictable enough: total destitution, especially in old age, crime, domestic violence[5] and a notorious disposition among Glasgow men to seek refuge in alcohol. The consequences for children living in such environments were no less predictable: 'A 1904 investigation of those areas of the city which had the highest infant mortality found that 22 per cent of the infants showed strong evidence of malnutrition and only 9 per cent could be described as "well nourished".'[6]

Charitable enterprise abounded, not counting the final public backstop against destitution, namely poor relief inside or outside the Poorhouse. The charities in general aimed at improvement as well as relief, although it is clear that their impact was far from transforming the plight of Glasgow's poor or abolishing destitution. Nevertheless they formed part of the same pattern of municipal, local and voluntary endeavour that was

[4]And more in the case of women wage-workers. An 1891 report refers to 'old and debilitated workmen, widows with little children and women and girls without male support'. Fraser and Maver, *op. cit.*, p.165.
[5]A newspaper report of the time on a domestic killing has a particularly chilling casual aside that Glasgow men were reputed to use their fists when assaulting their womenfolk, but Lancashire ones their clogs.
[6]Fraser and Maver, *op. cit.*, p.360.

seen in the fields of education, medicine (including treatment of the insane), building standards and public health — not to mention professional football, then regarded as supplying an improving recreation — during the last third of the nineteenth century. What was to become Queen's College had its origins in this same social environment. It is probably not coincidental either that the 1870s were a decade when the variety and cheapness of foodstuffs available in Britain increased considerably thanks to imports by fast, steam-powered shipping and, a decade later, commercial refrigeration.

Grace Paterson

The driving force behind the Glasgow School of Cookery, which opened its doors in 1876, was Grace Paterson. Born in 1843 to upper middle-class parents she appears, from what is known about her, to have been a striking and forceful personality in the mould of Elizabeth Garrett or Emily Davies. Women's educational opportunities were the forefront of her concerns, though they were not confined to that. Apart from her role in the creation of the Glasgow School of Cookery, she was one of the first two women elected to the Glasgow School Board, and tirelessly active in that capacity. She was also a member of an Association for the Higher Education of Women and involved in the establishment of Queen Margaret College in Edinburgh.

Her other and connected principal interest was in women's suffrage, but never being a part of what became the suffragette movement, she is described as a suffragist. It was through the agitation of the first female suffrage movement, the Association for the Return of Women to Public Boards, that her election to the Glasgow School Board in 1885 became possible. She died in 1925 and one

GRACE PATERSON, Principal, Glasgow School of Cookery, 1875–1908.

of her obituaries is headed 'A Noted Feminist'.[7] Obituaries also claim that
the School was founded 'on her initiative and under her direct supervision'[8]
though it is not clear exactly what form her initiative took. It must have
involved at any rate very considerable lobbying among the Glasgow elite,
without whose endorsement and financial backing the scheme could not
hope to be viable.

The concept of systematic education in domestic hygiene and nutrition
was not born in Glasgow but at the London International Exhibition of
1873, though that appears to have been responding to a current of public
sentiment most likely related to the urban public health advances of the
1860s. The result of the Exhibition's work was the establishment of South
Kensington National Training School of Cookery, whose first class was
enrolled in 1874. The class and philanthropic agendas behind the initiative
were stated clearly enough by *The Times*:

> ... not so much to teach good cooks how to cook better, as to show the
> great mass of the working people how to make the most of the food
> material which is nowhere so good, so abundant and so vilely cooked as
> in England.[9]

Encouraged by the work of J C Buckmaster, who had helped to organise the
demonstrations at the London Exhibition, a similar proposal was mooted
in Edinburgh in April 1875. The secretary of the organising committee was
Christian Guthrie Wright, also an establishment-orientated pioneer of
women's political and educational rights and friend of Grace Paterson.
Aristocratic ladies were recruited as patronesses. The Lord Provost chaired
the inaugural meeting and the Edinburgh School of Cookery (eventually to
develop into Queen Margaret College) was opened at the end of the year.
As with London the social agenda is far from hidden and the assumptions
were brutal. Classes were offered in Superior Cookery, Plain Cookery and
Artisan Cookery. According to the *Edinburgh Courant* of April 22:

> Cookery is among the middle classes practically a lost art.... As for
> women in still more humble circumstances, the question is one of

---

[7] *Glasgow Evening News*, December 1, 1925.
[8] *Glasgow Herald*, November 30, 1925.
[9] *The Times*, July 7, 1875.

really vital importance.... The gain physically, morally and pecuniary from an improvement in dinners of hardworking people is simply incalculable .... The greatest care, then, should be taken to avoid any appearance of exclusiveness in the course of instruction offered.

And from the *Scotsman* of October 19:

The real difficulty lies in reaching the working people. Classes that wives and mothers are expected to attend have, as a general rule, proved to be failures.

An advert in *The Bailie* of March 22, 1876 quoted prices for instruction:

Superior Cookery — Potage Ecossais — Tickets 25s per dozen
Plain Cookery — Scotch Soup — Tickets 21s per dozen
Cookery for the Working Classes — Broth — Tickets 3s per dozen

Grace Paterson had participated in the Edinburgh developments and it is to be presumed that there was co-ordinated activity on the part of the two women and their associates such as Janet Galloway and Louisa Stevenson to institute formal cookery education in their respective cities. In bringing about a similar development in Glasgow Grace Paterson worked closely with a Church of Scotland minister with a social conscience, F L Robertson, who, appalled by nutritional standards in his Glasgow parish, was willing to lobby influential people for projects to improve culinary standards among the working classes. Following an initial meeting convened by the Lord Provost, Robertson was appointed convenor to a committee for establishing a Glasgow School of Cookery. According to the minute of the public meeting:

At a Conference held within the Religious Institution Rooms, 172 Buchanan Street Glasgow on the 13th November 1875 — convened by the following Notice

It having been intimated to the Lord Provost that, before Mr Buckmaster BA FCS of the National Training School for Cookery, South Kensington, London, who is at present in Scotland, leaves for the South, a Conference should be held in Glasgow with a view to the organization of some scheme for instruction in cookery in the City:

and as the Lord Provost believes the subject to be of immense importance, he has convened a meeting of Ladies and Gentlemen favourable to the object, for the purpose of hearing an Address from Mr Buckmaster. The Conference will be held in the Religious Institution Rooms, 172 Buchanan Street on Saturday next, the 13th instant, at Two o'clock afternoon when the attendance of those feeling interested is requested.

Glasgow 9th November 1875.

In the presence of a large and influential Assemblage of Ladies and Gentlemen, William Taylor Esquire Ex-Preceptor of Hutcheson's Hospital, on the motion of the Revd. Mr F Lockhart Robertson, and in the absence of the Lord Provost of Glasgow (Mr Bain) by indisposition, was appointed Chairman —

The Chairman after briefly referring to the importance of the object of the Meeting and the benefits that would result to the Community by Cookery forming part of the education of the rising generation introduced Mr Buckmaster to the Meeting.

Mr Buckmaster delivered an address.

There were afterwards read letters from several parties regretting their inability to be present — a Communication from Miss Guthrie Wright the Honorary Secretary of the School of Cookery just established in Edinburgh was also read and of which the following is a copy

6 Lynedoch Place
Edinburgh 12 Novr. 1875

The Right Honble.
The Lord Provost of Glasgow
My Lord
The Executive Committee of the Edinburgh School of Cookery hear with much pleasure that you are taking the initiative [sic] steps towards establishing a School of Cookery in Glasgow and beg to express their sympathy in the undertaking. They have newly opened the Edinburgh school and have already met with much encouragement from all classes. They trust that the two schools will be on friendly terms, and that the example shown by the two chief towns, will speedily be followed by other towns in Scotland.

Being myself a native of Glasgow I take a warm interest in all
that concerns it.
I have the honour to be
My Lord
Your Lordship's obdt. Servt.
(Signed) C E Guthrie Knight
Hon. Sec.

On the motion of William McEwan Esquire Ex Lord Dean of Guild
seconded by the Reverend Walter C Smith a Committee of Gentlemen were
appointed to initiate the movement for the establishment of a Glasgow
School of Cookery with the Reverend F Lockhart Robertson as Convenor
and power to add to their number.

A cordial vote of thanks was passed to Mr Buckmaster for his
instructive address and to Ex Preceptor Taylor as Chairman.

The first prospectus appeared the following year. Financial responsibility
was in the hands of 23 Directors, headed honorifically by the Lord Provost
and containing a couple of MPs and professors as well as the Catholic
Archbishop of Glasgow and the secretary of the Abstainers Union. A sub-
committee exercised the real responsibility for premises, equipment and
finance of the embryo school. Actual running of the establishment was in
the hands of a Ladies' Executive Committee. Later on Grace Paterson
appears as the Honorary Secretary of this body. She was in effect the
School's Principal, though never formally having that title.

Margaret Black and the West End School of Cookery

Grace Paterson's role was organisational. She did not herself intend to
undertake teaching duties or their direct supervision, and so a suitable
individual was sought to fulfil these responsibilities. The sub-committee
mentioned above was in charge of this search; the dominant personality on
it was Baillie William Collins of the publishing company. Collins was a
zealot, a part of the Glasgow business and social elite, yet less than fully
integrated into its culture, for he was an activist of the Free Church (the elite
tended to be Church of Scotland or United Presbyterian), and initiator of
social reform projects — he had declared upon becoming Lord Provost that
property had its duties as well as its rights — and an uncompromising

WILLIAM COLLINS who was one of the first Directors of the Glasgow School of Cookery in 1875. He became Lord Provost of Glasgow in 1877. *By Courtesy of the Mitchell Library, Glasgow City Libraries and Archives.*

Glasgow School of Cookery students at the 1888 Great Exhibition. Glasgow School of Cookery ran a tea-room at the exhibition.

temperance advocate, or more correctly, prohibitionist. The temperance movement, with prohibition as its ultimate objective, was very strong in Glasgow at the time and had successfully conducted a long campaign for increasingly close restriction of the city's drink trade:

> Although the temperance movement was broad-based in its early years, it increasingly became the preserve of middle-class evangelicals, who, with characteristic determinist logic, believed that all of Glasgow's social ills could be overcome by total abstention. Even cholera could be eradicated.[10]

The drive was not unresisted, however. When Collins became a baillie there was speculation as to how his temperance principles would go down

---

[10]Fraser and Maver, *op. cit.*, p.418.

with his convivial colleagues, and he was the first teetotal Lord Provost when elevated in 1877. The woman chosen to attend the National School of Cookery in South Kensington for the purpose of earning its diploma was Margaret Black, whose family had strong friendship links with Collins, which was no doubt why she was selected. She had been married only briefly to John Black, a shawl manufacturer, when he was drowned in the River

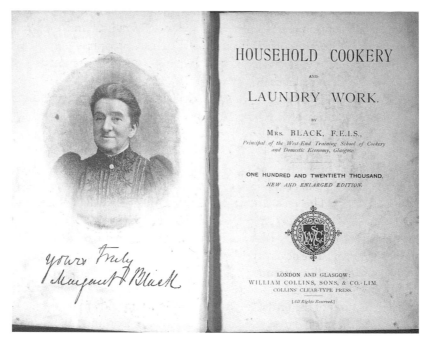

HOUSEHOLD COOKERY
AND
LAUNDRY WORK.

BY

MRS. BLACK, F.E.I.S.,
Principal of the West-End Training School of Cookery
and Domestic Economy, Glasgow.

ONE HUNDRED AND TWENTIETH THOUSAND.
NEW AND ENLARGED EDITION.

LONDON AND GLASGOW:
WILLIAM COLLINS, SONS, & CO. LIM.
COLLINS' CLEAR-TYPE PRESS.

[All Rights Reserved.]

MRS MARGARET BLACK, *FEIS*. Principal of The West End School of Cookery, 1875–1903. Previously she had worked at The Glasgow School of Cookery as a lecturer (1875–1878). This photograph has been taken from one of her many books, *Household Cookery and Laundry Work* (held in Glasgow Caledonian University Archive), which also shows her signature.

Kelvin in 1874 and thereafter, from the age of 44, his widow directed her energies towards social improvement in a number of spheres. She was later, in 1891, elected to the Glasgow School Board as a temperance and free educationist candidate, was secretary of the Women's Liberal Association, an office-bearer in the National Temperance Association and a parish councillor. In 1885 she was elected a Fellow of the Educational Institute of

Scotland. Evidently she possessed energy and determination of a similar sort to Grace Paterson's.

Possibly the personality differences of two able and self-confident individuals may have had something to do with the fact that after less than three years with the Glasgow School Margaret Black departed to set up her own rival establishment under the name of the West End School of Cookery. However, it is possible to guess at other considerations behind the rupture. As noted, Margaret Black was very much a part of the Free Church evangelical tradition, religiously and even socially radical and Liberal in politics, but culturally conservative. Grace Paterson by contrast was an early feminist and suffragist. So far as her religious affiliations are concerned, there is a suggestive silence in surviving references, including her obituaries in 1925, and a slightly later *Evening News* report of December 1 of that year makes no mention of her funeral. She was certainly not ostentatiously provocative in her public work, but the possibility that she was privately a secularist of some kind cannot be excluded, and this would certainly have generated friction with someone of Margaret Black's outlook.

The surviving School minutes referring to the schism are tantalisingly uninformative. The record of a meeting on June 27, 1878 of the sub-committee of Directors notes that 'Miss Paterson was requested to communicate with Mrs Black as to the apportionment of work in the coming session'. The next meeting of this group, on September 16 (at which Lord Provost Collins attended), however, records that:

> The Minutes of the last Meeting having been read and approved of, Mr Robertson reported to the Meeting that Miss Paterson and he had had an interview with the Lord Provost and Mrs Black, anent the resignation of the latter, when they had been informed that owing to private engagements which Mrs Black had already entered into, she would be unable to resume her former position as a Teacher in the School. At a subsequent interview however Miss Paterson had been informed that Mrs Black was disengaged on two forenoons every week and that she was open for engagement on those two days if the Directors thought fit. This was reported to the Meeting, when after a somewhat lengthy discussion, it was resolved to accept the resignation of Mrs Black.

The President of the Ladies' Committee, a Mrs Donald, tendered her resignation at the same meeting, which agreed to ask her to reconsider. The meeting was adjourned shortly afterwards and reconvened the following day, when it was agreed to accept Mrs Black's offer of part-time assistance — the minute noting that the committee was 'expecting and feeling sure that Mrs Black will conscientiously do her best at those classes and that they would endeavour to make it pleasant for her'. Immediately after this business a resolution was passed to the effect that the Directors should meet more regularly and that to 'save time at the meetings a slip of paper should be given to each member naming the subjects which are to occupy their attention'. The proposal appears to have been to introduce the practice of written agendas.

This is the last entry in this minute book, although it was only one-third filled at that point, and subsequent minutes are missing, resuming only in 1907, so the further dealings between the School and Margaret Black are unclear. What is clear however is that she had support from Lord Provost Collins (despite his position among the Directors of the Glasgow School) when she opened her own establishment later in the year. Collins further demonstrated his backing by publishing the numerous textbooks on cookery and household management written by her. There may also have been an element of intra-class rivalry. The Directors of the West End School appear to have been drawn from a less elevated sector of the business and professional class than Grace Paterson had been able to recruit. They included a drysalter's agent, a grain and flour merchant, a grocer's supplier, and a minor textile manufacturer.[11] The necessary preparations had been completed just prior to the famous collapse of the City of Glasgow Bank in that year, otherwise it is probable that the project would never have obtained sufficient funding.

Neither school, it is scarcely necessary to add, could have afforded purpose-built accommodation. Instead they leased existing premises, in the case of the West End School at first on an *ad hoc* basis. The Glasgow School was better provided, with its first permanent home in a building called the Albert Hall in Bath Street, which was furnished and equipped especially for the purpose, with a public opening in February 1876. In the course of time further premises were added or exchanged in the case of both establishments and both consequently remained physically scattered.

---

[11]Ellice Miller, *Century of Change 1875–1975; one hundred years of training home economics students in Glasgow*, Queen's College centenary pamphlet, 1975, p.13.

The two schools in context — other 'tertiary' developments

Nutritional education in Glasgow may have had a modest beginning but, as is evidenced by the backing which its pioneers secured from the elite of the day, it was no solitary idiosyncratic ambition. It represented one aspect of a process of extending formal education to penetrate the fabric of a society in which the initial phases of industrialisation had been completed and the impact of new technological developments based upon electricity, chemical science and the internal combustion engine were starting to be felt.

The 1870s were in the first place the decade of the Education Acts and the foundation of the School Boards. A corresponding expansion in teacher education followed and in the last third of the century grew beyond the capacity of the two existing Glasgow training establishments (one belonging to the Church of Scotland, the other the Free Church), Dundas Vale and Stow.[12] Initially the University was called in to take some of the pressure off but in the first decade of the twentieth century the Provincial Committee[13] of the Scotch [sic] Education Department (SED) combined them into Jordanhill College, eventually established on a greenfield site with freshly-built expanded accommodation.

Overshadowing every other form of non-university post-school education in the city however was the venerable and powerful Glasgow and West of Scotland Technical College (from 1877–87 Anderson's College), dating from the last decade of the eighteenth century and which had until 1877 insisted on calling itself Anderson's University, after its founder John Anderson, one of James Watt's teachers. It had abandoned the pretension only for the sake of détente with its ancient rival. In 1903 the Executive Committee of Grace Paterson's school approached the College with an affiliation proposal — but was rejected on account of the School's shaky financial circumstances. The College in its form of that period was itself the result of a re-amalgamation of Anderson's establishment with a College of Science and Arts which had emerged from the Glasgow Mechanics' Institution, itself a breakaway from the Andersonian in the 1820s. The

---

[12]Ironically, they were founded by the same individual, the philanthropist and educationist David Stow. Dundas Vale was his original creation, but belonged to the Church of Scotland. When he joined the Free Church at the disruption of 1843, he established the other close by.

[13]There were four of these, one for each of the areas covered by the old Scottish universities.

Mechanics Institution's premises between 1831 and 1859 stood, ironically, on the site later to be occupied by Glasgow College of Technology.[14]

A college of commerce also existed within the city, which operated for a time under the rather misleading title of the Glasgow Athenaeum. Its origins stretched back to the 1840s when, according to the *Chamber of Commerce Journal* of 1933–34, a number of young businessmen formed the Glasgow Educational Association to promote commercial education equivalent to that available in the University.[15] They first leased rooms from the Andersonian but soon acquired their own building, the opening ceremony being presided over by no less an eminence than Charles Dickens, after which the organisation took on the Athenaeum title from the fact that it also supplied reading rooms, a coffee shop and so forth. In the 1880s its educational activities were successful enough to result in the acquisition of grander premises and a separate designation as the Glasgow Athenaeum Commercial College. It achieved recognition as a central institution in 1903 and adopted the title Glasgow and West of Scotland Commercial College in 1915. In the '60s it became a constituent of Strathclyde University.

What was to become the Glasgow School of Art and to be based in one of the most important architectural achievements of the twentieth century, Charles Rennie Mackintosh's masterpiece, had come into being in 1840 as the Glasgow Government School of Design. The idea behind its establishment was to improve the standards of design in manufacture in order to make Glasgow more competitive in the European market — a familiar story.[16] In the late nineteenth century it was renowned as one of the country's premier art and design establishments. It benefited from considerable state backing and was educating artistic tendencies of exceptional importance.

Another development into tertiary education out of the Glasgow Athenaeum, which gave some attention to music and the fine arts, was the present Royal Scottish Academy of Music and Drama. When in 1888 the commercial aspect was hived off, the Glasgow Athenaeum became a limited

---

[14]For Strathclyde University and its predecessor institutions see John Butt, *John Anderson's Legacy: The University of Strathclyde and its Antecedents, 1796–1996*, Tuckwell Press, 1996.

[15]According to John Butt this was the reconstitution of an earlier body of the same name which *inter alia* had been associated with the foundation of David Stow's Normal School. *Ibid.* p.170.

[16]An earlier 18th century attempt to found a fine arts college had proved abortive.

company, and in the 1890s departments of music and art were formed into schools and the department of elocution and dramatic art was established. In 1903 the Glasgow Athenaeum (Limited) went into voluntary liquidation but re-emerged as the Glasgow Athenaeum (Incorporated). In 1928 the School of Music became the Scottish National Academy of Music. The 'Royal' prefix was added in 1944 and the name changed to the Royal Scottish Academy of Music. The College of Dramatic Art was established in 1950 and in 1968 the two were combined to form the present institution.[17]

From rupture to re-amalgamation

That both Schools were able to survive throughout the years following their foundation indicates that they were meeting a significant demand, though neither of them enjoyed a very secure financial position. As noted, they had both begun with the intention of educating young working-class women in culinary skills as a contribution to the improvement of family life among lower-income groups, 'That by and by they will be able to prepare nice meals economically for their husbands. That drunkenness and wife-beating will belong to the barbarous past'.[18] That approach however was not very successful, for although the daytime courses for better-off women were priced to subsidise the cost of evening classes for working women, these latter failed to catch on, even when offered *gratis*. Lack of available time and a degree of class suspicion might well account for that.

Consequently a fresh strategy was adopted by both establishments, namely to promote culinary education within the board schools, which proved a successful initiative. It began with the two Schools sending out their staff to conduct classes within the board schools, and soon developed into a system whereby the Schools trained domestic science teachers to work in the board schools. No doubt the eventual presence of the two pioneers on the Glasgow School Board accelerated the development. In 1876 representatives from cookery schools in Glasgow, Edinburgh, Liverpool and Leeds formed themselves into the Northern Union of Training Schools of Cookery to institute uniform standards and common examinations for teachers of cookery.

---

[17]Catalogue of Deposited Records, Glasgow City Archive, p.433, Ref. TD571–655, currently in Strathclyde University.

[18]*The Bailie*, March 1, 1878, p.7.

According to the syllabus of the Glasgow School for 1897–98,

> The Executive Committee are prepared to provide Teachers of Cookery, Dressmaking and Sewing Millinery, Housewifery and Laundry Work, for County Council Classes, to undertake Classes in Private Houses, Ladies' Schools, Institutions, Board Schools, etc., and to organise Public and Private Classes in other towns and villages in all the Five Subjects.

The use of the 'domestic science' designation in place of 'cookery' becomes applicable from the 1880s when the Scotch Code of the SED[19] provided for teaching of needlework, which was extended to laundry in 1891. Alongside any improvement in family circumstances likely to result from this form of education, the creation of a supply of able female domestic servants was a consideration that was certainly not, as surviving syllabuses demonstrate, absent from the minds of the contemporary middle class in an era when the employment of servants marked the most visible dividing line between the middle class and others.

During this period development of cookery, domestic economy or domestic science was proceeding. Apart from those already mentioned in Scotland, institutions were established in Dundee (1876) and Aberdeen (1891). Two other minor establishments also existed in the Glasgow conurbation, one of those, privately financed, being located in the then separate burgh of Govan.

A determining event of the Schools' future, almost as significant as their foundation and the turning point which consolidated their existence as a part of the Scottish education system, was their reunification in the first decade of the twentieth century. The initial catalyst was a political one, arising from the election of the last Liberal Government in 1906 following that party's landslide victory and the social reform programme upon which the administration embarked. The programme depended to a very great extent upon the agency of local authorities. The renowned 'Children's Act' of 1908 provided *inter alia* for medical inspection in schools and the provision of school meals to 'necessitous' children. The motives behind this legislation may not have been purely philanthropic. At a time of growing international tension the existence of a reservoir of fit potential soldiers for

---

[19]The SED's history is itself of great interest, first being established in London in 1872, then disappearing between 1878 and 1885 before revival as part of the responsibilities of the newly-created Secretary for Scotland (Secretary of State for Scotland from 1926).

the future was a significant consideration on the part of the authorities (one section of the establishment was also agitating for conscription on the European model and 'national efficiency'). The medical condition of two-thirds of volunteers for the Boer War had been appalling.

Sentiments springing from the same set of attitudes were being voiced in relation to women. The *Glasgow Herald* of February 19, 1910 reported a speech by Professor Darroch (his Chair was in education) of Edinburgh University to the effect that 'a recent writer had laid down that education must be concerned with all the living forces that go to mould a nation, and that one of the greatest, perhaps the greatest, of these living forces is that by means of our educational agencies we should produce a race of physically healthy, intelligently minded and morally earnest wives, mothers and housekeepers'. The 1908 Act's Scottish equivalent as well as covering these dimensions included a provision for the domestic education of schoolgirls.

By this time the schools' formal titles had been expanded. The Glasgow School now called itself the Glasgow School of Cookery and Domestic Economy, and the West End School, The West End Training School of Cookery. Both occupied different scattered buildings; the former, with assets of £1,118, employed eight teaching staff, and the latter, whose assets amounted to £477, five. Margaret Black had died in 1903 and direction of the School had passed to her niece Mary MacKirdy. Grace Paterson retired in 1908. Her successor was a Miss Ella Glaister.

MISS ELLA GLAISTER, first Principal of The Glasgow and West of Scotland College of Domestic Science, 1908–1910, and originator of *The Glasgow Cookery Book*.

The following are extracts from the syllabus of the Glasgow School from the late 1890s to the early 1900s:

Pupils requiring a Special Course of expensive and elaborate Entrees and Savouries, must pay at the rate of 5/- a Lesson

SPECIAL PRACTICE LESSONS FOR COOKS in High-Class COOKERY, on Fridays, from 10 a.m. till 1.30 p.m. Fee, 5/6 per Lesson.

Special arrangements are made for training of Cooks, and Certificates are granted to Cooks who make the necessary attendance at Practice and Demonstration Lessons.

Cooked Dishes are for sale at the close of each Lesson and orders will be taken for dishes to be cooked in the school. Cooked Food will be delivered to any address in Glasgow.

LECTURES ON HOUSEWIFERY

…This Course is intended to meet the requirements of Ladies desiring instruction in Household Management, Girls leaving School, intending Emigrants, Housekeepers, etc.

(Session 1897–98) [at this point the School employed a male lecturer along with its five female teaching staff — a Mr James Knight MA BSc, who lectured on the physiology of digestion and chemistry of food].

The Committee are prepared to send Teachers of Cookery to give lessons by the week to Servants in private houses. The Teacher is to reside in the house when convenient, and to undertake the cooking of all meals.

STUDENT RESIDENCE

The Residence and Housewifery Centre at 121 Bath Street is intended for lady Students coming from the country to attend the Housewifery or other training classes being carried on by the School. Board and lodging from £1 to £1 10s per week according to accommodation [later syllabuses added the requirement — 'Each intending student is required to send letters of personal recommendation from two well-known householders to whom she is personally known'].

HOUSEWIFERY TEACHING DIPLOMA

This Diploma qualifies its holder to teach housewifery in Elementary Day and Evening Continuation Schools, Technical Classes, &c. The course includes instruction in Cookery, Laundry Work, Sewing, Practical Housekeeping, Household Accounts and Domestic Expenditure, Sick Nursing and Hygiene, Elementary Science, with Theory and Practice of Education and practice in Demonstration and Class Teaching in all the

above subjects. The minimum time for training is 1000 hours [the fee was £30].
(Session 1899–1900)

TRAINING FOR HOUSEWIFE'S CERTIFICATE — FEE £20

The Housewifery Course is intended for young ladies as part of their ordinary education. Many girls, though highly educated in other branches, are entirely ignorant of Household Management, and begin housekeeping with little or no knowledge of what they are undertaking. In this Centre general education may be supplemented by thorough instruction in all that the mistress of a well ordered home requires to know.

LECTURES AND DEMONSTRATIONS ON HOUSEHOLD MANAGEMENT

Ten Lectures ... [including] Management of Servants — their allowances and division of work.
(Session 1905–06)

Candidates for Training in Cookery Laundry or Housewifery must hold the Intermediate Certificate or its equivalent, else they will be required to pass an Entrance Examination in Composition, Reading, Spelling, the first four rules of Arithmetic, Vulgar Fractions and Simple Proportion.
(Session 1907–1908)

Under the new Scottish educational regime domestic science colleges were to join the ranks of the 'central institutions', a term which came into use from 1901, and designated establishments funded directly by the SED. Only one domestic science college would be recognised in each city, a situation which made it imperative for the two Schools to discuss amalgamation, despite longstanding mutual rivalry and suspicion.

The shape of future developments being evident, discussions began as early as the beginning of 1907, but soon stalled. In February of that year the Glasgow Provincial Committee for the Training of Teachers brought together the Executive Committees of both the Schools to discuss amalgamation. A joint committee emerged in April, but was deadlocked before long by disagreements over representation, and an independent arbiter was sought, in the person of the Chairman of the

Technical College Board of Governors, Sir William Copland, under whom the great rebuilding of the Technical College had recently taken place.[20]

The committee succeeded in framing articles of association, but still failed to agree on the composition of a governing body. Nevertheless circumstances forced the amalgamation forward and at the end of the year a rather elaborate strategem, proposed by the representative of the SED, was found to get round the problem. An Association of up to 500 members was formed under the title 'The Glasgow and West of Scotland Technical Institute for Women' (a revealing title) and was accorded responsibility for the election of a Governing Body. Coincidentally its initial meeting, on December 19, 1907, took place on the same premises, the Religious Institution Rooms, as had been used when the Glasgow School was initiated over 30 years earlier, though at a different address.

Alongside 21 Governors elected from the Association six were appointed from various leading bodies in Glasgow and surrounding districts such as Glasgow Corporation, the respective School Boards of Glasgow and Govan, the Merchant House and adjacent county councils.

According to a *Glasgow Herald* report:

> The Chairman said they had met to launch a new association.... Educational institutions, he said, had undergone considerable change in Scotland in general, and in Glasgow in particular. He referred to the palatial buildings in George Street of the Technical College, the School of Art in Renfrew Street and the Agricultural College. They had also seen considerable changes in the Glasgow Athenaeum, which had been altered into a commercial school of the first order for Glasgow and the West of Scotland. Up till now the domain of the ladies had practically been omitted — he referred to the science of cookery and domestic economy. ...Both schools had trained a large number of teachers and the [Glasgow] School Board had drawn on both schools when they desired teachers. He touched on the attempts to amalgamate the two schools, and pointed out that the Education Department could only recognise one central school and with that object the Association had been formed.[21]

---

[20]See John Butt, *op. cit.*, pp.101–105.
[21]*Glasgow Herald*, December 20, 1907.

The Chairman of the meeting and of the Board of Governors that it elected was a Dr Paul Rottenburg, an individual of interesting background. Originally from Danzig, his family origins were in the German aristocracy and his brother was at one point Bismarck's Secretary of the Interior and subsequently Rector of Bonn University. Coming to Glasgow to enter his uncle's trading firm, he subsequently became its head and, as a naturalised British citizen from the 1870s, a major figure among the Glasgow commercial establishment. He was a Chairman of Vogt Engines and President of the Chamber of Commerce from 1897–99; convenor of its foreign affairs committee, its records show him to have had a particular interest in Glasgow's imperial role. He was also a director of the Scottish Amicable Life Assurance Company and the Merchants' House and had connections with societies for fine arts, music and philosophy. According to his obituary he was also instrumental in establishing the Glasgow Homeopathic Hospital.[22]

At the time the amalgamation proposal was raised Rottenburg was chairman of the Glasgow School's Executive Committee and was elected Chairman of the Board of Governors which took on the direction of the Association. The committee which it appointed to handle the details of the amalgamation met representatives of both the Schools, which agreed to be taken over by the Association. The name adopted by the joint institution at the beginning of 1908, having dropped the Glasgow and West of Scotland Technical Institute for Women designation, was the Glasgow and West of Scotland College of Domestic Science (Incorporated) — which would seem to be on the face of it a less ambitious title and a recognition of limitation to domestic spheres:

> After discussion, it was agreed that the Association should be called 'The Glasgow and West of Scotland College of Domestic Science (Incorporated)' and the Memorandum and Articles of Association were approved, subject to any adjustments required by the Board of Trade, which were left in the hands of Mr McCallum, who was instructed to apply to the Board of Trade for the necessary Licence, and on obtaining it to have the Association registered.[23]

[22]*Glasgow Herald*, February 4, 1929.
[23]Minute of initial meeting of the 'Glasgow and West of Scotland Technical Institute for Women', January 23, 1908.

D<small>R</small> P<small>AUL</small> R<small>OTTENBURG</small>, first Chairman of the Board of Governors of the Glasgow and West of Scotland College of Domestic Science in 1908–1915. *Thanks to Glasgow University Archive for the photograph.*

A few months later the merged establishment was recognised as a central institution.

Its new status made it eligible for grants to make up income deficits when expenditure had been approved by the SED. It also made its students eligible for travelling and maintenance grants from local authorities. It is not recorded whether Grace Paterson's resignation from her role as Superintendent and Office Secretary (ie principal) in March 1908 (she retired in June) was connected with the imminent merger. Her successor, Ella Glaister, the daughter of a professor of forensic medicine at Glasgow University, then had the responsibility of implementing the merger at staff level. It may not have been an easy undertaking, for she resigned after two years to take up employment by the SED as Inspectress of Domestic Subjects.

It is clear that the apprehension of the West End School that it would end up as the junior partner in a merger was well founded, for the question of representation on the new Board of Governors had been the initial impediment to the amalgamation. In the event Rottenburg, of the Glasgow School, became the Chairman of the new College's governors. He came from the Glasgow School side, as did the new head. It is unimaginable that Mary MacKirdy did not have some feelings about the loss of status she had suffered along with her School and that frictions were not generated on the part of staff who had effectively been taken over by a rival.[24] Given that the teaching staff of the new institution, scattered over several sites, still constituted a small group, the relative anonymity which might have diluted injured feelings in a larger institution was absent. Ella Glaister's successor was Dorothy H Melvin, who had also been on the staff of the Glasgow School at the time of the amalgamation — again Mary MacKirdy was passed over. Dorothy Melvin remained in charge of the College until 1946 and lived until December 1963. Her obituary notes:

Our Principal had a vision of the future which rebelled against such narrowness of outlook. In the purely academic field such attitudes [female

---

[24]As early as 1911 the existence of the former West End School was being written out of the script. A flattering profile of the College in the *Glasgow Herald* of March 25 states: 'Though it has been in existence for thirty years, being originally known under the less imposing name of the Glasgow School of Cookery', and the thumbnail historical sketch which follows suggests only one predecessor institution.

confinement to domestic functions] tended to make the leaders of women's education belittle the skills of the home but Miss Melvin was to be a notable member of a group of remarkable leaders in the Domestic Science Colleges who saw the subject as part of a wide cultural education and also as the basis of training for expanding socially useful careers for women.[25]

As with its predecessors, the new College could be regarded as possessing a double function — the training of teachers of domestic science for the schools and continuing to give instruction to the general public (and domestic servants). These latter could if they wished take diplomas in single subjects such as cookery, laundry work and housewifery, needlework, dressmaking or millinery, although from 1910 these were abolished and only diplomas for complete courses were awarded.

   Even before the First World War alarm at shortages of domestic servants was being combined with anti-feminist bile. An item from the *Glasgow Evening News* of June 18, 1913, under the title 'Woman's View' begins:

> Back to the home is more and more the cry of the present generation in relation to the education of girls. Only once have I heard a really good argument in favour of burdening us with the Suffrage .... Men are no longer the breadwinners of the nation; women are for the present their competitors. I do not know when the business began, but the Higher Education movement gave a great impetus to the altered relation of the sexes, the changed outlook of women. Twenty-five years ago when it all began, many men and women saw the trend and vainly tried to stop the craze for over-educating incompetent girls with the minds of a nursery governess, but excellent memories for cram subjects, and today such men [sic] and women as survive are finding justification in the overcrowding of trades and professions, and the ever-growing feeling that women are best placed when they are doing women's work.

The writer goes on to commend the College for providing systematic instruction in the domestic arts, then, under a subheading 'Wanted, Domestic Servants', she (he?) continues:

---

[25] *Former Students' Newsletter,* June 1964, pp 18–19.

While women of the educated classes are spending considerable sums in order to learn to acquit themselves as housewives, and while the girls and women of the artisan classes are being afforded ample opportunity of learning the business of domesticity, it is disquieting to be told that 'it is becoming increasingly difficult to get girls to enter domestic service … and the result will be that people will be required to serve themselves to a greater extent than they do at present, although probably improved organisation and the use of mechanical appliances will render the employment of domestic servants less necessary [an unnamed 'educational authority' is cited as the source].

THE

Glasgow Cookery Book

ISSUED BY

The Glasgow and West of Scotland College of Domestic Science (Incorporated)

FOR USE IN

THE COLLEGE.

PRICE · 3/6 NET.
Per Post, · 3/11

All Rights Reserved.

GLASGOW:
PRINTED BY N. ADSHEAD & SON,
11 AND 9½ UNION STREET.
LONDON: S. G. MADGWICK, 26 IVY LANE, LONDON, E.C.

The famous *Glasgow Cookery Book*, the student's handbook that made its way into many kitchens throughout the world. Various editions of *The Glasgow Cookery Book* are part of Glasgow Caledonian University's Queen's College Special Collection, held in the Caledonian Library and Information Centre (CLIC).

The SED appears to have felt that the College (and its Edinburgh counterpart) was too concerned with professional training at the expense of practical domestic education (an early instance of academic drift), and insisted on curriculum alterations.[26] At the time — 1910 — the College had 1218 students on its books including trainee domestic science teachers. An additional 503 were either student teachers of general subjects or elementary teachers upgrading their qualifications. (Miscellaneous attenders at public lectures are not included in these figures.)[27] A small number of students were resident — eight to be precise.

[26]Minute of the Glasgow and West of Scotland College of Domestic Science (Incorporated) [ie the Association], June 15, 1910.
[27]*Ibid.* October 27, 1909.

The New Building and the War

Recognition of the College as a central institution allowed it to apply for a building grant, but only equivalent to the sum it could raise under its own efforts. A report commissioned by Rottenburg estimated the required cost as being £30,000 (roughly £3 million in current values). The Association (which was the College's legal owner) decided at its General Meeting of October 1909 to launch an appeal, noting that it would have previously been inopportune to do so on account of economic recession. It still did not prove to be easy, and the Lord Provost had to be recruited to chair a public meeting in the City Chambers at which the University Principal was also on the platform. Subscription appeals were printed in the *Glasgow Herald*, the *Scotsman* and the *Citizen*, as well as the *Daily Record*, the *Evening Times* and the *Evening Citizen*. This raised £6,121. The Corporation allocated a Grant of £3,000 from the Glasgow Common Good Fund and a variety of other donations brought it to over £11,000 by October 1911 and £16,439 by October 1913.

A site was selected in Park Drive beside the West End Park (now Kelvingrove Park) with light and access on three sides and good transport facilities. Borings disclosed that underneath was one of the old coal workings scattered all around the west end of Glasgow so that extra expenditure would be required to make the foundations secure. On the other hand, for the same reason the selling price of the site was reduced. Draft plans were submitted at the end of 1912 after 'nine similar institutions had been visited and surveyed',[28] and by then the estimated overall cost (excluding the site) had risen to £40,000. The accommodation in the new building approximately doubled that of the existing scattered premises and was designed to possess internally 'the restraint and simplicity of a hospital … simple, practical and economical as can be, consistent with permanence and efficiency'.[29]

It is perhaps worth noting in passing that the closing years of the nineteenth century and the period up to the First World War saw in Glasgow a remarkable expansion of building in the non-university 'tertiary' sector of the time. The Technical College constructed its new George Street premises between 1903 and 1910 (the total cost was just under £354,000,

---

[28]Architect's Report, December 23, 1912.
[29]*Ibid.*

nearly nine times that of the College of Domestic Science building), 'the largest building in the kingdom devoted to education' — in fact the biggest such complex in Europe.[30] Rennie MacKintosh's masterpiece was going up at the same time and the new College of Education building at Jordanhill was likewise under construction. Interestingly, all four projects had a severe struggle to raise the funds which were required. When the economy boomed costs rose, when it was in recession donations contracted.

Building work at Park Drive commenced in 1913 and continued in the months following the outbreak of war (which, after all, was initially expected to be a short one). By the early months of 1915 the building was approaching completion and equipment was beginning to be installed when the Governors were confronted with a request from the Red Cross that the building should be turned over to it for the duration to be used as a hospital. In the circumstances the request amounted to a demand which could not be refused and an agreement was soon concluded whereby uncompleted building work was to continue, and the Red Cross Society was to maintain the building during its occupancy and pay the College £1,000 per annum compensation. On June 28 the Lord Provost opened the Woodside Red Cross Hospital.

A few days later prejudice against anything with the remotest German connections (dachshunds were being assaulted for example) drove Paul Rottenburg and his wife out of their positions as College governors despite the fact that the former had been a naturalised British citizen for over 40 years and had 'played a large part in the transfer of the new building to the Red Cross'.[31] In his resignation letter he wrote that 'I have to realise that under existing conditions I owe it to both College and Government Department of Education to tender my resignation'. Ida Rottenburg similarly wrote that 'Existing circumstances, however, leave me — I am truly sorry to say — no other choice'.[32] Some Governors at least had the grace to propose that the resignations be declined, but this was defeated by nine votes to five. 'Respect, esteem and sympathy', however, were publicly expressed.[33] The mover of the unsuccessful amendment was Dr Henry Dyer, a Life Governor of the Royal Technical College as it was then, and

---

[30]John Butt, *op. cit.*, pp 104–105.
[31]Minute of the Glasgow and West of Scotland College of Domestic Science, July 6, 1915.
[32]*Ibid.*
[33]Governors' Report, December 1915.

An early photograph of the Glasgow and West of Scotland College of Domestic Science, 1-6 Park Drive. At the left of the picture, 7, 8 and 9 Park Drive can be seen prior to the building work of 1935/36 that added them to the College. The original College building was almost completed in 1915 when it was taken over by the British Red Cross and used as Woodside Red Cross Hospital for the duration of World War I.

the pioneer of technological education in Japan, where he had been the first Principal and Professor of Civil and Mechanical Engineering in the Imperial College of Engineering, Tokyo, between 1873 and 1882.[34]

In this manner the College of Domestic Science began its incorporation into the war effort.

[34]John Butt, *op. cit.*, p.87.

Chapter Two

_____

The College of Domestic Science, 1915–1945

The College during the War

Owing to the takeover of the new building by the Red Cross, teaching had to continue in the old scattered premises. This too began to be directed towards wartime purposes. Military and civil authorities soon began to draw upon the College's expertise: advice was sought regarding cooking practices in military camps, and military cooks were trained by the staff. Similarly, the College advised on running canteens in munitions factories and trained personnel for that purpose.

What happened to the institution in various aspects of its functioning between 1914 and 1918, from the takeover of the building to the remit given to its instructors and voluntary undertakings by its students (such as sponsoring military hospital beds and war savings schemes), exemplified the civilian mobilisation that was an unprecedented feature of this war in all the major belligerent countries and was the essential underpinning for continuance of the slaughter.

By the spring of 1917, in consequence of the German U-boat blockade campaign, serious food shortages were manifest. A degree of food rationing was introduced, a state of affairs likely to result in peculiar demands on the time and energies of domestic science teachers. In Scotland, the College appears to have played a central role and its work to have extended beyond Glasgow. A Food Economy Campaign was inaugurated in April with representatives of the College Governors on the directing committee. Between May and July, with all members of staff utilised, 70 lectures had been given throughout Scotland. Experiments were begun with recipes using ersatz constituents and these were demonstrated in public lectures. The *Bulletin* of March 31 reported:

> Miss Waldie, head teacher of the Glasgow and West of Scotland College of Domestic Sciences, gave an interesting demonstration of food saving… yesterday afternoon. The subject of the demonstration was bread baking and the use of flour substitutes. Mrs Waldie said that home baking was a great economy at the present time. By supplementing flour with cereals which were not restricted, bread and scones for family use might be made by the home baker without exceeding the official rations. Split peas, lentils, haricot beans, barley, rice, maize and rye might be used to supplement flour in baking.

Recipes included barley loaf, turnip scones and carrot pudding.

The records show no reflection in the life of the College of the social and political turmoil that rocked Glasgow during the war and immediate post-war years, from the great rent strike of 1915 organised by women protesting against iniquitous rent rises on the part of landlords taking advantage of accommodation shortages created by the expanding war industries, through the industrial conflicts in these same industries which brought the term 'Red Clydeside' into the historical and political vocabulary, to the riots which accompanied post-war strike action. However, the College was certainly recruited to try to preserve working-class domestic morale and as early as October 1914 the staff were being asked to advise on cheap menus suitable for working-class households in time of war and instructing students in this branch of work. Later on, when the authorities must have been extremely concerned at the possible effect of food shortages on volatile working-class sentiment in Glasgow:

> In conjunction with the Glasgow Infant Health Visitors' Association the Patriotic Food League [an organisation strongly supported by the College], which has already done much useful work in Glasgow, is starting a new campaign this week. Cookery demonstrations will be given in the kitchens of working class housewives in six districts — Calton, Garngrad, Hutchestown East and West, Govan and Partick …. [The instructors] will work only with utensils provided in the houses where the demonstrations are given, for it is realised that this is the most practical method of teaching economical cookery. It has been left to members of

the Infant Health Visitors' Association to select suitable kitchens in each district, the housewives themselves being asked to give invitations to their neighbours so that as many local women as possible may have an opportunity of profiting by the demonstrations. The charge for admission will be a penny per head, and the food cooked will be left with the hostess. It is hoped that similar demonstrations will be arranged in other districts later on.[1]

It is not explained how any numbers of an audience could have been fitted into a Glasgow single end while leaving room for the demonstrator. Presumably only more commodious kitchens were selected. It would seem also unlikely on the face of things that this initiative had much impact on the attitudes of Glasgow's working-class women.

The Inter-war Years

The College emerged from the war into a world in which many features of the social and cultural landscape had been washed away by the deluge, and further trauma was soon to follow in the shape of chronic economic depression and acute slump. The institution's development between 1919 and 1939 was determined in many ways by the effort to reposition itself in the face of such changing circumstances. Following a brief and hectic post-war boom, the Scottish economy foundered as the traditional industries upon which it was founded were overtaken by dramatic contraction in world markets and collapse in demand for their products. Coal mining, iron and steel manufacture, engineering and above all shipbuilding were the principal victims. Everything that had favoured Glasgow in the late nineteenth century now turned around to its disadvantage. Mass unemployment appeared as a permanent feature of the Glasgow and west of Scotland scene. The political and industrial confrontations for which the city was renowned in the immediate aftermath of the war soon died away, although they left behind a legacy of electoral radicalism. In the general election of 1922 a bloc of Glasgow left-wing Labour MPs were returned to Westminster: the Clydesiders. In the thirties the Labour Party at last won control of Glasgow Corporation and thereafter has seldom failed to rule the municipality.

---

[1] *Glasgow Herald*, October 4, 1917.

When during 1919, therefore, the College was at last able to occupy its new premises, the first necessity for its Governors and Principal was to adapt to the changed demands likely to fall upon it with the ending of the war-related contracts which had occupied much of its attention during the conflict, and the altered social environment which the war had brought into being. Unquestionably the College was part of Glasgow's middle-class culture, of which its location in one of the more salubrious areas of the city might be viewed as a symbol. A list of its staff members for session 1919–20, 20 full-time and seven part-time, shows that they all lived at 'good' addresses, most of them in the more affluent suburbs. The same was true 13 years later. A press reference of a much later date notes that apart from its role in training domestic science teachers for schools, systematised from 1918 under the new Education Act, the College was then regarded by some as a kind of finishing school for middle-class young ladies.

> The image of the 'Dough' school has radically changed over the years …. From being looked on as a kind of finishing school to which 'nice' families sent their daughter between school and marriage, it is now accepted as a training ground for a variety of professions based on, but often far removed from, the traditional skills of cooking, sewing and cleaning.[2]

Upon the resumption of 'normality' and the occupancy of its premises, the College was immediately faced with two significant problems. The lesser of these was the condition in which the building had been left by the Red Cross following its use as a military hospital. This does not appear to have been very satisfactory, for the Governors complained that much of the fittings and equipment had been damaged to the extent that they could no longer serve their intended purpose.

> Mr Watson [the architect] also stated that the removal of the Red Cross furniture and a more careful inspection of the premises had disclosed much more serious damage and wear and tear than was apparent during the occupation …. Among the cases of serious damage were basins and

---

[2] *Times Education Supplement*, September 24, 1965. The College's own retrospective view of its position in the '20s shows a somewhat different picture: 'There were the days of economic crisis, called the Slump, when the urgency was to help mothers to budget and to prepare reasonably nourishing meals for next to no money, and with no thought of saving time and energy' (Governors' Report, 1961–62).

tubs, practically all of which were broken and cracked, showing usage altogether beyond ordinary wear and tear … doors and fittings had been severely used and damaged, mantelpieces badly damaged, and tiles in fireplaces smashed or removed and most of the fireplace kerbs damaged … and amongst the most material of the items will be the painting of the interior of the building.[3]

Miss Dorothy H Melvin with Glasgow and West of Scotland College of Domestic Science students outside Park Drive in 1920. Today the building is Glasgow Caledonian University's Park Campus.

On account of escalating costs of materials and labour occasioned by the brief post-war boom, the Governors found themselves under financial pressure and called upon the Red Cross Society to make up the difference between pre-war and post-war costings. (Additional building work was also continuing, which further complicated the position.) A chilly correspondence

[3]Governors' Minute, March 11, 1919.

resulted, during which mutual threats of legal action were exchanged, the issue only being resolved as late as 1922 (by which time costs had fallen again) under an agreement whereby the Red Cross made an *ex gratia* donation of £2,650 in return for being absolved by the College from legal obligation. The difficulties over completing the building work had been compounded by the fact that in addition to enhanced costs the workforce, doubtless influenced by the labour militancy of the times, did not hesitate to take strike action whenever they felt it was warranted.

The second problem was a lot more serious. The Education (Scotland) Act of 1918 wound up the School Boards and transferred responsibility to Local Education Authorities. These, however, were separately elected from the Corporation and in Glasgow constituted a merger of the existing School Boards. In place of one Governor each from the Glasgow and Govan School Boards to the College, two were appointed from the new body. The Act also envisaged 'the extension of the school age to 15 [and] compulsory attendance at continuation classes up till 18'[4]— provisions which might have expanded the College's clientele but which were of course abortive, the second never being implemented. The Act prescribed minimum national salary scales, but some Authorities instituted higher ones, and Glasgow nearly doubled the pre-war remuneration. However 'Higher Institutions' (the terminology used by the SED, now retitled the *Scottish* Education Department) did not come under this remit.

Consequently the College found itself in the potential dilemma that unless it could match what the Authority was paying, its staff would be on smaller salaries than the local authority teachers whom they had taught; not exactly a happy position for attracting high-quality staff. The Governors appealed to the SED to increase its grant to make up the difference, but received a dusty answer. It was the era of the Geddes Axe, so named from the Whitehall civil servant Sir Eric Geddes who drew up the spending cuts that the government began to implement as depression closed in and its tax base contracted. The most that the SED was willing to offer was funding to cover increases on the scale implemented by the Edinburgh Local Education Authority, which were considerably less generous than those of Glasgow. The difference was not insignificant. For Miss Melvin, the Principal, the increase would have been from £330

---

[4]*Glasgow Herald*, March 15, 1919.

per annum to £550 on the Edinburgh scale, but £940 on the Glasgow one, a fairly substantial salary for the times. For an ordinary lecturer at the College it would have meant a rise from £160–170 to £300 maximum on the Edinburgh scale, up to £400 on the Glasgow one.[5] In response to the Governors' pleas the SED officials scarcely bothered to be polite:

> Your understanding of the position is based upon a complete misapprehension …. If Central Institutions cannot pay their own way under normal circumstances, they have no claim to financial help from the central authority unless an adequate contribution is provided by the locality. If the locality is not prepared to do its part, recognition as a Central Institution will have to be withdrawn.[6]

Miss Dorothy H Melvin, *OBE, JP,* Principal of The Glasgow and West of Scotland College of Domestic Science, 1910–1946.

The suggestion being made was that Glasgow should cover the difference, but the Governors got only marginally greater satisfaction from that quarter.[7] The Authority offered £3,000 for the year 1920–21, which did avert the immediate crisis, but thereafter its grant declined by stages to £200 by 1924. In the end the long-term problem appears to have been met by fee increases, which must have narrowed the recruitment base of the College's students.

The College Prospectus of 1919–20 summarised the areas of its work as follows — it is worth noting that the same paragraph appeared in the 1944–45 Prospectus:

---

[5]Governors' Minute Book, 1917–23, pp.242–243.
[6]J Struthers to Jas A M'Callum, June 25, 1920.
[7]M Macleod to College, October 25, 1920.

The object of the College is to provide, at moderate cost, thorough instruction, theoretical and practical, in Cookery, Laundrywork, Housewifery, Dressmaking, Needlework, Millinery, and allied branches for those desirous of becoming expert in Household Management, for Professional Housekeepers, Cooks, Laundresses, and Dressmakers, and for those proposing to become Teachers of Domestic Science subjects. It also provides short courses and public lectures and demonstrations ... and in addition, the correlated subjects of Chemistry, Hygiene, Home Nursing, First Aid and Infant Management, Drawing, Design and Bookkeeping, Upholstery, Simple Household Repairs, &c.

Interestingly, the cookery included vegetarian cookery, but overtones of the old class divisions still remained, for the practical lessons were graded, among other categories, as artisan, household and high class.

   These subjects were offered in a range of Diploma and Certificate courses, one of which was training for domestic service, for which the College offered employment-finding assistance on completion of the course.[8] The minimum age for commencing this Certificate was 16, for Diploma courses it was 18 and required satisfactory standards in basic education, preferably the Full Leaving Certificate of the SED.

Students training as teachers must wear College uniform — blouse and short skirt. Aprons and sleeves of a uniform pattern are obtained at the College. Neat plain white collars [in those days these were detachable] and black sailor ties must also be worn, slippers must be worn, no jewellery is allowed. An overall of the same material as uniform must be worn for chemistry and housework.

However, it was not long after the end of the war that perennial upper-class worries about the shortage of domestic servants were combined with the new spectre of mass unemployment to produce a specialised scheme to train unemployed girls specifically for domestic service. According to a report late in 1919:

The Ministry of Labour are going to make an effort to solve the domestic servant problem and details of a practical scheme of training, which will

---

[8]The College was also prepared to send out a cookery teacher to give lessons to servants in private houses.

be brought into operation soon and which will go a long way to solving the existing difficulty were supplied to a *Citizen* representative to-day. ...

It has been decided to open a special class at the School of Domestic Science and Training [sic] in Park Drive, and it will be open to girls who are at present in receipt of out-of-work donation or girls who at some period have drawn out-of-work money. It is pointed out, however, that the class can only be taken up by girls who have been genuinely unemployed.[9]

A short press item the following day made certain assumptions about the journal's readership:

HOPE FOR MISTRESSES
Those of us who would wish to employ what the Americans describe as 'hired help' but cannot get it, have heard with interest of the scheme of the Ministry of Labour for training unemployed girls as domestic assistants.[10]

A few months later the *Bulletin* was coming back to the theme, with a page of photographs of 'Scottish ex-War Workers' as they were described, at the College 'in discharge of their duties, which include the hundred and one jobs required of a maid'. The accompanying article, headed 'Training Domestic Servants: Ministry of Labour Scheme in Glasgow' reported that the majority of the 40 students were ex-munition workers but that 'several are girls from offices and other employments who have been attracted to domestic service by the various advantages which the life has to offer under the improved conditions that are now general'. The aim of the scheme, the reporter noted, was to turn out 'not specialists, but well-trained and competent general servants for duty in middle-class households'.[11] A related sentiment was voiced in November 1921 in an address by the Duchess of Atholl to the students, who 'deprecated the choice allowed to girls in the supplementary courses of taking up commercial subjects as an alternative to domestic'.[12]

[9] *Evening News*, October 23, 1919.
[10] *Bulletin*, October 24, 1919.
[11] *Bulletin*, January 14, 1920.
[12] *Times Educational Supplement*, November 19, 1921.

The issue kept recurring. An editorial in the *Evening News* of August 28, 1926 argued for the professionalisation of domestic service along American lines, commenting that 'we are slow to adapt ourselves to any kind of domestic service that does not imply servility and "living in"'. The following year, in December 1927, the Duchess of Montrose, presenting certificates at the College, commented, according to the *Bulletin*:

> ...that today one heard much about unemployment, and yet when one wanted a maid for domestic work it was almost impossible to get one — especially for laundry work. The one idea of most girls seemed to be to go into a shop or factory, or to do some work that was previously done by a man.

Surely, continued the speaker, this must go a long way to account for at least some of the unemployment. She was glad to hear that they had already trained and placed in situations in Scotland over 5,000 girls.[13]

This expression of aristocratic opinion provoked a response the following day from the *Evening Citizen*:

> The Duchess of Montrose apparently does not understand the domestic service problem. At least, one would gather as much from the remarks she made at the closing exhibition of the Glasgow House training class yesterday. She bemoans that girls nowadays prefer to get work in a shop or a factory rather than be domestic servants. In doing so she merely stated an obvious fact without attempting to give reasons why this should be or how it can be altered.
>
> If asked to explain the reluctance of girls nowadays to become domestic servants, many people would say they have been demoralised by high wages paid during the War. But the War happened thirteen years ago and has been over for nine. Large numbers of girls who should be going into domestic service never earned high wages during the war. They were mere children. But they were at school. They were enjoying the glorious heritage of free education. As a result many girls who would duly have become domestics have been attracted into other spheres in the belief they will have greater freedom and better conditions of employment.

---

[13] *Bulletin*, December 14, 1927.

Not only are they attracted into the shops, offices, factories, etc., but they are repelled by the drudgery which characterised to far too great an extent the domestic service of pre-War days.

The article then goes on, however, to blunt its critique:

If domestic service is made sufficiently attractive there will be no scarcity of applicants. As Sir Andrew Pettigrew said, there is no stigma attaching to domestic service, and there is 'nothing which contributes so much to the happiness of a household as ready, willing and efficient service by those engaged in the domestic work of the household'. He might however have added — 'and sympathy, understanding and appreciation by the mistress of the merits of the servants'.

The press coverage of the College's activities reveals one instance of direct involvement in the socio-political turmoil of the time. The *Evening News* of May 6, 1921 carries a lengthy piece headed 'WOMAN'S VIEW' and 'concerned with practical points supplied by courtesy of Miss Melvin', instructing readers on how to save coal so as to beat the coal strike then in progress. A headline on the reverse page of that number reported a crisis in the Glasgow docks over the refusal of dockers, in sympathy with the miners, to unload cargos of Welsh coal. (A further headline refers to another ongoing political crisis of the time — an IRA shooting in Glasgow High Street.)

A brief press item from 1926 notes the Chair of the Governors at a diploma presentation day refuting what was referred to as recent 'ill-informed press criticism' of the institution, stating that the College had been called a blind alley leading nowhere. It has not proved possible to locate the criticisms in question.

Premises extension
The College did not remain satisfied for long with its new building alone. Nowadays the campus occupies the site on its own but when initially constructed there were three occupied dwelling houses adjacent to it. One by one, up to 1934, the College acquired them all. The first was in 1923, but, on account of what had happened in Glasgow during the war years, it was required to wait 10 years before this could be used. The great rent strike of 1915 had resulted in the passing of the Rent Restriction Act,

which protected the position of sitting tenants. When the first of the
dwelling houses (No 7 Park Drive) was sold at public auction due to its
owner's bankruptcy, the College acquired along with it a sitting tenant
who refused to move in spite of all persuasion and offers of alternative
accommodation. Not until 1933 was the College in a position to convert
and utilise it. Ad hoc arrangements had been made to use as a hostel and
student union facility the second purchase (No 8): once all three were
available it was decided to develop the three as a unitary extension, which
was eventually opened in October 1936. When completed it included
teaching accommodation, the updated Union premises and extended
residential accommodation; raising the available spaces for such students
to 96 in total.

The Principal of Glasgow University was among the official party and the
rather patronising comments he made are revealing for what they indicate
about the way that the College's role was viewed by the higher education
elite:

> Sir Hector Hetherington said that not only Glasgow University but
> others known to him suffered from the inconvenience of cramped
> accommodation, and his University certainly looked with envy and
> admiration upon the Domestic Science College with its handsome
> addition…. While at the University they were mainly concerned with
> pure science as an end in itself, the College was concerned with the
> fundamentals of science in relation to human society, and he wished it
> long continuance of this service towards the welfare and happiness and
> amenities of home life.[14]

The Chair of the Governors by this time was Sir Andrew Pettigrew, who had
occupied the office since 1924, having been voted a Governor in 1919. He
was one of the founders of the department store Pettigrew and Stephens
(among the first of its kind). After chairing the Executive Committee of the
Scottish National Exhibition at Kelvingrove in 1911 he was given the Chair
of Scottish Literature and History at Glasgow University — a somewhat
unusual career move. Apart from his academic commitments he occupied
a great many positions in the business and voluntary networks of the time

---

[14] *Glasgow Herald*, October 30, 1936.

Miss Dorothy H Melvin (seated front right), Sir Andrew Pettigrew, Chairman of the Board of Governors, 1924-42 (seated right), and others at an evening function, 1931, held in the Ca' Doro, Glasgow.

and remained the Chair of the College Governors until his death in 1942, at the age of 85, having married (for the third time) four years earlier.

His predecessor, who had taken over from Paul Rottenburg, was Sir Samuel Chisholm, again a businessman, and also a former Lord Provost, likewise widely involved in charitable enterprise. His attitudes and politics were a reflection of the times: Liberal, Temperance, and with a background in the United Presbyterians, they were in the same tradition as Provost Collins, and not least Margaret Black. He had been a passionate advocate of municipal enterprise in utilities, particularly library services, electricity and telephones, stigmatised by its enemies as 'municipal socialism'. Chisholm 'rejected accusations that the Corporation was empire-building at the expense of the private sector'.[15] A series of London *Times* articles in 1902

---

[15]W Hamish Fraser and Irene Maver, *Glasgow 1830–1912*, Manchester University Press, 1996, p.472. This also contains a portrait of Chisholm.

'identified the Glasgow administration as one of the most extreme examples of civic collectivism in the United Kingdom. The accusation was directed in particular at Lord Provost Chisholm, whose dual pursuit of the drinks trade and private landlords aroused a bitterly hostile reaction among assorted vested interests in Glasgow'.[16] His successor Pettigrew was likewise a Liberal and temperance advocate — evidently it was part of the College tradition. Chisholm himself, however, clearly ended up in the Lloyd George rather than the Asquith camp, for he is reported as having been a fervent Coalitionist and to have chaired a meeting for Bonar Law, the Conservative leader in late 1919.[17] He too died in office and at an advanced age — in his case 87.

Corporate Student Life

Not least of the consequences for the College of its occupancy of the new building was that it brought the students together as a body and enabled them to develop the kind of collective identity that students in better-

Glasgow and the West of Scotland College of Domestic Science students, 1926.

favoured establishments had traditionally enjoyed. A Student Union was formed in 1920, initially under the title of the Literary Society and Students' Union. At the general meeting held on January 12 to make

---

[16] *Ibid.*, p.474.
[17] GWSCDS press cutting book — source and exact date not identified.

preliminary arrangements, not only students were present, but representatives of staff and Governors. When the inaugural meeting proper took place a week later over 350 were present. The nature of the office-bearers appointed is striking. It was perhaps not surprising that the Chair of the Governors should have been made Honorary President, and interesting that the Honorary Vice-President should have been the Principal of Queen Margaret College, as an indication of outside links.

What would astonish a modern observer, however, is that the functioning office-bearers were all members of staff, not students. The President was Miss Melvin, the College Principal, the Vice-President Mary MacKirdy and the Secretary a Mr Walter Jamieson, a visiting lecturer in Chemistry. The Treasurer at least was a student, though she was assisted by two other people, one of whom was the other Miss MacKirdy. Attitudes were clearly paternalistic and must have evinced a marked lack of confidence in the students' ability to run their own organisation.

Membership was open to all past and present diploma and certified students. One of its remits was to mount lectures on varied subjects of interest, both professional and general. In the first year these included Professor Noel Paton on 'Activities of the Ductless Glands'; Andrew Barclay on 'Insects as Carriers of Disease' (illustrated with lantern slides); the Rev T Hunter Boyd on 'The Smaller Republics of Europe' (the post-Versailles states); and a Dr Steel on 'Love and Literature'. The formation of the Union was reported extensively in the local press (presumably the College had effective media contacts) and the Governors' report for session 1919–20 stated that the Union was growing rapidly and referred to components such as a hockey club, a swimming club, a golf section, a dramatic society, choir and debating society.

As noted above, permanent Student Union premises were provided with the extensions to the building which occurred during the '20s and '30s — though owing to impediments not initially until 1929,[18] with new and improved accommodation only in late 1936. The proposal for these premises had first been advanced in 1925 with College playing fields being projected as well. The students themselves set about raising funds, with a target of £10,000 — a very considerable sum in 1925 — but again the staff

---

[18]'The Students' Union Club … has now been completely furnished and equipped, and is forming a source of comfort and happiness to students and former pupils' — Governors' Report, February 1930.

took overall charge of the project. Fund-raising activities included whist drives, badminton tournaments, mannequin parades, sales, dances and entertainment evenings. The culmination was a two-day bazaar in late 1927, postponed from the previous year on account of 'adverse conditions due to the Coal Strike and other causes',[19] and which included fortune telling, a spook's tunnel and a Wild West saloon. Miss Melvin's introduction to the bazaar programme embodied a number of the cultural presumptions of the age:

> Noted Statesmen, Divines and Educationalists have spoken so often of the tremendous importance of this side of College life, whereby students complete a liberal education which the purely academic and technical alone cannot give.... The wholesome discipline of team work in out-door sports and games produces a healthy body and mind and the Union House would provide proper facilities for former and present students for recreation and for mutual education in self-government and discipline, and where all might learn the lessons of forbearance and consideration for others so necessary if their lives are to be of full value to their country and to themselves.

Playing fields were acquired, and by February 1930 the recreation ground at Chesterfield Avenue, Kelvinside was completed with a hockey pitch, three tennis courts and a pavilion. The badminton and recreation hall, also projected in the original plan, finally came into existence along with the improved Union premises in 1936. In 1934 a Yachting Club was established and sailed with success in the annual University and Public School races in the Gareloch on the Clyde estuary. In the summer 1939 races the College crew won outright (the Young Challenge Trophy in the Universities' Section), beating Oxford University, the holders for the previous four years.

The Student Union had no sooner been set up than it commenced to publish a magazine, the initial number appearing in January 1921. Again this was extensively reported in the local press, and according to the *Evening News* of January 17, was 'eminently newsy, personal, varied and it has what is often lacking in similar publications — a keen sense of fun'. Once again it was run by the staff not the students, though the latter did the writing and

---

[19]Governors' Report, January 1928.

contents included articles, reports, poetry, photographic competitions and personal news. The original cover, which was designed by a student, Margaret Duncan, was of exceptionally high quality, though subsequent numbers were of poorer calibre. In fact the magazine appears to have lasted for only a few years and to have disappeared before the end of the decade.

Consolidation and Educational Developments

It is something of a historical irony that just at the time at which the City's economic base collapsed, an institution which had struggled precariously for its existence in the days of prosperity had by the mid-'20s achieved a safe and stable institutional existence. In the initial post-war years falling rolls as the depression began to bite added to the financial problems the management was encountering over building costs and staff salaries, seeing a decline from 1,237 students in 1919–20 to 914 in 1922–23. Elementary student teachers receiving instruction similarly declined from 362 to 67, and these courses were under threat for a time.

The situation would doubtless have been worse had the College not from 1919 also provided Ministry of Labour training courses for former war workers in cookery, laundry and housework and for war widows in dressmaking (the assumptions behind the Ministry's thinking are themselves revealing). The College also served as a central training place for unemployed girls under the schemes of the Central Committee for Women's Training and Employment. However, by session 1923–24 student numbers, 1,062 in that year, began to rise again and continued to do so consistently until the outbreak of the Second World War. In the 1938–39 session the number was 1,450.[20] By contemporary standards these do not appear very large figures, but it is worth remembering that as late as 1960 Aberdeen University had only 2,000 students and St Andrews considerably fewer.

Unemployment did not spare teachers of domestic science. With public funding under constant pressure centrally and locally, the subject was scarcely a priority for education authorities. The Principal's answer was to encourage her graduates to be flexible and pursue other forms of employment that their training fitted them for. According to Dorothy Melvin's obituary which appeared in the *Former Students' Newsletter* for June 1964, 'many

---

[20]Governors' Reports. The figures for attendances by the public at open lectures and demonstrations grew from 694 in 1931–32 to 2,486 in 1938–39.

people found that their gifts lay in Institutional Management and Industrial careers, and trainings for such employment were developed and strengthened'. The introduction of trained dieticians in hospitals was another field of employment opening up for College graduates.[21]

The comparative stability and status that the College had reached was reflected in the Golden Jubilee celebrations of 1925. The senior bailie (in the Lord Provost's absence) hosted a reception in the City Chambers with a guest list of around 1,000 and a platform of eminent personages. The following day the College itself opened a three-day exhibition, at whose opening the Lord Provost appeared in person, accompanied by the Countess of Glasgow. The *Glasgow Herald* of May 13 reported of Sir Andrew Pettigrew's inaugural speech:

> ...was it not wonderful, he affirmed, that a school formed 50 years ago with the conception of being able to render help to the poorer people in simple home cooking should have developed into the scientific instrument it was today. The College also equipped young women who did not desire to be teachers to be good housewives and good mothers. Another important branch was the institutional work of equipping women to take charge of house-keeping, catering and cooking in the great institutions which were growing up around them.

Attendance during the subsequent three days reached over 3,200 people.

Just before her retirement Dorothy Melvin, when asked what she considered to be 'the biggest change in domestic training from the early days' replied that it was 'the development of nutrition research and the scientific approach generally'. In the 1925–26 session a course was launched for sister tutors and dieticians, intended for trained nurses and intending dieticians, though open to some other categories in addition. It included physiology, hygiene, biology and bacteriology along with cookery, laundry and some book-keeping — a comprehensive syllabus. The courses in this field developed into certificate and diploma courses and eventually postgraduate diplomas and certificates in dietetics.

Among the driving forces for these initiatives was Mary Andross, a graduate of Glasgow University. During part of the war she had worked for

---

[21]A number of newspaper reports of the diploma ceremony in November 1932 referred to this aspect.

the Ministry of Munitions Inspectorate on Poison Gases. Appointed to the College staff in 1925 she applied analytic procedures to determine the effect of cooking on the nutrients in everyday foodstuffs. Her most notable contributions were to the study of changes in food proteins, especially during the cooking of meat and eggs. Her published work in the inter-war period included 'Dietetic Survey on Women Students'; 'Milk in Adult Nutrition'; 'Testing Height-Weight Formula in Women'; 'Losses on Boiling Milk'; 'What to Eat and Why'; and 'Report on Argentine, New Zealand and Australian Chilled and Frozen Meats'. Her appointment was the eventual outcome of the resignation of Walter Jamieson, who had taught the students chemistry, not on the College premises but in North Kelvinside School, his salary being paid by the Local Education Authority. As a result of his withdrawal it was decided to appoint a full-time College lecturer in chemistry, the SED intimating that 'they would have no objection to the College's request to appoint a lady lecturer'. This, with the appearance of equipped laboratories, was the beginning of a science department. The first incumbent was a Miss Agnes Alexander, replaced three years later by Mary Andross.

Electricity and other publicity
The Principal appears to have held a strong appreciation of the new domestic power source, electricity. A national organisation, the Electrical Association for Women ('EAW'), was formed in 1924 aiming to disseminate information on the 'safe, wise and efficient use of electricity', provide a platform which would allow women to comment on style and design, and give women a voice in the community, especially since electricity was to have a major role in the development of the modern home. The minutes indicate that Miss Melvin began serious purchase of electrical equipment from the early 1920s. Day and evening classes were run in electrical housecraft and electrical repair. The equipment included cookers, refrigerators, mixers, peelers, lighting equipment, irons, kettles, toasters, wafflers, and a selection of electrical laundry devices including washing machines. All students studying for the College's Diploma I and III qualifications were obliged to follow a course covering the work of the EAW Certificate examinations and an electrical laboratory was equipped with samples of most household apparatus for dismantling plugs, sockets and so forth.

Miss Dorothy H Melvin with the Duke and Duchess of Kent during their visit to
The Glasgow and West of Scotland College of Domestic Science on 28 May 1935.

In the 1929–30 session the College installed a demonstrative and
experimental switchboard for the instruction of both students and the
general public. According to the *Daily Record* of November 12, 1930:

> The College of Domestic Science in Glasgow has installed an electrical
> switchboard on which students can blow out bulbs, repair fuses and learn
> how all the different branches of electricity, as applied to the home, are
> worked without disturbing the rest of the current and without danger, as
> all the plugs are safety ones. The practice switchboard is the first of its kind
> to be installed in Scotland, and was the idea of Miss Melvin, principal of
> the College, who read of the working of a similar one in Newcastle-on-
> Tyne College, the only other place in Britain to have one.

In 1937 the College hosted the EAW's Summer School, a five-day course
of electrical housecraft aimed at assisting teachers of domestic and/or
electrical subjects to enlarge their knowledge of the principles of electricity
and its domestic application. The Director of the EAW was Caroline

Students at a lecture, c1931.

Students in the model flat at Park Drive, c1931.

Students in the science lab, 1937.

Students in an upholstery and sewing class, c1931.

Haslett, who had been trained in electrical expertise during the war, including a period in a boiler works in Annan. She was Secretary of the Women's Engineering Society and the first woman Companion of the Institution of Electrical Engineers: 'it might come to women of the future running the power stations and the men the homes, Miss Haslett declared amid laughter of her audience'.[22]

Later in the course of the summer school a speech by a woman bailie, Jean Roberts, was reported in the following terms:

> The business of housekeeping was not one out of which profits could be made, and therefore no-one had been particularly interested in the welfare of the housewife [this remark suggests that she must have been a Labour councillor]. In the absence of outside attention she had come to the conclusion that the housewives must make their own saviours.
>
> For a number of years she had been trying to urge Glasgow Corporation Electricity Department to give washing machines to Glasgow housewives on hire purchase terms.
>
> Replying, Miss Melvin, Principal of the College, remarked that the College was the first to have an electric cooker, and she thought they could now claim they had the largest number of electrical appliances.[23]

A degree of discomfort at a perceived shift in gender roles — or at least the potentiality of such — is clear in these reports. The College's work was focused on what was regarded as the traditional sphere of female responsibilities; all its regular students and virtually all its staff were women. Yet it also aspired to be at the cutting edge of the new technologies of the day as well as developing new forms of training and educational experience. The perception that this process could eventually call into question the hitherto accepted allocation of roles and that advancing technology would undermine the sexual division of labour, is present in the reported exchanges. The College had also in the 1920s established a Chefs' Club — at the request of the restaurant trade — to train institutional chefs, and this was open to both men and women. At the diploma ceremony of November 1933, the Moderator of the Church of

---

[22]GWSCDS press cutting book — source and exact date not identified.
[23]GWSCDS press cutting book — source not identified.

Scotland, who was making the presentations, declared in his speech that 'Men should know how to cook'.[24]

In the same context it is worth mentioning a report which appeared in the *Evening Times* of October 20, 1933 on the 'Engaged Girls' Course', more popularly known as the 'Brides' Course', and which had run at least since 1910. The mixture of sentimentality, sexism and social reference is revealing:

> Love laughs at depression, and bad trade cannot hinder the matrimonially inclined! Crisis or no crisis this has been a 'bumper' year for weddings in Glasgow, and there is prospect of an even greater spate of brides and bridegrooms in the comparatively near future. One straw which shows the way the wind is blowing is the increase in the number of girls who have enrolled for the 'Engaged Girls' Course' at the College of Domestic Science....
>
> No longer can husbands complain of indigestion; no longer do they limp about with 'lumpy' darns in their socks, no longer do they search fruitlessly for a clean collar. The 'Engaged Girls' Course' produces efficient house-keepers who know their job thoroughly and are particularly good at 'feeding the brute'.

A less fortunate encounter with heating technology than the electrical experiments occurred in February 1930, and again the Ministry of Labour training course in domestic service was involved. One of the students, Agnes McDermid, was instructed to light the fire in one of the College kitchens. A frozen boiler exploded as a result, severely injuring the unfortunate student. Her skull was fractured, her nose broken, the hearing in her right ear destroyed and her arms and legs burned. The College's attitude was less than admirable — it denied liability, but in a jury trial at the Court of Session she was awarded £650 damages. The domestic service training scheme was mentioned again a year later in a jokey piece under the byline 'The Girl Next Door', with the remark 'Meet Jenny, the unemployed factory girl who is training for domestic service!'[25]

The College newspaper cuttings book contains a lengthy article dated July 19, 1932. Its source is not specified, though it is probably from the *Glasgow Herald*. It does not directly relate to the College, nor to domestic

---

[24] *Glasgow Herald*, November 18, 1933.
[25] *Glasgow Evening News*, April 20, 1931.

science, so it is of some significance that the College should have thought it worth preserving. It is striking how remarkably the sentiments expressed reflect those frequently voiced from the '60s to the present, for all the post-war revolution in tertiary education. Headed 'EDUCATION IN SCOTLAND' and with subheads 'THE PRESENT PROBLEMS', 'OVERCROWDING AND WASTE OF MONEY' and 'TRADITION MISHANDLED', the author, a 'Special Correspondent', claims:

> ...since the Universities are, in the ultimate resort, affected [by school graduates' wish for status and security] there is overcrowding of these ancient institutions, leading to tendencies to mass production, absence of the requisite leisure for the staffs to pursue their special studies, and, what is worse, a growing supposition on the part of the public that something is surely wrong with institutions that allow thousands of persons to go forth with a degree which, in former times, was something very distinctive, but is now becoming 'cheap', even though standards as a whole have been adequately maintained.

The author goes on to suggest the alleged phenomenon could be a cause of social and political discontent:

> The Universities were at the very peak of their numbers about 1927, before the economic blizzard set in. The post-war rush to the Universities has had little to do with conditions in industry and commerce. It is a social phenomenon to the encouragement of which the 1918 Act gave timely help by the lavish [sic] use of public money on secondary and University education which, while impoverishing local exchequers, to say nothing of the Treasury, has now bred an amount of disappointment that now finds vent in social unrest whenever the full force of unemployment is felt. In other words, the 1918 Act is now proved to have been as grandiose as it is expensive and was formed in that super-idealistic frame of mind which stern reality shows to be unsupportable in the workaday world.

A less neanderthal response to chronic unemployment was in fact developed by Mary MacKirdy, in her role as a member of the Women's Committee of Community Service, who established clubs in Glasgow's east end for unemployed women and the wives of unemployed men. At the Bridgeton club, according to Miss MacKirdy:

When we started the girls were depressed and did not seem to have the heart to be enthusiastic about anything. There is a big difference now. They are fit, for one thing, and many of them have brought along their mothers, or their children, or both. It has become a family affair. All the classes are well attended. We teach cookery, dress-making, swimming, gymnastics, country dancing, and singing, and we have not sufficient instructresses to cope with the demand. All this has been done with funds raised by the Glasgow and West of Scotland College of Domestic Science, plus the enthusiasm of the members.

She concluded that:

To be of real value, these clubs must not be regarded as emergency refuges for working people. They must be a normal part of the community … what is needed now is an enthusiastic group of people to start new clubs.[26]

Three years later the Lord Provost, Pat Dollan, a renowned figure in the labour movement, suggested that a branch of the College should be established in every ward of the city, comparing its educational work with that of the WEA (Worker's Educational Association).[27] Nothing ever came of the scheme, but Miss Melvin must have sympathised, describing domestic science as 'the Cinderella in the educational world and the purely academic women had often acted as the "wicked sisters"'.[28]

As well as the EAW summer school, the College was involved during the inter-war years in a number of other major public events occurring in Glasgow, the visit of the British Association for the Advancement of Science in 1928 and the Empire Exhibition 10 years later. At the first of these the College hosted a reception for the delegates and friends involving about 500 people. Following the greetings a Mr George Eddington replied on behalf of the Association with the rather patronising remark that 'no other branch of science provided more comfort and happiness for the human race'. As a result Miss Melvin, along with her Queen Margaret counterpart, was invited to attend the British Association meeting in South Africa the following year.

[26] *Glasgow Weekly Herald*, February 2, 1935.
[27] *Bulletin*, November 19, 1938.
[28] *Cumberland News*, December 17, 1938.

Miss Dorothy H Melvin with a group of ladies at a formal celebration in 1929. Miss Melvin is third from the left.

The Empire Exhibition of 1938, opened by royalty, was intended as a response to the depressed condition of the area and reflected current government concerns, initiated after 1932, to create an imperial trade bloc. The exhibition was not an outstanding success. Total attendance at 12.6 million was substantially less than the 15 million break-even figure and it lost £128,000. The deficiency was put down to unfavourable conditions and anxiety at possible European conflict[29] (the Munich crisis occurred while it was running). It may be speculated too that an exhibition of such a kind at a time of economic depression struck a false note (there was a degree of economic upturn in England by 1938, but not in Scotland). The College was involved in running a stall, placed in the Women of the Empire Pavilion. Its focus was on dietetics. Two 10-minute films were also made in the College for the occasion, but not on any nutritional subject. One dealt with upholstery, the other with millinery.

---

[29]P and J Kinchin, *Glasgow's Great Exhibitions: 1888, 1901, 1911, 1938, 1988*. White Cockade, c.1990, p.129.

It was near the same time, in September 1937, that Mary MacKirdy finally retired from the College staff, following 42 years' employment with the institution and its predecessor School. In 1935 she had been appointed a Fellow of the EIS. Her resignation, however, did not mark the finish of her career, for at the age of 62 she became a Nutrition Supervisor for the Community Service in Scotland. A College prize was instituted in her honour.

The Second World War

Angus Calder has characterised World War II as 'The People's War'. The term has political resonances, with reference to the conflict between fascism and democracy, but it also refers to the heightened level of popular consciousness and participation in public affairs, an appreciation of war aims, that marked this conflict distinctly from the previous one, as well as the even greater level of civilian mobilisation which accompanied it, especially after the fall of France in May 1940 and the establishment of Churchill's Coalition Government. The extent of the emergency was reflected in the extension of conscription to young women for war work, agricultural employment or the women's auxiliary services.

Given the centrality of food supply and other basic essentials to this mobilisation, apparent in such developments as the imposition of a universal rationing system and the creation of a Ministry of Food, it might well be expected that the College would be placed in the forefront of institutions required to train its personnel and propagate its purposes. Such indeed was the case. This time the building was not requisitioned, although until 1943 a barrage balloon unit of 14 men was billeted on the premises, in the badminton hall. An Emergency Committee of the Governors was appointed soon after the declaration of war to handle day-to-day organisation, and the immediate general policy was set out at a Governors' meeting on September 11:

> The Secretary reminded the Meeting that on the instruction of the Governors he had in May written to the Scottish Education Department asking whether the College should remain open in the event of war. They had replied without giving any instructions or advice but had indicated that the College should at least make arrangements for continuing the training of students training as teachers.... After discussion and

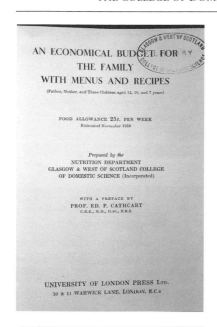

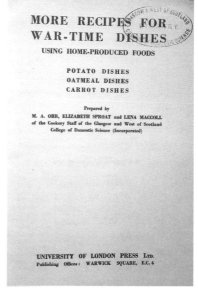

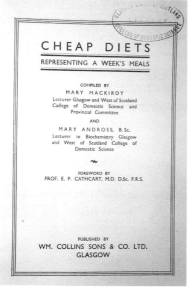

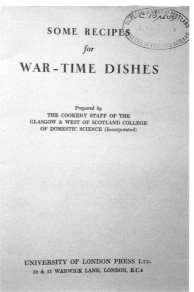

The Glasgow and West of Scotland College of Domestic Science World War II food publications. All four of these publications are part of Glasgow Caledonian University's Queen's College Special Collection, held in the Caledonian Library and Information Centre (CLIC).

consideration, the meeting agreed that it would be advisable that the work of the College should be carried on and the Secretary was instructed to telephone the Scottish Education Department.

A tunnel below the building (presumably from long-past mining works) which had been discovered in the course of its construction and now housed heating pipes, was converted into an air-raid shelter, and corridors were sandbagged.

Not surprisingly, a particular specialism was the training of military cooks, but the College itself provided from 1941 a military canteen for troops passing through St Enoch's railway station — a distinctive hexagonal construction decorated in the College colours of blue, white and purple. Up to 1945 it served over 1.5 million people. Red Cross work also featured from the first year of the war in the form of making bandages and medical garments and training workers in the skill to do the same in other centres.

There was no less strong an orientation towards the civilian population, and the following aspects give a picture of what was involved. As in World War I, staff went out to teach cookery in the kitchens of deprived areas, suitable addresses being obtained from the City of Glasgow Society of Social Services, and these demonstrations continued into mid-1941 when the MoF established a Food Advice Centre which took over the work. In the College itself there were evening demonstrations every week covering such topics as Catering Without Coupons, Expanding the Meat Ration, and Vegetables, Salads and Potatoes in Variety. From 1942 vegetables were grown in the College playing fields at Chesterfield Avenue, including experimental work with herbs and less common vegetables. A dried egg display was held in the College in February 1944, illustrating the multiplicity of uses to which dried egg could be put.

Beginning in July 1940 the College undertook to preserve fruit and vegetables brought in by the public and to do it in public so that the process could be imitated subsequently by those who brought them. Both bottling and canning were demonstrated. The scheme was then carried into the counties of western Scotland. In that year about 10,000 lbs were saved, around 1,700 lbs being done in the College itself:

Housewives will be able to have their fruit canned for storage until winter under a scheme started by a team of experts who will set out next week on a tour of Scotland. The leader of the scheme is Miss Andross BSc,

Lecturer in Dietetics, of the Glasgow and West of Scotland College of Domestic Science, assisted by teachers of domestic economy. They have offered their services free to can and bottle fruit during their tour. The demonstrations will take place in schools, lent for the purpose by the Scottish Education Department.[30]

Mary Andross was also responsible for another striking initiative in experiments with sources of Vitamin C, which she undertook in conjunction with the West of Scotland Agricultural College. The source she identified was dog-hips, wild rose fruit, and she recommended the method by which the syrup should be fed to infants and young children — though contrary to some public expectation the liquid, unlike orange juice, was not issued free but obtainable only through the shops, where it was in brisk demand.[31]

Miss Mary Andross, nutrition expert at the Glasgow College of Domestic Science, has made some remarkable discoveries about the properties of the dog rose hips, and hospitals all over the country are planning to take up this 'fruit' in a big way. Most exciting thing about it is that its vitamin C content is far higher than that of oranges — the puree contains 600 to the oranges' 30 and even the preserve rates 90.[32]

The College was mentioned in an *Evening News* report containing extensive suggestions on fuel saving, noting that 'saving of fuel is one of the economies that has always been an integral part of teaching at the College'. They included techniques for getting the most out of an iron with minimum electricity (an electric iron was assumed, rather than the flat irons heated on stove or range and still commonly in use); advice never to wash hands under running water; heating water in an oven previously used for cooking; economising on baths; oven-cooking simultaneous with baking; banking up fires — and advice to go to bed rather than light a fire in the evening.[33]

As the war drew towards its close, courses were opened with the purpose of re-integrating women service personnel into a domestic environment. These included a training scheme in home management established early

---

[30] *Calton Gazette*, July 6, 1940.
[31] *Daily Express*, February 4, 1942.
[32] College cutting book — source and date not indicated.
[33] *Evening News*, May 26, 1942.

in 1945 for ATS women. Reports in the local press revealed the cultural presumptions behind it:

GIRLS STEP FROM KHAKI INTO APRONS
Training for Demob Day
After years in the open air, drilling on the parade ground and toughening-up under military discipline, ATS girls of all ranks are finding ordinary domestic work infinitely more trying and a greater strain than any of their wartime duties.[34]

Today's ATS may provide tomorrow's perfect housewife. She will be a good planner, furnishing her home tastefully and comfortably, a good cook, an ideal mother and a competent person in the sickroom.... That's why the ATS Education Authorities are holding courses in home-making, one of which is in progress just now at Glasgow and the West of Scotland College of Domestic Science ... Their course also includes lectures by experts on such things as infant care, housing, choice of civilian clothes and budgeting.[35]

But one perennial issue appears at last to have been laid to rest. The *Times Educational Supplement* as early as 1942, discussing post-war developments in education and under the heading 'DOMESTIC SCIENCE COLLEGES', considered the broadening of their syllabuses and commented 'The household of many servants has gone, never to return'. A round-table conference in the College the following year was stressing the importance of wives and mothers having sufficient time to be good citizens as well and that their voices should be heard on public matters.[36]

Jean Haining
College staff, students and graduates were naturally involved in the women's service organisations (the College had maintained a large Voluntary Aid Detachment from the '20s), and not only in Britain but in a variety of foreign theatres. None of them suffered such a grim fate as a graduate who was involved in a different kind of undertaking. Jean Mathieson Haining,

---

[34] *Glasgow Evening Citizen*, March 9, 1945.
[35] *Glasgow Evening News*, March 9, 1945.
[36] *Evening Citizen*, October 23, 1943.

born in 1897 in Dumfriesshire, had graduated (and was a prizewinner) in the early '30s. The fact that she entered as a mature student — she had previously, following a business course, worked for the Paisley thread firm of J & P Coats — was due to her decision to undertake missionary work for the Church of Scotland among East European Jews[37] and to gain appropriate qualifications.

Following her College graduation she worked in a radium institution in Manchester, then after a further period of training at St Colms Women's Missionary College, took up in 1932 her post as matron of a girls' home of the Scottish Mission in Budapest — she had learned to speak the language perfectly. The school had around 300 girls, many of them Jewish, and about 50 boarders, likewise with many Jewish girls.

The Hungarian regime was of an ultra-right complexion, reasonably characterised as fascistic, established after the counter-revolution of 1919 and led by Admiral Horthy (though the country

JANE HAINING (right) (Jean Mathison Haining), an Institutional Housekeeping student at the Glasgow and West of Scotland College of Domestic Science in 1930/31, who died at Auschwitz-Birkenau. (Jane Hainings's last letter from Auschwitz can be referred to at the National Library of Scotland ref. Acc. 9548, G. 46a). *Photograph courtesy of John MacWilliam.*

had neither coast nor navy following the Versailles settlement). It became a close ally of the Third Reich during the '30s and a German satellite in World War II. Even after the outbreak of war, however, Jean Haining opted to remain in the country and continue her responsibility as matron although she now lacked diplomatic protection and was subjected to constant police surveillance.

---

[37]On the face of things this seems a very unusual choice, members of the Jewish faith not appearing to be very likely converts. However, one of the authors recalls a contemporary in his school in the late '50s who had a similar ambition.

Anti-semitism was rife in Hungarian society and politics but the Horthy regime, despite representations from Berlin, at least protected its Jews from physical molestation. In the summer of 1944, however, as the Red Army advanced towards the borders of Eastern Europe the Nazis invaded their ally, deposed Horthy and installed a regime run by Fernec Szalasi's Arrow Cross, a fanatical Nazi-style organisation and entirely co-operative puppet. Roundup of Hungarian Jews for deportation began, supervised by Adolf Eichmann: Jean Haining and her pupils were swept into the net. She was by then in poor health, having undergone two bladder operations earlier in the year. Deported to Auschwitz, she died there two months later. Whether she perished in the gas chamber (as her charges certainly did) or from the routine brutality of an extermination camp there is no way of knowing.

 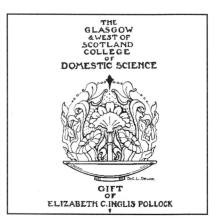

Bookplates for the Glasgow and West of Scotland College of Domestic Science Library. The bookplates were the work of Margaret De Courcy Lethwaite Dewar (1878-1959), one of the Glasgow Girls. Miss Elizabeth C Inglis Pollock had a long connection with the College and was latterly a Governor (1933-50). She gifted £150 to the College at the time of her resignation in 1950, which was invested and used as a book fund.

Chairs of Governors and Patrons

Sir Andrew Pettigrew's death in 1942 resulted in the chair being assumed by Osbourne Ronald Hatrick, who had been a Governor since 1927, originally representing the Trades House. His main business connection was with a firm of manufacturing chemists founded by his grandfather. Apart from members appointed from a variety of Glasgow institutions, Governors were elected by the Association, which continued as the legal owner of the College. By 1935 Hatrick was Convenor of the Property and Finance Committee and was made the first Vice-Chairman, only a few months before Pettigrew's death and his own subsequent elevation. However he did not remain in office very long, resigning in 1946 for health reasons.

Since its foundation the College had possessed aristocratic patrons such as the Duchess of Montrose and the Marchioness of Ailsa, but in 1944 it received the royal accolade when the heir-apparent, Princess Elizabeth, agreed to join the list. Osbourne Hatrick described it as 'a mark of royal recognition for the work which the College had been doing in the West of Scotland'.[38] This royal connection was to continue through the remainder of the College's independent existence and give rise to unforeseen complications at the time of its amalgamation.

[38] *Glasgow Herald*, December 21, 1944.

Chapter Three

The College of Domestic Science, 1945–1975

The experience of Glasgow following the Second World War was incomparably different from its fate in the years after 1918. To be sure, there was to be no restoration of its late Victorian position of industrial and commercial domination and pretensions to civic independence. There was, however, to be full employment—labour shortage indeed—and seemingly miraculous revival in the traditional industries. During the immediate post-war years production continued to be mobilised to the utmost, no longer to support the war effort but to cover the threatening trade gap, or rather balance of payments deficit. 'Export or Die!' came to be the Government's watchword. The immediate crisis was overcome thanks to Marshall Aid and devaluation, but thereafter the dynamism of a developing world economy centred on the US and initiated the 'long boom' of the '50s and '60s. In these favourable circumstances, reinforced by government regional policy, not only were new industries implanted in Scotland, but even the traditional ones enjoyed an Indian summer.

Full employment was accompanied with social programmes of extended welfare, most dramatically those of slum clearance and rehousing on an extended scale, which in the case of Glasgow created the enormous estates on its perimeter, bereft of social facilities and due before long to turn into major social problems on their own account. But they appeared to be a good idea at the time, and were only one aspect of the drive and planning of a government which purported to have social welfare and the extinction of pre-war deprivation as its lodestone and priority. Of course wartime austerity continued into the late '40s, taking the edge off the favourable social transformation and bringing about the Labour Government's loss of office in 1951, but in the following decade the public sacrifices of the wartime and post-war era blossomed into the consumer society and the epoch of 'never had it so good'. Combined, these processes were to result in radically altered social and cultural norms whose long-term effect upon the College was to turn it into an entirely different kind of institution.

Though in 1945 certainly much altered from what it had been on its foundation 37 years earlier, the features of continuity were more marked than those of change and it was still recognisably the same institution as in 1908. Thirty-seven years later virtually nothing was left of the old structures (except the building) — not even the name.

Post-war Developments to 1960

The transition from wartime to peacetime conditions was doubtless less dramatic than on the previous occasion as the degree of social continuity between the war and post-war years was much more marked. The foundations of the post-1945 welfare regime were laid during the war and these included expansion and renewal in both the secondary and tertiary education spheres. There was also the continuum of austerity. In the words of the College AGM for session 1961–62, 'Then there were during and after the last war, years of scarcity and "make do and mend"'.

The College had 1,453 students (full-time and part-time) on its books in the 1944–45 session, which rose to 2,039 by 1946–47. Thereafter overall numbers fell back (1,521 in 1952–53) — this appears to have reflected changes in the curriculum and the steady move towards a more professionally exacting portfolio (with the phasing out of more marginal qualifications and non-certificate courses) rather than declining popularity. Many of the students were drawn from the private girls' schools in Glasgow. Full-time permanent staff numbers rose from 37 to 47 between 1945 and the mid-'50s, increasing only very slightly over the following two decades. The annual student magazine was restarted soon after the war, but again, as with its original manifestation in the '20s, doesn't appear to have continued for very many years.

A feature of the post-war entrants was a number of overseas students. According to Dorothy Melvin speaking on her last Diploma Day as Principal:

A return to peace-time conditions had resulted in a number of students from other countries joining the College, among them girls

from the Gold Coast [Ghana], Turkey, Poland, and Belgium ...
There was at present a great demand for women with training in
domestic science.

The trend continued over subsequent years. Doubtless the revenue these
overseas students brought in made its modest contribution to coping with
the critical balance of payments difficulties of those times.

   As well as incomers the College also catered at this time for outgoers, for
in 1949 it ran courses for intending women emigrants to Canada. This was
connected with an organisation called the Scottish Committee on Women's
Training and Employment set up during the inter-war period to provide
'settlers' courses for girls about to emigrate to the Dominions and which was
revived following 1945 with the support of the Ministry of Labour and
National Service.

   A less successful initiative was an attempt to teach cookery to the boys in
Greenock Borstal, with the outcome as reported being that:

> Miss Gibson reported that the teacher from the College who had
> attended to give instruction at the Greenock Borstal School had arrived
> in the midst of an insurrection among the inmates and had a very
> uncomfortable time. The teacher was not willing to go back and Miss
> Gibson did not think the course should be conducted by the College. The
> meeting agreed and instructed Miss Gibson to inform the School
> accordingly.[1]

Nevertheless the College did provide a film for the Gateside Women's
Prison in Greenock. Elsewhere, in an interesting attribution of public
problems — in this case industrial ones — to private nutritional discontents,
the then director of the Royal Technical College, presenting the awards at
the College's graduation, noted that strikes were frequently occasioned by
disputes over canteen catering and claimed that they provided a convenient
pretext for discontents that really arose from unsatisfactory relations at the
bench or in the home. The expertise provided by the College could help to
overcome that sort of thing, supposedly.

---

[1]Property and Finance Committee Minute, October 22, 1948.

Syllabus and Courses

The post-war teaching of the College came to be concentrated in three major areas, trends which were consolidated in the late '40s, though their roots can be traced back to the inter-war period and beyond. The three were home economics, as domestic science had begun to be retitled (although the College continued to use the old title into the '70s) and which represented the College's central and permanent commitment; dietetics, which, as indicated above, Miss Melvin had identified as the key new development during her years as Principal; and institutional management.

MISS DOROTHY H MELVIN with a group of Glasgow and West of Scotland College of Domestic Science students in 1946.

The years following 1945 saw a shortage of domestic science teachers, which was attributed to the fact that the profession was entirely staffed by women and tended to suffer significant loss through marriage, accentuated by the falling age of marriage in an era of full employment and rising incomes, even though the marriage bar which prevailed until the war had by now been removed. A Special Recruitment Scheme was instituted in

1954 to encourage mature students to train as teachers. According to the
Governors' Report for 1959–60:

> First of all we wish to continue to develop, for those who will be teachers,
> a training on an ever-widening basis, equipping them with good standards
> of skills, but with much else. There is an increasing need for an informed
> scientific understanding of nutritional problems and of all the ways in
> which modern science and technology is affecting the work of the home.
> Equally important is a knowledge of social and economic conditions and
> community development so that teachers may follow the trends of their
> time and adapt the teaching of children and also of adults to contemporary
> needs.

Some forms of the contemporary needs are indicated in the Governors'
Report for 1954–55:

> Last year it was reported that the College had been asked to introduce
> certificate classes to meet the needs of men and women already in the
> Catering industry. This is a branch of technical education which is
> developing very rapidly in this country because it is found to be meeting
> a very great need as good cooking standards are essential at all levels of
> industrial and trade catering. Such education is also an essential part of
> new apprenticeship schemes established for different branches of the
> industry.

The College's initial course in dietetics was the first of its kind in Scotland
and its diploma, first appearing in the 1925–26 session, the only one
available in that country, being directed at trained nurses who wished to
qualify as tutors to probationers. In 1936–37 it became a postgraduate
diploma and certificate course and evolved throughout the war years and
was consolidated between 1945 and 1954 under the title Diploma in
Dietetics. The subjects included: chemistry, hygiene, phonetics, educational
methods, book-keeping and business affairs, cookery, electricity, biology,
physiology, dietetics and medical lectures.

From session 1954–55 the name remained, but the structure changed so
that the diploma was offered in two parts, Part I consisting of alternative
professional training and Part II being the specialised dietetic training
within the College. The course was then open to science graduates and

holders of a teaching diploma as well as state registered nurses. According to the 1954–55 prospectus entrants required:

> passes in five subjects in the Scottish Leaving Certificate or passes in four subjects, one of which must be on the higher grade.
> English must be included,
> or
> passes in the General Certificate of Education in five subjects at Ordinary Level or three at Ordinary and one at Advanced Level. English or English Language must be included....
> It is advised where possible one of the certificate subjects should be mathematics.

Miss Isobel S Gibson with Glasgow and West of Scotland College of Domestic Science dieticians in 1948.

Part II of the course, now specifically the College's remit, consisted of three terms' training in nutrition and diet therapy, physiology, biochemistry, bacteriology, and also short courses in chemistry, hygiene, phonetics, educational methods, book-keeping, business affairs and electricity. Twenty additional lectures were given by hospital consultants, and finally (as before) students were required to do six months' training in the dietetic department of a recognised hospital before receiving the diploma. Holders were eligible for membership of the British Dietetic Association and qualified hospital, school or institutional dietitians, or research workers in the nutritional field.

Social forces similar to those influencing the qualifications in domestic science and dietetics can be seen at work in the third major stream of the College's work, that of institutional management. The expansion of the welfare state and the expansion of commercial catering in a society of growing affluence brought along with it the expansion of institutions requiring to be managed and administered upon scientific and systematic lines. These courses were designed for students who wished to qualify for posts as managers in large-scale catering establishments, hospitals, industrial canteens, hotels, restaurants, the school meals service or other undertakings of a similar nature. It was reported at the AGM for session 1947–48:

> National Institutional and Catering Management Certificate:—
>
> The Institutional Management Association has instituted and examines for this new national certificate. The main difference between the new course and the former one is that after the examination at the end of a two years' College course, the student must spend a year in approved employment and pass another examination before qualifying for the Certificate. Formerly the Institutional Management student was granted separate certificates for different branches of study.[2]

The subject was a very popular one in the College, frequently being oversubscribed, no doubt because of the extensive employment prospects which it offered.

Staffing
At the beginning of the post-war period the academic structure comprised the Principal, heads of department, second mistresses and staff teachers.

---

[2]Governors' Report.

The Glasgow and West of Scotland College of Domestic Science student fashion show, 1957.

The Glasgow Caledonian University student fashion show, 1997.

The departments in question were Cookery, Laundrywork, Housewifery, Dressmaking and Millinery, Needlework, Science and Institutional Catering. Ten years later the post of second mistress became principal lecturer and new posts of senior lecturer were added (coincidentally or otherwise this structure replicated that of the English non-university tertiary system rather than that of the Scottish universities). The differentiation beneath head of department however seems later to have disappeared, the academic staff simply appearing under the title of lecturer.

The late '40s saw the retirement from College teaching of a significant number of its pioneers, among them the Principal herself, who departed in December 1946, describing the history of the establishment as 'a small enterprise in common-sense philanthropy'.[3] Her successor, in the obituary she wrote on Miss Melvin's death in 1963, noted that:

> In the purely academic field such attitudes [of contempt for domestic affairs] tended to make leaders of women's education belittle the skills of the home but Miss Melvin was to be a notable member of a group of remarkable leaders in the Domestic Science Colleges who saw the subject as part of a wide cultural education and also as the basis for expanding socially useful careers for women.[4]

The main College building was later named in her honour, though 'Melvin Building' later fell out of use.

Her successor was Isobel Scott Gibson, born in Glasgow in 1897, the daughter of a mathematics professor and herself a graduate of the College and of Glasgow University, with a BSc in Applied Science. She was obliged at first to cope with continuing scarcity and rationing but subsequently directed the developments referred to above and put a lot of work into the establishment of a proper library. A paragraph from a newspaper profile on her retirement contains the interesting comments:

> 'When I first started my college training teaching was practically the only field open to us. Now there are many more opportunities for our students — domestic administration in hostels and so on, dietetics, and, newest of all, industry.'

---

[3] *Glasgow Herald*, May 5, 1947.
[4] Isobel Gibson in *Former Students' Association Newsletter*, June 1964.

MISS ISOBEL S GIBSON, *OBE, JP, BSc*, Principal of The Glasgow and West of Scotland College of Domestic Science, 1947–1962.

Nevertheless Miss Gibson herself still believes that teaching is the most important job to be done. Homecraft properly taught in schools, she feels, can influence for good the whole family structure. She goes so far as to say that schoolboys should learn certain aspects of homecraft too — 'This is already being done in Scandinavia and America', she points out, and emphasises that it needn't mean teaching boys what they regard as 'girl's work', but 'simply equipping them to play an equal part in the partnership of marriage'.[5]

She was also a leading light in the affairs of the International Federation for Home Economics (defined as the exact and reasoned knowledge of all problems relative to the home and family; research and dissemination of research concerned with food, clothing, shelter, health and human relationships). It was founded in Switzerland in 1908 under the inspiration of a Swiss State Councillor with the unlikely name of George Python, and was the principal force behind the encroachment of this title at the expense of 'domestic science'. Isobel Gibson served as its President from 1958 until 1963, the first from Britain.

With the change in Principal the time was thought opportune for a change at the top of the staff hierarchy:

> The convenor explained that Miss Mackinnon and Miss Greta Melvin would soon be retiring and that Miss Gibson and he had discussed whether advantage should be taken of the occasion for some reorganisation of the staff. They were each of the opinion that as Miss Mackinnon had undertaken duties as Deputy of the Principal the time was opportune to institute the position of Vice Principal.[6]

With agreement from the Scottish Education Department one was advertised for, but the applicants proving unsatisfactory, a former College graduate, Miss Etna Jane Taylor, was head-hunted from Jordanhill College, where she was Principal Lecturer in Domestic Science.

Dorothy Melvin was not the only long-standing member of staff to depart during the late '40s. Her sister Margaret, always known as Greta, who had been Head of the Housewifery Department for some 31 years retired in 1948, the last of the original staff to go. The first of the institutional management courses had been started in her department, and was credited in the tribute minuted upon her death at the end of 1972 as having laid the foundations for the then existing Department of Social Science.[7] Yet another of the Melvin sisters, Muriel, also taught in the

[5]*Glasgow Herald*, December 21, 1962.
[6]Property and Finance Committee Minute, January 23, 1948.
[7]Governors' Minutes, January 24, 1973.

College after having transferred from the Glasgow School, though she left at the end of the First World War.

Meantime Mary MacKirdy, though she had retired in 1937, continued to preserve her links with the College. When the Bridgeton's Women's Institute, of which she was Convenor, was wound up in 1950 a gift of £200 from its assets was made to the College. *Her* sister, Janet, was also on the College staff, and when she retired in June 1947 was Second Mistress in the Housewifery Department — though she was not formally thanked by the Governors at her retirement nor at the AGM for 1961 was any reference made to her recent death.

KAY MATHESON, a former Glasgow and West of Scotland College of Domestic Science Group 1 Diploma student who was involved with the taking of the Stone of Destiny (Christmas 1950), pictured with Ian Hamilton (right) and Gavin Vernon (left). *Photograph courtesy of the Daily Record, c1951.*

So far as Chairs of the Governors were concerned, the marathon lengths of service of the early days were no longer to be found, though in some cases they continued to be of impressive duration. Hatrick as noted retired in

1946. His successor was John F Carson, who held the position for seven years and his successor, A I Mackenzie, stayed in office for 12. His retiral, 90 years after the foundation of the Glasgow School and 57 after the establishment of the College, finally saw the appointment of a woman to the Chair of what had remained during that time an institution staffed by women with an almost exclusively female intake. Princess Elizabeth, on ascending as Queen in 1952, continued as patroness, and as monarch was, as protocol required, necessarily the sole patron.

A footnote to these years relates to the episode of Christmas 1950 when Scottish nationalist students removed the Stone of Destiny from Westminster Abbey and transported it to Scotland (it was returned in 1951). One of the four was Kay Mathieson, who was a student at the College between 1946 and 1949. According to her companions the project could never have succeeded without her nerve and resolution.[8]

The Tertiary Revolution

By the early '60s pressures were building up within the post-school British education system that were to force it into changes and adaptations of a wholly unprecedented sort — though at first the main direction of the new strategy was to try to retain as many as possible of the characteristics of the existing system within an enormously expanded structure catering for immensely greater numbers.

In the first place a combination of improving secondary education and rising levels of income throughout the '50s had generated growing demands for access to higher education, available since the '40s regardless of income level and qualifying graduates for a range of expanding employment opportunities.[9] Secondly, the first tarnish was beginning to show upon the post-war economic miracle. Economic growth was characterised by the stop-go cycle, mild hiccups compared with what came to be experienced after 1973, but regarded very seriously at the time. It was also clear that foreign competitors, including former enemy countries, were drawing

---

[8]See Pat Gerber, *The Search for the Stone of Destiny*, Cannongate, 1992, and *Daily Record,* July 4 and October 22, 1996.

[9]'in 1938 only about 4 per cent of children aged seventeen in Great Britain were at school; in 1962 the proportion was 12 per cent.... These changes, reinforced by the steady rise in national prosperity, are now making their impact on the demand for higher education.' Robbins Report, pp. 11–12.

ahead of Britain in technological development and industrial productivity. The early '60s saw among government and political leaders feverish pursuit of a range of measures to address the underlying deficiencies of the productive economy. They varied from the establishment of the National Economic Development Council, to Harold Wilson's exhortation, to the 'white heat of the technological revolution', to application for admission to the EEC, to a revolution in higher education.[10]

The blueprint for the latter was the Robbins Report, though it is worth stressing, in view of its subsequent fame, that this document did not by any means stand alone. The Committee which produced it was instituted in 1961 'to review the pattern of full-time higher education in Great Britain and in light of national needs and resources and to advise Her Majesty's Government on what principles its long-term development should be based'. However five years earlier a White Paper on *Technical Education* had been published with the aim of promoting colleges of advanced technology in England and Wales and significantly improving the existing central institutions in Scotland. The Brunton Report, appearing in 1963, the same year as Robbins', proposed closer links between educational institutions and industry.

Robbins' main remit did not concern institutions like the College, though the Committee did take note of further education along with higher education, and there is in fact within the Report a passing reference to the Scottish colleges of domestic science (and all three gave evidence):

In Scotland nearly all full-time advanced further education is carried on in fifteen colleges known as Central Institutions which are financed directly by the Secretary of State for Scotland (excluding the Royal College of Science and Technology, Glasgow, which is treated as a university throughout the report....) Some are polytechnics, while others such as the Colleges of Art and the Colleges of Domestic Science, offer a narrower range of courses.[11]

---

[10]'But, in general it is not seriously open to doubt that if in any country educational investment in general and higher education in particular falls appreciably behind what is being undertaken elsewhere ... general earning power is liable to be affected ... the danger seriously threatens this country in the future'. *Ibid.*, p.207.

[11]*Ibid.*, p.33.

The Robbins recommendations had implications for the College as a Scottish central institution. These were covered by Nos 61 and 62. After predictably recommending the promotion of the most advanced to university status, it recommended:

> The others should either have some form of association with the Royal College of Science and Technology in its new role as a university *or should follow the arrangements proposed for the Regional Colleges in England and Wales* (emphasis added).

The recommendations in question were:

> 67. The Regional Colleges should develop a wider range of advanced full-time courses.

This was the one which was to be of immediate import for the College.

> 69. There should be opportunities for others, in some cases after federation with another technical college or a Training College, to become in due course parts of universities.

That might be regarded as prophetic, although nobody in 1963 would have taken seriously the idea of the Dough School becoming a component of a university.

In fact the line of the Robbins recommendations was beginning to be implemented even before the Report appeared, as the creation of Strathclyde University out of the Royal College was well under way. It achieved formal university status in 1964, doubtless to the satisfaction of John Anderson's ghost. Following the Report (leaving aside the transformation in England and the appearance there of the polytechnics under Anthony Crosland) Heriot Watt was similarly elevated and Dundee hived off from St Andrews, while Stirling was created as an entirely new foundation.

The College in Transition

The immediate influence of the forthcoming regime was felt in the entrance requirements for diploma students which came into effect from 1962 with a new Scottish Certificate of Education. Entrants through the Scottish educational system required a Certificate of Attestation of Fitness from the Scottish Universities Entrance Board or alternatively combinations of subjects in the Scottish Certificate of Education with a minimum of two passes at higher grade — there was also provision for entrance via the General Certificate of Education.

The new perspectives are embodied in the Report for the 1961–62 AGM:

> Now there is a very different picture: women working outside as well as inside the home, time more scarce than money, better housing standards, hire purchase, labour-saving devices and convenience foods, a growing consciousness of the place of art in everyday life, a different use of leisure. These are only some of the things to be reckoned with and always with the knowledge that present conditions may be no more static than those of former years.
>
> The changes in the houses of the country lead to a new industrial demand. Housewives who buy labour-saving equipment, modern man-made fabrics, and convenience foods are important consumers and there is now a place for women to act as a link between manufacturer and housewife and help to put goods on the market. They ... must have sufficient scientific and business knowledge to understand the manufacturer's problems. The College now offers a three-year training in Home Economics for Industry and Commerce and Journalism.
>
> Dietetics has entered a new phase, with the passing of the Professions Supplementary to Medicine Act which provides for Registration and for regulations for professional education and conduct.
>
> ... A new diploma course [in Institutional Management] of three years spent in College is now established.
>
> Of recent years encouragement has been given to older people with varied experience to train for the teaching profession. In 1962 a one-year conversion course has been offered to holders of the Certificate of the Institutional Management Association, the training being done at Jordanhill College of Education and in this College.

The plans which the SED had for its central institutions, corresponding to the Robbins perspectives, was to give priority to training at higher levels. Lower level tertiary education was being hived off to the local authority colleges which began to be constructed during the same period.

The days of the old short classes and demonstrations were numbered. It was not without heart-burning that the staff watched the classes being absorbed, in some cases at least, by the new young Further Education Colleges, which were rising in the city around it. To this day, many of the public remember College because of what would now be termed its 'interest' classes. None the less, those interest classes had an educational goal which from eye-witness accounts appears to have been fulfilled. Always the aim was the raising of home standards as it had been in the days of Grace Paterson and Margaret Black.

So wrote Ellice Miller in her centenary pamphlet on the College's history.[12] In the earlier part of the '60s some certificate courses (and even some public demonstrations) still remained but from session 1967–68 only diploma and post-diploma courses were offered:

> Discussions on the future policy of the College have been undertaken with officials of the Scottish Education Department and if the College is to take its place as a College of Higher Education then normally only courses of at least three years' duration should be undertaken. As a result of this policy, combined with the urgent need to train the maximum number of Teachers[13] and Institutional Managers, it was confirmed that September 1966 would be the last entry date for students taking the Household and Catering Management Certificate.[14]

The demonstration and interest classes were discontinued and the traditional craft courses were abandoned or handed over to the further education ('FE') colleges. It was not so much a question of academic drift as of a powerful and rapidly rising tide.

As early as 1960 the Governors had declared that, 'Equally important is a knowledge of social and economic conditions and community development so that teachers may follow the trends of their time and adapt their teaching of children and also of adults to contemporary needs'. By 1967 it was reported that, 'A fundamental review of the pattern and content of teacher training

---

[12]*Century of Change 1875–1975*, p.60.
[13]At the time there was a severe shortage of teachers in the Clydeside area. Any person with a teaching qualification who sought employment was automatically offered it.
[14]Governors' Report.

courses has been undertaken' and in 1973 the name 'Domestic Science' was changed to 'Home Economics'. According to the General Meeting:

> The importance of this lies in our greater freedom to develop the subject matter of Home Economics, to identify its elements and to study in depth selected subject areas.
>
> At the end of three years the College Diploma in Home Economics will be awarded to successful students and those who wish to teach will then proceed to the College of Education for their professional subjects and teaching practice. The others will enter the fields of commerce, industry and social and community services.

The definition of 'Home Economics', as expressed by the United Kingdom Federation for Education in Home Economics, has distinct ideological overtones:

> Home Economics considers the family as the most important unit of society and concerns itself with the development of each individual in the family, the education of the family as such, and the strengthening of values inherent in family life. It deals with the household and family life in all its aspects; moreover it concerns itself with assisting the family to adapt itself to the evolution of technological, economic and social conditions. It influences the attitude of family members towards the community and the nation by developing social responsibility and prepares them effectively to participate in family living.[15]

For the students costs were high — books, uniforms, scissors, knives and utensils all had to be individually purchased and material and foodstuffs were also extremely costly in the year of specialisation.

There were changes and refinements also in the Dietetics Diploma in the course of the '60s, though not of a far-reaching nature. So far as

---

[15]These overtones are even more apparent in the Diploma address for domestic science graduates in Aberdeen in 1967:

> Dr Foss stressed the importance of education of young women 'who may by their greater influence on society and by their instinctive desire for creativity, reverse the present trend towards destruction of all that is basically good in mankind'. He said in reference to the importance of training for domesticity: 'I believe that happy, purposeful family life is the greatest force for good in the community'. *Times Educational Supplement*, October 20, 1967.

institutional management was concerned, a diploma course was introduced
in the 1961–62 session and thereafter developed with expanding content
to reflect the changing needs of large-scale catering and industry. In the
late '60s it became a Higher National Diploma and was taught under four
headings: food services, administration of house services, social and
general studies and applied sciences. A mark of the expansion in subject
area taking place in the late '60s was the appearance of a new department:
'The subject known as Social Science had had a lecturer since early in the
sixties, but in 1970 a Department of Social Science and Communications
was formed'.[16]

The figures for overall full-time student numbers show an actual *decrease*
between the early '50s and the late '60s (777 in session 1953–54 as against
495 in session 1967–68) while the number on diploma courses continued
to grow (192 in 1953–54 as against 478 in the latter session), demonstrating
the trend which placed virtually every full-time student on a diploma
course. The number of part-time students fell from its highest figure of 735
in 1955–56 to 311 in 1966–67. In other words what had taken place was
a concentration of the institution's work — smaller intakes but more
extensive and deepening education for the students who did come in. The
137 students who enrolled in 1967 was a record first-year intake for
domestic science teacher training, not only for Glasgow but any Scottish
college.

The New FE Colleges

These deserve to be considered in some greater detail, both as a contrast to
what the College was becoming as its character was transformed, and
because they were to have a bearing on the beginnings of the other
component of the eventual Caledonian University, Glasgow College of
Technology. They were created partly to accommodate the lower-level
courses which were being hived off from the aspirant establishments, the
Royal College and the College of Domestic Science, and partly as a
continuing assertion of civic pride on the part of the municipality, whose
dilemmas are examined at greater length below.

Some of them did have comparatively long historical roots, others were
creations of the '60s. Among the former category was Stow College of

---

[16]Ellice Miller, *op. cit.*, p.62.

Engineering and Allied Trades, to give it its full title, which was named in honour of the same David Stow who had been instrumental in the foundation of the teacher training establishments. It dated from the inter-war years and when opened under the Corporation's authority in September 1934 was described as the largest and probably the most modern trades school in Britain, with approximately 1,700 students. It was opened by Sir Godfrey Collins, the great-grandson of William Collins, and in the circumstances of the 1930s its creation can only be regarded as a triumph of hope over then current realities.

The other institution in the same category was the Glasgow College of Building and Printing, whose origins went back to 1927 and whose initial title as the Stow Technical Institute also referred to this ubiquitous individual. It provided evening classes in, *inter alia*, carpentry, joinery, boilermaking and welding; the engineering related courses being transferred later to the new Stow College and the Institute being renamed the Stow College School of Building and Allied Trades. In the early sixties educational revolution its scattered premises were consolidated into a 13-storey tower block, taking along with it a small printing school (the Stow name now disappeared). Its initial complement of students was 3,752, with 280 of these being full-time on advanced courses at diploma level.

The new creations were the Central College of Commerce and Distribution (a somewhat confusing title, liable to give rise to the misconception that it was a central institution) which did retain a minor link with the past by incorporating a long-standing school of hairdressing; and the further education colleges at Langside, Barmulloch and Anniesland. The existing College of Commerce, a central institution, merged with Strathclyde University. The Central College's new building was erected literally across the street from the Building College, as part of the academic precinct that the Corporation was intentionally establishing in the redevelopment of the Townhead area (previously a zone of extreme multiple deprivation) and which was also to involve Strathclyde University and the future College of Technology. 'It is adjacent to other senior colleges of further education, in close proximity to the commercial and financial centre of the city, and convenient for transport services.'[17] It opened its

---

[17] *Glasgow Chamber of Commerce Journal 1962–3*, August 1962, p.359.

doors to students in September 1962 and was formally opened by Lord Craigton in May the following year.

On April 24, 1964 Harold Wilson, still Leader of the Opposition at that point, opened three of the colleges — Building and Printing, Langside and Barmulloch — simultaneously. The actual ceremony was performed in the Building College, the other two being linked by close-circuit television — presumably in celebration of the white heat of the technological revolution. As a central institution the College of Domestic Science possessed a considerably higher academic standing than those colleges, especially in the light of the '60s developments, though in ordinary public perception it doubtless stood on a fairly similar level or even lower — 'a set of crusty old spinsters, locked in some timewarp of antiquated values, attitudes and manners.'[18]

Staffing at the College

Isobel Gibson, Principal since 1947, retired at the end of 1962 just before the major transformation began to gather momentum. Her successor was Juliann Calder, who was born in either 1911 or 1916 and graduated with an Honours BSc in Chemistry from Glasgow University in 1936, then qualifications in primary and secondary teaching from Jordanhill College in the following year. Her relationship with the College began in 1940, when after schoolteaching in Kinross and Glasgow she was appointed as a science lecturer, with Mary Andross as her Head of Department. The appointment was made in a very informal fashion. A lecturer was leaving to get married (the marriage bar was still in

MISS JULIANN M CALDER, *BSc (Hons), Med, FEIS, FAHE, MHCIMA, FSA Scot*, Principal of The Glasgow and West of Scotland College of Domestic Science, 1963 until March 1975 when the title of the college was changed to The Queen's College, Glasgow. She remained Principal until 31 August 1976.

---

[18]Andrew Greig, 'The Do. School: Memoirs of a former Head of Department' in *Caledonian Perspective*, Glasgow Caledonian Alumni Magazine No.2, Spring 1996.

effect and applied to central institutions as well as schools) and 'brought along a friend of hers who might like to apply for the post. We liked the friend'.[19] Having joined the staff she decided to take an MEd, which was done in record time and with distinction. She had a particular interest in plastics and was on the Committee of the Society of the Chemical Industry as well as innumerable other boards and committees connected with her profession.

The first woman Chair of the College Governors was Mrs Margaret B Cross, who served from 1965 until 1968. Conversely male appointments to College personnel, other than boilermen, janitors and part-time lecturers, also began in the '60s. The first was Harry Rose, who occupied the newly created post of Senior Administrative Officer, beginning in January 1969. It was necessitated by the growth of administrative work as the institution's responsibilities expanded beyond what could be managed by the existing system of Secretary and Treasurer, a professional man appointed from among the Governors (that post continued to exist, but its incumbent acted as Secretary to the Governors only). Previously Harry Rose had been Chief Clerk at the Technical College in Coatbridge and became responsible for much of the day-to-day work passing through the Secretary's office:

The new appointment has proved to be most valuable. The reorganisation of the committees of Governors with Mr Rose acting as Clerk has enabled the administrative work of the College to be dealt with at greater speed and allowed the circulation of information to be carried out more efficiently.[20]

When Harry Rose took over as Secretary and Treasurer a practice was ended which went back right to the origins. All previous incumbents both of the Glasgow School and the College had come from the legal firm of Hill and Hoggan. Since the formation of the College there had only been four, and the Annual Report for 1971–72 indicated:

The Governors wish to record their appreciation for the long and excellent service given to them by Hill and Hoggan, who have been law agents in Glasgow since the early eighteenth century.

[19]Mary Andross, *Former Students' Magazine*, 1963.
[20]Governors' Report, 1969–76.

The new firm of Mitchell Johnston Hill and Hoggan will undertake the legal affairs of the College and this continues an association which spans nearly a century.

The first full-time male academic member of staff to be appointed was Andrew Greig, a graduate of Glasgow University in Economics and Politics and formerly a lecturer in economics and management studies at Napier College in Edinburgh. In September 1969 he commenced as Head of the Department of Institutional Management, newly created and combining catering studies, business studies and accommodation services. He published a reminiscence following his retirement, and in it remarked that 'The College ... was out of sight and mostly out of the minds of citizens in and around Glasgow ... should I go to the Do. School in the West?' He goes on to record that one member of his staff did not hesitate to let him know that the appointment of an outsider and a man at that was a major mistake and that his expertise, management skills, existed abundantly in the College, where it had been taught for years in relation to home and household management. 'The deficiencies of men, and their inappropriateness for certain kinds of work, was also made very clear.' However this was untypical, and though he was a 'natural object of curiosity' was otherwise treated with courtesy and sensitivity. There was of course no male lavatory for academic staff and he had to seek out that used by the boilermen and storemen. A vignette of the College style is also included:

> The teaching staff with few exceptions lunched together at a fixed time. There was a top table at which were seated the Principal, Vice-Principal, Secretary/Treasurer and the five Heads of Department. ... The top table was served by two maids, dressed in appropriate black. The rest of the staff had to shift for themselves and could start eating once it was apparent that the top table had begun. The provision of such a personal service, superior to that found in many a high class restaurant, was a new experience for me.[21]

He goes on to record that he found taking tea with the women Heads following lunch a difficult experience, owing to lack of common interests

---

[21]Andrew Greig, *op. cit.*

for small talk, but nevertheless refutes the stereotype of the 'crusty old spinsters locked in a timewarp'. The College staff, he notes, came from a variety of backgrounds, some were married, some had seen war service, some had come from other sectors of education and industry, others had travelled extensively.

MISS JULIANN M CALDER, MISS DOROTHY H MELVIN and MISS S ISOBEL GIBSON (left to right) all together at the 1962 Diploma Day.

Governing Body and Academic Council

A less high profile but significant change occurred in 1974, affecting the manner in which the College was governed. The SED issued new regulations which reconstituted the Governors as a Governing Body and widened its membership, although the Association continued to elect six members. Students now achieved representation on the Governing Body, with two representatives, one being the Student Representative Council President, the other drawn from the Student Association. Teaching staff were represented as well, and there were representatives from the Senates of both the city's universities. The first Chair under the new regime was George Parker, an accountant and one of the Association-elected members. An Academic Council had already been formed in 1973, again according to

SED regulations, and apart from senior members of staff included six elected rank-and-file members. One of those described the experience as initially a meeting where those assembled listened to Miss Calder, and information not previously available was shared with the Council members. However before the Principal retired it had become more of a working and debating collective. The controlling structures of the College were therefore by the '70s being brought more into line with the academic mainstream.

Expansions

The reorientation of the College's work and growing numbers of advanced students resulted in the extension of the institution's physical space. Most of the student accommodation in Park Drive was reconstructed for teaching purposes and new larger purpose-built Halls of Residence, costing around £300,000, with room for around 120 students took its place in Dorchester Avenue near the College playing fields. The complex was named Gibson Hall in honour of the former Principal. It was entirely gas-heated.

The Hall also incorporated self-contained flats for staff members as well as

> ... two self-contained home-management practice flats for students who live there on a limited budget for a week or longer while attending normal classes. The exercise forms part of the normal training of Teaching Diploma students.
>
> The purpose of the flats is to simulate as nearly as possible the condition of ordinary working women with homes to look after, and they supplement the home management flat which has been used for many years at the college.[22]

The first students moved in in the autumn of 1967 and the complex was formally opened by the Queen in July 1968.

A major building programme was put in hand around the same time in expanding the existing building with new wings and extensions. Planning had begun as early as 1962 and new laboratory space was opened two years later. The main work fell into three phases beginning in 1968. Phase II, which ran from the spring of 1971 to the summer of 1973, involved a far-

---

[22]*Builders Standard*, June 1968.

THE QUEEN formally opened Gibson Hall on 5 July 1968. Gibson Hall was named after MISS ISOBEL S GIBSON, College Principal, 1947–62. On the platform were MISS CALDER, Principal 1963–76, pictured left with MRS QUAILE, Chairman of the Board of Governors, 1968–71, pictured right. The bouquet was presented by the SRC President MISS FRANCES McGINNISS.

reaching reconstruction of the original building and was the source of great disturbance to all staff, academic, administrative and manual, as well as students, from disruption, noise, plaster dust and innumerable minor inconveniences. In Ellice Miller's words, 'it has sometimes seemed to staff and students that during most of the last decade training has been achieved with a constant background of banging hammers, if not interminable pulsating of pile drivers'.[23] The outcome was vastly improved accommodation, though also a rather unlovely jumble of architectural protrusions at the rear of the main building. The new complex was formally opened by Willie Ross, the then Scottish Secretary (he had also in 1972 opened the Glasgow College of Technology) on September 12, 1975.

He said that the former Domestic Science College had taken its place in the history of Glasgow for the uplifting not only of cooking but of

[23]Ellice Miller, *op. cit.*, p.62.

home life itself. He welcomes the diversification of the college into the field of social work, and the recognition of the need for students and teachers to enter the home so as to show people the value of home life based on the kitchen.

As his remarks show, Willie Ross was a very traditionally-minded individual, the stereotype of Old Labour's outlook in its Scottish manifestation.[24]

He had not in any case been the College's first choice. In March that year Buckingham Palace had given its assent to a request by the Governors for the College to have its name altered to the Queen's College in its centenary year:

> The name 'Domestic Science' has gone out of use and been replaced in the international field by the name 'Home Economics'.

> Throughout the years the College has developed courses which were originally based on the skills of Domestic Science but which have evolved into quite different professional activities. For instance Dietitians, Institutional Managers and Caterers require completely different courses from that offered in 'Home Economics' and it is difficult for young people to realise the variety of opportunity available in a College whose name suggests a limited field of study.

> … there is some evidence that future developments and recruitment may be impaired because of the limited field suggested by our name.[25]

Not surprisingly the Governors hoped that the Queen herself would perform the opening ceremony, but the invitation was declined since she was otherwise engaged. The next choice was Alistair Hetherington, the editor of the *Guardian*. He too turned down the invitation and only then was the Scottish Secretary suggested by the Principal — with an initial response by the Governors that perhaps Ross's politics were not in accord with those of the College. However Miss Calder noted that he was an educationist as well as a politician, so in the end he was invited and accepted. At the centenary dinner, during which greetings were read on behalf of

---

[24] *Glasgow Herald*, September 13, 1975.
[25] Governors' letter to Sir Martin Charteris, the Queen's Secretary, December 23, 1974.

representatives of the founders' families, the toast was proposed by Magnus Pyke.

Council for National Academic Awards ('CNAA') degree

The social work teaching to which Willie Ross referred, was then at the point of being introduced. A Social Sciences Department was established in 1969, with Dr William Roach appointed as its head in 1970. The initial form which Social Work teaching took was a certificate course for long-serving unqualified social workers who had to be nominated by their employers, and to enter Phase II of the three-phase course had to be over 35 years of age.

At last in 1976 approval was received from the CNAA for the College's first degree course, a BSc in Dietetics. The submission was prepared during 1974 in collaboration with Paisley College of Technology and in February 1975 submitted simultaneously to the Dietitians' Board and the CNAA. The former visited the College in February 1975 and the latter in October. Eighteen students represented the first intake in September the following year. The two Colleges operated with a Joint Board of Studies for a degree which involved nine terms of study in one or other of the colleges and three of placement.

> It is an objective of the course that graduates should be able to apply this knowledge of fundamental science, social science and dietetics in the service of people from widely differing social, cultural and economic backgrounds. For this reason the course aims to develop in the student the critical ability to evaluate and adapt his [sic] own disciplines and contribution to the differing situations calling for the services of a dietician.[26]

In the space of a decade and a half the physical shape, the educational purposes and the staffing complement of the institution (not to speak of the name) were all transformed in line with the new shape that tertiary education was assuming in the public drive to produce a more highly educated workforce and citizenry. The College's character at the point at which it changed its name is probably best described as a monotechnic

---

[26]From the Course Regulations, Schedule 1.

institution of higher education. Its similarities in essence to its Edinburgh counterpart, now known as Queen Margaret College, were close, though undoubtedly the Edinburgh institution had the advantage in every respect — from buildings (it had moved in 1970 to a magnificent new greenfield campus) to numbers and prestige.

Chapter Four

The Origins of Glasgow College of Technology

Although this College did not open its doors until 1971 its complex and convoluted roots stretch back into the educational revolution of the '60s. Its early days as a functioning institution could not have differed more from those of its eventual partner. Instead of birth in relative obscurity out of the workings of private philanthropy, making use of temporary, hired and shifting premises it emerged in glory as a new purpose-built complex standing in generous green space (despite its city centre location) and furnished with scores of academic personnel as well as state-of-the-art equipment (despite its chronic underfunding compared with equivalent institutions).

Establishing a modern centre of higher education from scratch is no small undertaking, and has happened only very occasionally. To be sure, a number of entirely new British universities (not counting institutions which received promotion to that status) were created during the 1960s. They comprised Sussex, Essex, East Anglia, York, Lancaster, Canterbury and Warwick.[1] Stirling was the only Scottish example. The fact that it all happened so recently and remains a taken-for-granted aspect of present academic circumstances obscures the reality that this sort of thing could only be a once-in-a-millennium occurrence. It was possible only because the full powers and resources of the state were deployed to support the enterprise.

[1] The University of Bath was new in effect, but formally was an existing institution migrating from Bristol to a greenfield site. Keele was entirely new, but dated from the '50s.

Even rarer is such a development arising from a local authority initiative. No municipality ever created a full-blown university of course, but even lesser institutions of higher education were scarcely within their scope. In fact there are only four instances, two of them Scottish. The earliest example was Hatfield College of Technology, founded in the '50s, followed by the John Dalton College of Technology in Manchester, which commenced operations in 1964. Its establishment was motivated by exasperation on the part of Manchester Corporation at the tendency of the city's three previous institutions, going back to Owens College in the nineteenth century, to jettison their non-degree and part-time courses as they pursued the route to university status. To cope with demand in Edinburgh for higher education outside the standard university system, Napier College, owing its existence to the city's Corporation, was opened in 1965 following the elevation of Heriot Watt. The fourth example was Glasgow College of Technology.

To understand its origins two sets of circumstances have to be kept in mind. The first, which has been referred to above, was the national development of higher education occurring in the '60s. In the middle of the decade this was given a further impetus. Harold Wilson not long after his election victory in 1964 appointed Anthony Crosland as his Secretary of State for Education. Crosland had very definite ideas about the nature of the good society which he saw as evolving out of the social revolution he was convinced the Attlee governments had brought about. He thought of higher education as valuable in its own right, realised that even beyond the Robbins Report projections a big unsatisfied demand remained, and he shared the general belief in its importance for economic expansion and competitiveness. In consequence his was the inspiration behind the creation of the English polytechnics.[2] The plan, embodied in a White Paper of 1966, by which time the Robbins student projections for 1970–71 had already been exceeded, was something of a compromise between desire for enhancement of status on the part of colleges doing advanced work, the sensitivities of existing universities (particularly new ones), and financial constraints. It did not of course apply to Scotland.

The second circumstance affecting the College's foundation is more particular to the locality and related to the overall position which Glasgow itself had arrived at by the time of the national educational revolution. The city which emerged

---

[2]See especially Eric Robinson, *The New Polytechnics*, Penguin, 1968, particularly pp.35–41.

from World War II was physically not very different from what it had been 60 years previously, but it was an epoch away from the peak of industrial dynamism and civic self-satisfaction of the late nineteenth century.

Its leaders, like their counterparts in the Scottish Office or Whitehall (though they might quarrel over methods), were conscious of expectations that the future had to be dramatically different from the inter-war years of depression and demoralisation; that economic planning was the key to sustained growth and full employment; and that welfare and amenity directed by central or local government represented the way forward from the blights of the past. Sydney Checkland entitled the relevant chapter in *The Upas Tree* 'The City Reshaped'. Comprehensive planning was to be the instrument, beginning with the Clyde Valley Plan of 1946. Housing was the immediate priority, with large numbers of the city's population occupying the most unacceptable housing, amounting to about 10 per cent, decanted to peripheral estates or new towns. 'Some councillors still hankered after the days of the second city of the empire, but most accepted the logic of reduced densities leading to overspill'.[3]

Nevertheless at the end of the '50s much still remained to be done. 'The Corporation decided that it must undertake a major operation on the inner parts of the city. It adopted a policy of Comprehensive Development... Between 1957 and 1960 Glasgow produced plans for one of the most ambitious slum clearance schemes in Europe, culminating in the 1960 Development Plan'.[4] Between 1960 and 1975 the city's population was reduced from just over a million to a little over 825,000 — more than a fifth of its inhabitants were removed by overspill policy. Many others whose homes were demolished were to be housed in the new tower blocks or high rise flats. At the same time the shape of the city was further altered by an enormously ambitious road-building scheme involving urban motorways, expressways, a new bridge and the Clyde Tunnel.

Certain aspects of this planning were to have direct implications for the future College. More generally, the desire to create a new and improved city, manifest also in significant cultural developments of the period, could not leave tertiary education out of the picture — the new further education colleges have already been noted. However, just as these undertakings were

---

[3]S G Checkland, *The Upas Tree: Glasgow 1875–1975*, University of Glasgow Press, 1976, p.70.
[4]*Ibid.*

getting into their stride the first serious signs of post-war economic decay were starting to emerge. Glasgow's incipient de-industrialisation was not altogether unintentional, for firms as well as people had been encouraged to relocate from the Comprehensive Redevelopment Areas, but this did not involve large numbers. A much more serious issue, reflecting a national and not merely regional problem, was the clear uncompetitiveness of much of British industry in international markets and the deficiencies of British entrepreneurship. The problems were reflected at one level in the fact that most of the firms which did locate themselves in the Clyde valley during the boom years were owned overseas or at least elsewhere in Britain. More dramatic was the clear crisis in the shipbuilding, locomotive and engineering industries which started to be apparent even in the early '60s. The great North British locomotive works closed down in 1963. Financial collapse and closure were endemic in shipbuilding by 1965, leading early in 1968 to the amalgamation of the remainder into Upper Clyde Shipbuilders, a publicly owned concern.

It was a very different chapter of the Glasgow story from that of the late nineteenth century. One response was to try to diversify by replacing employment in the manufacturing sector with the promotion of tertiary employment and doing it via public enterprise, either directly or by establishing the conditions in which private undertakings (shops and offices in the main) could flourish, especially in the Central Business District. This form of comprehensive planning had a direct bearing upon the decision to establish a major new educational institution.

To the north and west of the new Strathclyde University stood the Townhead district, an area of notorious slum housing and multiple deprivation, and on its edge the Buchanan Street passenger and goods railway station, one of Glasgow's four mainline stations. In the aftermath of the Beeching Report only the major station, Central, was automatically safe. Debate took place as to which two of the other three should close — Buchanan Street and St Enoch drew the short straws and a great deal of space was left for redevelopment. On account of its closeness to Strathclyde University and other educational establishments, the Townhead area was zoned and designated for educational development, the long-term idea being to create a precinct with only a small quantity of new housing and dominated by tertiary education as Strathclyde expanded and other institutions were established.

The concluding factors were first of all demand — the existing or anticipated demand for higher qualifications of a predominantly vocational nature both full- and part-time, which the universities would not be providing; and finally the question of civic pride. The principal English cities (and less principal ones too) were to have their polytechnics, under local authority control; Edinburgh had Napier College, and Paisley College of Technology brought educational cachet to Paisley on Glasgow's border even though it was a central institution and not owned by the local authority.[5] If the status quo of the mid-'60s prevailed, Glasgow would be the only major British city without a municipally-owned institution of higher education. It has to be said however that the city fathers were not at first unduly agitated by that prospect — presumably they felt that two universities and several central institutions sufficed for the city's prestige. The initial intention was simply to establish two high-calibre further education colleges to deal with academic overspill from the existing ones by absorbing their upper-level courses. The decision to transform this into a plan for a polytechnic-type institution of higher education took place comparatively suddenly and seems to have been motivated by the realisation that changing circumstances threatened to leave Glasgow behind in an exciting new national development. That development was the extension of CNAA degrees.

The New Colleges

Regrettably, a great deal of detailed documentation is missing which would have given a clearer picture of how the decision was made to establish the two new colleges and then combine them; likewise records of how recommendations were administratively implemented are also missing. For although the minutes of Glasgow Corporation and its sub-committees from the '60s are extant, the supporting papers that would have explained the detailed thinking and considerations behind the decisions have, with one important exception, not survived. The outline that can be deduced from the minutes themselves therefore has to be filled in so far as possible from personal reminiscence and less immediate sources such as newspaper reports.

The future of two further education colleges within the city, the Central College of Commerce and Distribution and Stow College of Engineering,

<hr>

[5]It was first established as a technical college in 1897 and received central institution status in 1950 — again indicative of the educational developments taking place at the time.

was relevant to the new institutions which began to be planned from as early as 1964. Virtually from the moment it opened the Central College was under pressure as courses were transferred into it both from institutions further down the line such as Langside College, and from the opposite end of the tertiary spectrum, Strathclyde University, which had decided to discontinue final professional courses. According to a document submitted to the Further Education Sub-committee, 'Within two years of the date of opening, the Central College of Commerce and Distribution was fully occupied and accommodation could only be found by using [five] annexes.'[6] In view of Strathclyde Senate's decision 'lasting damage can be done to the structure of Higher Education for Commerce in the city.'[7] The same document noted that a new Central College of Commerce had been fully planned and an architect appointed. Stow College, though over a much longer period, had likewise outgrown its original function; its building was cramped and lacked the space for the equipment necessary for the higher level courses it was developing, not all of them in engineering. 'The assumption, implicit in existing government policy, that higher education in the technical colleges was a temporary expedient, was generally accepted even by the few who recognised that it existed at all'.[8] This comment was intended to apply to the English situation, but can be readily translated into Scottish terms.

At a meeting of the Sub-committee on Properties of the Education Committee on January 29, 1965 it was reported that a site of approximately six acres for a new College of Technology had been incorporated in the Comprehensive Development Area Plan submitted to the Secretary of State for Scotland. Meantime a site of approximately three acres was required for a second college, evidently the college for commercial education.[9] On January 18, 1966, following further consultation and study of maps and models, the Planning Committee agreed that a site to the north of Buchanan Street goods station, formerly zoned for industrial purposes, be rezoned for educational, while part of the goods station area, intended for educational use, should be changed to public building purposes — it involved a slight shift in location, but in essence

[6]Document submitted to meeting of Glasgow Corporation Sub-committee on Further Education, June 18, 1965.

[7]Ibid.

[8]Eric Robinson, op. cit., p.29.

[9]Glasgow Corporation Education Committee Minutes (Sub-committee on Properties), January 29, 1965.

the Education Committee had its wish. The envisaged College of Commerce would stand approximately where the railway line entered the Buchanan Street passenger terminus. (At this point the station was still operational.)

In 1968 the construction of the College of Technology was underway, at a cost of around £3 million, and the decision taken to retitle it 'College of Science and Technology'. A Principal was sought and no fewer than 37 applications received. From a short list of six the choice eventually fell upon Dr Reginald J Beale, aged 46, who was at that time the Vice-Principal of Borough Polytechnic in London. His salary was £4,450, giving an indication of the change in relative values since that period — the salary of a Head of Department was £3,365. A sidelight on the appointment is provided by the fact that at the full Education Committee meeting a Cllr John Mains protested that the sub-committee which had made the appointment was inquorate, and in fact had consisted of only two individuals instead of the five there should have been. He was answered by the Convenor who agreed that the facts were true as stated, but the decision had been homologated (a word then much beloved in local government circles) by the Sub-committee on Further Education and Youth Employment and so was in order.[10] As Principal-in-waiting of the future College of Commerce, now also starting construction, the Corporation appointed Mr Frank Ebbage, the current Principal of the Central College.

Reginald Beale was born in 1922. His early career was in ship design — small craft such as torpedo boats as well as sailing yachts. He then studied for a degree in mechanical engineering at a London polytechnic, followed by lecturing and work for his PhD at Queen Mary College, London University. After a short period as a research fellow in the area of heat transfer he became Head of the Heat Transfer Laboratory at GEC, working on such projects as fuel elements for the nuclear reactor at Hunterston. Following this he was Head of the Nuclear Design Department at Atomic Power Construction, concerned with the design of the Trawsfyndd power station. He returned to the academic field as Head of Department of Mechanical Engineering at Hendon College of Technology and progressed to appointment as Vice-Principal of the Borough Polytechnic in London.

[10] *Glasgow Herald*, December 21, 1968.

The Working Party and the Amalgamation

As far back as 1955 there had come into existence the National Council for Technological Awards (sometimes known as the Hives Council after its first chair). It marked a very significant innovation and was to have a momentous future. Its remit was to approve technological courses of honours degree standard in approved colleges, though 'in deference to university interests … the award was not to be a degree but a diploma — the Diploma in Technology or Dip Tech as it was familiarly known.'[11] Approval was to be dependent on the colleges designing courses which satisfied the Council's standards following inspection. Following Robbins the NCTA format was adopted in the Council for National Academic Awards, which incorporated the former body and under Robbins' proposals replaced the Dip Tech with bachelors' degrees. NCTA-approved degrees were all sandwich ones, but with the establishment of the new body in 1964 under a royal charter all types were brought under its remit.

The construction of the new colleges, which had been conceived outside the CNAA framework, was well advanced when the Corporation became sufficiently concerned to authorise a working party to examine the prospects of bringing CNAA courses to Glasgow. It met for the first time in August 1968 — a few months prior to Dr Beale's appointment as Principal of the College of Science and Technology. Convened by Edward Miller, the Depute Director of Education, it contained the Principals of the Central College (Frank Ebbage, who chaired it), of Stow College, Langside College, the Glasgow College of Nautical Studies and the Glasgow College of Printing. Their eventual report, which appeared in May 1969, was produced as a fairly elaborate booklet, giving a sense of the importance accorded to it. Its remit was stated as being:

> To consider and evaluate the various means by which CNAA courses can be offered in colleges of further education in Glasgow; to consider the implications of offering such courses for the administration and government of the college(s) concerned and other colleges within the city; and to make recommendations.

After sketching the history of non-university tertiary education in Glasgow the report noted that Glasgow's 'civic interest in the promotion of further

---

[11]Eric Robinson, *op. cit.*, p.26.

education' was now represented by five major monotechnics, six district colleges working at lower levels and three small specialised centres. The commercial college and college of technology under construction were referred to in this report as monotechnics-to-be.[12]

It was noted that up to that point no further education college in Scotland was offering a CNAA degree and that 'Here is the opportunity for Glasgow to maintain the reputation it deservedly holds as a pioneer and leader in further education... serious and urgent consideration must now be given to the provision of CNAA degree awards within the further education system of the city'.

The report explained that to qualify for CNAA accreditation a college, whether polytechnic or not in character, was required to possess a large measure of autonomy 'with a minimum of detailed control by the maintaining authority', because only under such conditions could staff of the requisite calibre be attracted. It then went into some detail in explaining how such a devolution of control and academic autonomy might be instituted; that autonomy would necessarily include staff participation in college government, and in addition 'conditions commensurate with the level of work undertaken by teaching staff and adequate allocation of time for effective and efficient conduct of these duties'.

A major difficulty in this regard which the working party identified was that since degree level work was mainly carried out in universities and central institutions where salaries were much more attractive than in further education, the most highly qualified staff recruited to further education tended to transfer after a short period to posts in universities, central institutions or industry. If CNAA courses were to be instituted staff would require time 'for essential professional duties outside the classroom'. The following were mentioned: 'systematic meetings between staff, with representatives of industry and commerce, with external examiners and CNAA officials'. Essential tasks, which would include formulating, planning and preparing course structures, schemes of work and other organisational and administrative arrangements, research, consultancy and attendance at short courses would make 'considerable demands on the time and energy of staff'.

---

[12]A third was Glasgow College of Food Technology, built near to the College of Commerce and still functioning in its original role.

The report then listed the range of areas where improvement would be needed — library services, teaching accommodation and equipment, and staff workrooms, which required 'far greater provision than hitherto pertaining in colleges of further education'. 'Rooms accommodating from two to three staff seem to be preferred, and rooms for more than six do not find favour with the Council.' Dining accommodation, student common rooms and student social facilities were also mentioned. The working party had visited some colleges mainly concerned with CNAA courses — Brighton, Enfield, Lanchester in Coventry, Hatfield and Rugby College of Engineering Technology. It reported on college government in these institutions, library facilities, course structures, working environments, relationships with local authorities, and under 'Staffing' reported:

> Staffing was obviously most generous and matched the needs of the course in every respect. Staff work loads were in keeping with the levels of work being undertaken and took into consideration the whole range of educational duties. Thus, reading and preparation, research and publication, planning, committee work for courses, industrial liaison and student visits, tutorials, projects and laboratory supervision were all included in addition to the basic class contact hours, which could be very low indeed. The calibre of staff, judged by qualifications (usually higher degrees), industrial and business experience, and research experience was of a high level. The principle of appointing staff in advance of requirements and allowing study leave and return to industry for staff was generally accepted. The establishment of ancillary and supporting staff was, of necessity, very liberal.

The conclusion drawn by the working party was that with the initiation of the CNAA procedures, and its insistence that 'students for its degrees should study in an atmosphere comparable with that of a university and should, in general, enjoy similar facilities', it was necessary to concentrate such expensive resources in a relatively few selected establishments, and they pointed out that in England and Wales the polytechnics, while remaining part of the further education system, were officially given special status. Extension of CNAA practices to Scotland would require upgrading of selected local authority colleges and 'progressive modification' of the existing central institutions.

Observing that in Glasgow colleges with higher level courses tended to be specialised and monotechnic (though one may note the amalgamation in 1968 of the colleges of music and drama), the working party drew a comparison with England, where, it claimed, there was a move away from such structures in order to gain the economies and advantages of polytechnic organisation. It endorsed with enthusiasm the creation in Glasgow of an institution of that sort:

Such an institution would have considerable academic freedom and autonomy in government and would be capable of offering to students facilities to study both intensively and extensively at the highest level and to participate fully in the life of the institution. It would be possible economically to employ and deploy highly specialised staff thus helping to create a climate of advanced study wherein staff could promote their own specialisms while contributing effectively to the requirements of advanced courses....

For students there would be the possibility of a much fuller student life including better facilities for study, comprehensive sports activities, a more liberal and wider contact with students in other disciplines, better refectory facilities and a stronger student body with which to identify themselves.

The recommendations therefore were for the development of 'a substantial programme' of CNAA degrees in Glasgow and the identification of suitable colleges to carry it through. In this connection the two new colleges were specifically mentioned; others indicated as having the possibility of later becoming associated were the Colleges of Building, Printing, Nautical Studies and Food Technology. 'Thus a college structure hitherto unknown in further education in Scotland, will develop and call for a different approach to staffing, especially on the aspects of remuneration and conditions of service.'

The report then recommended the formation 'as soon as practicable' of a single Board of Governors for the two Colleges, while apparently assuming that in other respects they would remain separate institutions and went on to make particular recommendations regarding the composition of the governing body, the principals, the academic boards, the students' associations, library services — which required substantial upgrading from existing plans — concluding with an unconsciously prophetic statement:

It must be stressed that in all these matters relating to the government of colleges, the spirit and intentions behind the principles of the proposals should operate 'de facto' along with the 'de jure' position if full benefit is to be derived and the colleges are to develop into major institutions of higher education complementary to universities.

Finally, it was remarked that 'The recommendations may appear formidable — so is the task ahead if CNAA courses are to be successfully operated and developed.'

It would appear that the decision to combine the two colleges into one must have been taken in the succeeding months. The full Education Committee finalised the proposals on April 3, 1970. The question then arose of what to do about the fact that two individuals had already been appointed as Principals of the separate establishments. It was agreed in the first instance that they should be offered posts as Depute Directors of the merged College, with the post of Director (rather than Principal), which conformed with polytechnic practice and carried a salary augmentation of £500, advertised separately. This decision was confirmed in August 1970, at which point the Town Clerk was authorised to proceed with the establishment of a Governing Council for the College.[13] In the event, however, Dr Beale became Director of the College with Mr Ebbage as one of his Depute Directors.

The minute of this decision (as throughout the working party report) refers to 'a polytechnic establishment', and that of the full Education Committee the following month 'a polytechnic organisation' whose Governing Council in order to meet CNAA requirements 'would have a very much greater degree of autonomy than the existing Boards of Governors of further education colleges'.[14] An Instrument and Articles of Government for the College was compiled on October 1 and the scheme approved by the Secretary of State on November 25, 1970.

Moving in
The initial meeting of the Governing Council took place on January 28, 1971. The Director's notes for his report to the meeting have survived, and begin with a definition of 'a polytechnic establishment of higher education' — ie one dealing exclusively with work above SCE higher grade or ONC/

---

[13]Glasgow Corporation Education Committee (Sub-committee of Further Education and Youth Employment), August 28, 1970.
[14]Glasgow Corporation Education Committee, September 18, 1970.

SNC and including provision for first degree and postgraduate work. He regarded 3,000 full-time or equivalent students as a reasonable capacity, with academic staff numbering 300–350 and non-academic staff 150. Noting that the present courses scheduled to move into the College were mainly vocational in aim he suggested, interestingly, that 'this vocational aspect may well decrease'. Ironically, in view of what was to happen later, the notes state that 'success and future of the college is really in the hands of the Governing Council' and that 'Academic policy [is] firmly in the hands of the Academic Board'.

Observing that the Instrument and Articles of Government were very similar to those of polytechnics south of the border and generally similar to Scottish central institutions, he mentioned 'immediate difficulties' as being those of forming an integrated academic community, attracting sufficiently good staff with experience of higher education — likewise administrative staff and technicians — and recognition by the schools, public, etc of the new College as a centre of higher education.

A document presented to this meeting consisted of extracts from a report by the Director of Education agreed by the Education Committee in March 1970, which laid down guidelines for class contact hours for staff engaged in degree provision as follows: lecturers, 10–15 hours per week; senior lecturers 8–10 hours per week; and Heads of Department 3–6. This, it was surmised, should leave adequate time for these staff members to conduct appropriate research, according to the requirements of the CNAA. Moreover:

> The new College of Commerce and Glasgow College of Science and Technology, which will combine to form the Glasgow College of Technology, were designed essentially as colleges of further education. Particular attention will require to be paid to the provision of adequate staff work room accommodation, small rooms for tutorials and interviews, dining areas, common rooms and rooms for social and recreational activities.[15]

This was spelled out more explicitly in a further document, so that 'senior staff each has his or her own room, and other staff should be generally sharing a room with one other person' — it is interesting to note that this

---

[15]Extracts from a report by the Director of Education accepted in principle by the Education Committee in March 1970.

still remained an unachieved target for the College (by then the Polytechnic) in the early 1990s.

Two eminent individuals were elected respectively as Chair and Vice-Chair of the Governing Council: Mr George H Moore and Mr Charles Oakley. George Moore came originally from the mining town of Abertilly, where he had been a mineworker, but which he left in the early '20s to serve for six years in the Royal Tank Corps, and following that had a variety of jobs in agriculture, engineering and salesmanship, during which he was engaged in trade union and Labour Party work. At the same time he continued studying with a renowned independent working-class network of the time, the National Council of Labour Colleges, taking courses in Economics, Sociology, Trade Union History, Political Philosophy, etc. In Glasgow by this time, he attended a course on Personnel Management and Industrial Relations.

During the Second World War he was employed by the Air Ministry as an engineer at various aircraft establishments, the final one being Prestwick. He was agent for more than one Labour MP and was himself elected as a councillor for Ayr Burghs. Following a spell of two years as Northern Organiser of the Tobacco Workers' Union, he finally settled in Scotland as the Scottish Secretary of the Industrial Orthopaedic Society and was elected as Councillor in 1955 to represent Cowcaddens ward, which he continued to do until his retirement from the Corporation in 1970. Holding various chairs within the Corporation structure, he was particularly interested in education, was Vice-Chair and Chair of the Education Committee and was responsible for the building and equipping of the further education colleges of the '60s. He was elected a Fellow of the Educational Institute of Scotland and ended his Corporation career as Bailie and Deputy Leader of the Labour group. It was because of his activities in the Scottish Trades Union Congress that he was nominated as one of its three members on the Council.[16]

He continued as Chair until his chronic ill-health, ultimately due to his period as a mineworker, deterred him from seeking re-election in 1980. He was then unanimously voted Honorary President of the College, and accepted the honour in person, but unhappily died in December of the same year. The main building of the College was renamed the George Moore Building in recognition of his dedicated service to the institution.

---

[16]GCT *Contact* No. 3, May 1977.

MR GEORGE H MOORE, *JP, DL, FEIS*, first Chairman of the College of Technology's Governing Council, January 1971 to September 1980. One of the University buildings is named after him.

Charles Oakley grew up in Plymouth, moved to Scotland and served a six-year apprenticeship as a naval architect in John Brown's shipyard at Clydebank. With shipbuilding prospects destroyed by the 1920s shipbuilding slump, he decided to specialise in technical education, qualified by courses at Jordanhill College and Glasgow University, while writing freelance articles for Glasgow's then three evening newspapers. According to his own account it was largely by accident that he became a psychologist, first at Aberdeen and then Glasgow University, the latter in industrial psychology, the lectureship having been established by the Glasgow Chamber of Commerce. He was a founder of the British Film Institute and the Chair of the Scottish Film Council for almost 40 years, as well as the founder of a very successful soup-making food company.

Seconded to the civil service during the Second World War, he was the Scottish Regional controller of the Ministry of Aircraft Production, and in the post-war years Scottish Controller of the Board of Trade — his last chief being Harold Wilson. He then returned to lecture at Glasgow University until his retirement in the early 1970s. During this period he wrote voluminously, both books and journalism, his best known volume probably being his history of Glasgow, *The Second City*. While undertaking these commitments, sufficient for any ordinary individual, Charles Oakley was also Convenor of the Chamber of Commerce's Education Committee, and in the 1960s President of the Glasgow Chamber and then the Association of Scottish Chambers — and these were only his main responsibilities.

He records that he hesitated before agreeing to be Vice-Chair of the College's Governing Council (he was already the Chair of Glasgow Central College of Commerce), and that Dr Beale, who had never previously been in Scotland, had hesitated likewise about accepting the Principal's position. Seldom can there have been an individual who combined in his person so fully the roles of academic, business leader and cultural expert. Following his retirement as a Governor, the newly-built Charles Oakley Laboratories were named in his honour in 1992.

The same meeting received a list of the courses to be transferred to the new College, covering full-time, full-time sandwich, block release, day release, and other part-time day — not counting part-time evening. A considerable number of separate courses were involved, 57 in all, ranging from the Optics and the London External BSc degrees, to certificates and diplomas in public administration, data processing, police studies, engineering and marketing. The first students arrived in April, 60–70

Dr Charles Oakley, *CBE, JP, LLD*, first Vice-Chairman of the College of Technology's Governing Council, elected January 1971. He remained an Honorary Life President of the College. In 1992 the Charles Oakley Laboratories were named after him.

ophthalmic students transferred from Stow College. By the end of the summer, staff in other disciplines were in the process of being installed. An advert in the *Times Higher Education Supplement* early in 1971 sought lecturers in biochemistry, human physiology, microbiology, general biology, economics, economic history, psychology, sociology, inorganic chemistry, physics, accountancy and costing, management studies, marketing, business administration, computer science, mathematics, communication, mechanical engineering and civil engineering. The prefatory remarks are interesting:

> The Governing Council invite applications for posts in this completely new polytechnic institute of higher education offering CNAA and London (External) degrees, diplomas and professional courses. Applicants must be able to offer one or more of the following...

The salary scale for the time was £1,400 to £2,600, plus £100 for approved teacher training. The detailed specifications of the appointments stated that preference would be given to candidates with higher degrees and research experience and that the successful applicants would be 'expected to face and overcome the inevitable problems that will arise from running new courses in a new college'. In spite of the references to 'polytechnic institute' however, the appointment letters made it clear that they were 'in the Further Education service of the Corporation' and that conditions of service would be 'in accordance with the Corporation's arrangements for full-time teaching staff employed in Further Education'.

The reference to new courses reflected an intention rather than a reality at that point. All of the courses for which these appointments were being advertised were already in existence, running in the further education colleges, and they, along with the initial corps of teaching staff, were transferred from there.[17] A more unkind description of what was happening would have been asset-stripping, taking away from these colleges the high level work that they had built up over the previous decade. Although it does not appear in the documentation, recollection among those involved makes it clear that there was much angst and bitter resentment generated among the staff at the affected colleges over who was going to be transferred to the enviable conditions of the new establishment with its higher education cachet and who was going to have to remain behind with the lower grades. Additionally, new staff were being recruited from outside to make up the required complement. Without any doubt, for its first students and staff the

---

[17] An intention to introduce a degree in nautical studies in collaboration with the Nautical College never came to fruition.

College opened on a wave of hope and expectation — it was seen as embodying the new educational perspectives that had been developing in the '60s, of a non-university sector of higher education which would run according to its own structures and agendas and would avoid some of the less commendable features of the traditional universities or indeed the newly promoted ones. It was also a time when, although resources were never as plentiful as academics would have liked them to be, they continued to be lavish in comparison with what was to come, and the recurrent traumatic squeezes of the future were never imagined.

Original sins?

It cannot be denied that although Glasgow College of Technology and its successor institutions fulfilled the hopes that had been placed in the institution initially so far as the provision of high-quality education was concerned, they have experienced a troubled history in terms of their management, staff reactions and interrelations with outside bodies. The question that suggests itself here is whether there was any element in the College's original character which predisposed it and its successors in such a direction, or whether the problems were contingent misfortunes that could have been avoided with better perception and guidance.

The truth, as so often in these cases, is almost certainly divided between the two, and so far as the inbuilt problems are concerned, they derive from the fact that the College was created near the very end of the period of institutional expansion in higher education[18] and the fact that two institutions very different in intention were planned on the same site and then rather hurriedly combined. Added to that were the additional complexities in the Scottish tertiary education system compared with England and Wales. The College, although established and funded by the local authority, and therefore constitutionally lying in the further education sector, was obliged on account of its educational objectives (like Napier in Edinburgh) to compare itself with central institutions in Scotland and polytechnics in England and Wales.

These considerations had serious consequences in relation to resourcing and turned the College into a poor relation in the field of Scottish higher education. Tensions and conflicts could not fail to be generated at various

---

[18]Expansion in other respects of course continued.

levels from such an environment, both between the College and its funding authorities and within the institution itself. They were exacerbated by a particular form of management style. There was however no necessary reason why initial difficulties of that sort should not have been transcended in subsequent decades given stability and controlled evolution in the higher education system at large. That however was exactly what did not occur, thanks to the shifts and perspectives of government policy which regarded higher education at all levels, but especially in the new institutions, as being likely to benefit from a more top-down and line-management style of governance that academics were liable to find congenial or regard as appropriate to the sector. Conflicting initiatives and reactions which in more fortunate circumstances might have faded away tended to become ingrained and conditioned over the years. The point is reinforced by the fact that the kind of problems which the institution faced throughout the '80s and '90s have been in no way confined to Glasgow College of Technology/ Caledonian University but have recurred regularly in various establishments of British higher education over the same period.

LORD NICKSON, MRS CELIA URQUHART, PROFESSOR HAMISH WOOD and PROFESSOR STAN
MASON at the graduation and awards ceremony, 25 November 1994.

Glasgow Caledonian University Coat of Arms, incorporating aspects of both the Coats of
Arms of the former Glasgow Polytechnic and The Queen's College.

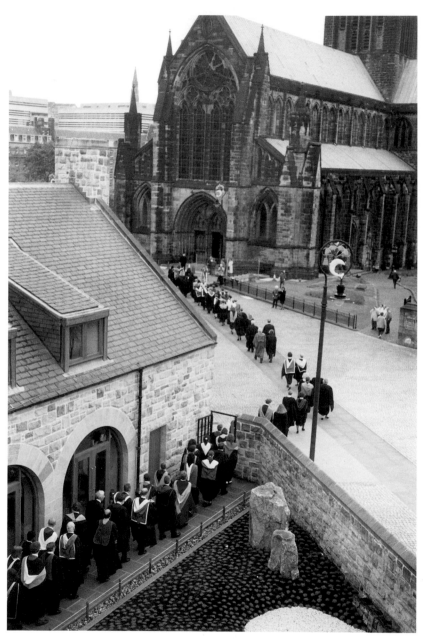

The inauguration ceremony procession entering Glasgow Cathedral through the St Mungo Museum of Religious Life and Art, 2 June 1993.

Glasgow Caledonian University's highest honour, Honorary Doctorate of the University
(D. Univ.) was given to NELSON MANDELA at a ceremony in Buckingham Palace on
10 July 1996. At this ceremony he received honorary degrees from eight Universities,
Glasgow Caledonian, Warwick, Bristol, Cambridge, Oxford, London, De Monfort and
Nottingham. Glasgow Caledonian University Chancellor, Lord Nickson, is pictured on the
far right.

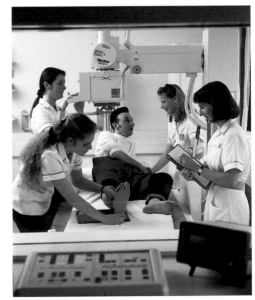

Radiography students at Glasgow
Caledonian University.
Photograph by Renzo Mazzolini.

Embroidery (and detail) for the
Glasgow Caledonian University
Chaplaincy, designed by Malcolm
Lochhead, Senior Lecturer in
the Department of Consumer
Studies. It was created under his
direction by the Glasgow
Embroiderers' Guild for
Reverend Christine Goldie,
University Chaplain, on behalf
of students, staff and visitors.
Photograph by Renzo Mazzolini.

Stow College, 43 Shamrock Street, Glasgow, one of the University's affiliated colleges and very much part of Glasgow College of Technology's initial development. *Photograph courtesy of Stow College.*

One of Glasgow Caledonian University's student halls of residence — Caledonian Court, Dobbies Loan, Glasgow. Opened in October 1995, this accommodation offers places to 320 students sharing self-catering flats.

Glasgow College of Technology — the George Moore Building.
Photograph by Stuart Menlaws.

One of the bars that make up part of Glasgow Caledonian University Students' Union.
This is The Refuge, part of The Asylum at City Campus.

Graduating students at Glasgow Caledonian University.
Photograph by Renzo Mazzolini.

Graduation day, showing the University colours. *Photograph by Renzo Mazzolini.*

Glasgow College of Building and Printing, 60 North Hanover Street — one of the University's affiliated colleges.
Photograph courtesy of Glasgow College of Building and Printing.

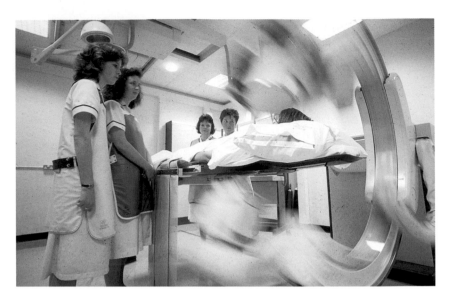

Glasgow Caledonian University students at work — Faculty of Health.

Above: Glasgow Caledonian University — a science lab.

Right: University students at City Campus.
Photograph by Renzo Mazzolini.

University students at work in the Norman and Janey Buchan Reading Room, officially opened on 17 May 1996, and a well-used part of Caledonian Library and Information Centre (CLIC). *Photograph by Renzo Mazzolini.*

Glasgow College of Food Technology, 230 Cathedral Street, Glasgow — one of the University's affiliated colleges. *Photograph courtesy of Glasgow College of Food Technology.*

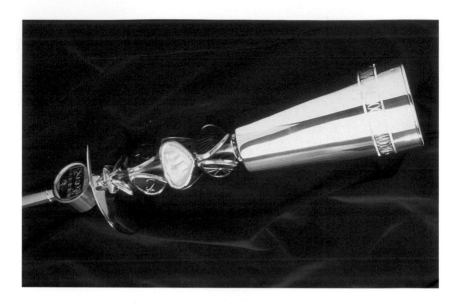

Above: The University Mace, gifted by the Universities of Glasgow and Strathclyde. The Caledonian Mace is the first mace this century to be produced in Scotland for a Scottish University. *Photograph by Stuart Menlaws.*

Left: The courtyard of the University's Britannia Building, officially opened on 30 August 1995. This £4 million Financial Services Centre was financed by an innovative partnership between Glasgow Caledonian University and Britannia Life Ltd. It was designed by Glasgow architects SBT Keppie and houses the Departments of Risk and Financial Services and Finance and Accounting, as well as the University Management Group. *Photograph by Renzo Mazzolini.*

Chapter Five

Queen's College, 1975–1992

The major reorientation that Queen's College was about to undergo from the middle of the '70s was symbolised not only by the introduction of a degree course but by the retirement of its Principal, and even more dramatic, the appointment of a man to be her successor.

The Principal retired at the end of August 1976 and one of the new extensions was named the Calder Wing in her honour. Geoffrey Richardson was 40 years old at the time of his appointment, a graduate in geography from Cambridge University, with schoolteaching experience in England and Australia. Before coming to Queen's College he was senior tutor at

The newly named Queen's College, Glasgow, with the new Calder wing, completed in 1975. The Calder wing was named after Miss Juliann M Calder, College Principal from 1963–1976.

Ilkley College of Education. A man of wide interests, he fished, ran three miles every morning, was principal clarinettist in the Cambridge University Orchestra and subsequently played in several musical societies, including a swing band. During the period of his Principalship he completed a doctorate at Glasgow University.

The appointment evoked a considerable degree of local press interest, a lot of it frivolous:

> A man is taking charge for the first time at Scotland's female bastion of haute cuisine. But no women's lib students at the old Dough School — now Queen's College, Glasgow — are expected to burn their cakes in protest [a nudge-wink reference to the alleged feminist practice of bra-burning].
>
> … Though he beat many women applicants to the post, Lancashire born Mr Geoff Richardson is not conscious of striking a blow for men's lib[1].

More seriously:

'I'm not a new, dynamic Principal putting right the old Dough School. Changes have been going on here for a long time, it's just that the pace is quickening.' A timetable for the quickening has already been established; this term is one of re-assessment for departments, individual members of staff and students — all of which will 'culminate in a staff conference in February [1977] to decide short and long term priorities.' The long-term priorities, according to Richardson, will be a general upgrading of the academic standards of the college. 'We are not a school and we are not a finishing school for girls in domestic arts.'

Dr GEOFFREY RICHARDSON, *MA, PhD, Cert Ed, Dip Ed Man*, the first male Principal of The Queen's College, Glasgow, 1 September 1976 to January 1991.

---

[1] *Sunday Express* August, 1976.

Whatever trepidation the Dough School staff may have had about the appointment of a man to lead their diversified and enlarged college, they couldn't have envisaged themselves faithfully following a track-suited, clarinet-playing, Lancastrian pied-piper round the new building in Park Drive.[2]

This piece was entitled 'In it for domestic dough'. Richardson strongly objected to the continued use of the 'Dough School' name and was said even to reprove taxi drivers who used it.

Management Developments

A member of the College's senior management, Andrew Greig, Head of Management Studies, did his MBA thesis on the planning and evolution of strategy in a small college, namely his own, in its efforts to solve its problems by adopting more systematic and explicit approaches to planning. What follows is based upon his findings.

One of the Principal's first moves was to set up a senior management team to provide more formal planning and devise a development plan. It was composed of the Principal himself, his Vice-Principal, Miss C M Lowe, the Secretary and Treasurer, Harry Rose, and five academic Heads of Department. The following problems were identified.

1. Market conditions as far as student recruitment was concerned had been relatively benign for some decades. The College held an advantage in the market for the training of home economists on high level courses as the only institution doing this kind of work in the West of Scotland. The College was identified in the public mind with domestic science and home economics, and in the 1950s and 1960s demand for teachers in these subjects continued to rise. However a decline had set in from 1974, only partially compensated for by increases in institutional management and social work.

2. Staff recruitment was beginning to be a problem. In the previous two decades it had not been difficult to find staff of the requisite calibre. Nearly all had come from home economics teachers in schools, people of similar

---

[2]*Glasgow Herald*, September 16, 1976.

background and training who shared the values of the College staff and for whom a college post was an attractive career move. In this context staff turnover was extremely low, with an average length of service of 11 years and some of 20–25 years. As courses began to change in character and become more multi-disciplinary, new kinds of staff were needed, often people of a different background and training who would not be attracted by the College ethos.

3. There were questions regarding the economic use of resources. The staff/student ratio of 1: 8.7 was too generous in relation to SED recommendations, which was 1:10 and more time needed to be spent on staff development and research. The system for internal resource allocation lacked sophistication.

4. Problems relating to the organisational structure of the College were serious, with evidence of deteriorating communication, frustration of attainment of group objectives and alienation of significant numbers of staff. Overall the existing organisational structure was no longer adequate to meet the needs arising out of changing circumstances, such as the increased range of courses, new subject inputs and the development of an increasing service function of departments for each other. Questions of research, course development and industrial liaison were also mentioned in this connection.

College achievements, strengths and weaknesses were assessed. The achievements included the reputation the institution had attained throughout the world for training home economists; growth in numbers; expansion in physical terms; diversification of course provision; and staff expertise. Strengths included the regard in which the College was held by the SED, long term links with former students and second and third generations of students coming from the same families, and the readiness with which College staff were called upon for consultancy work.

However, serious weaknesses were also identified, some of them the obverse of the College strengths. The values with which it was identified — discipline, meticulous order and attention to detail — while appealing to part of the public did not do so to another and relatively growing section. The expertise of the teaching staff in their subjects, though admirable in terms of technical operation and manipulative capacity, lacked an academic dimension.

This would lead to difficulties when the College wanted to offer degree programmes incorporating these subjects. There was also a shortage of staff expertise for the development and teaching of new courses.[3]

A further consideration at this stage, which was not internal to the College but had its repercussions, was the economic climate of 1976. It was the year of a major financial crisis when the Chancellor of the Exchequer was induced to approach the IMF for a large loan which was only granted on condition of substantial cuts in public spending. Education was affected like every other area: staff/student ratios were set to worsen, expansion plans to be cut back. At Glasgow College of Technology there were even fears that the institution might be closed down, though these were doubtless alarmist exaggerations. However, so far as Queen's College was concerned it did undoubtedly add another complication to what was already an ambitious and delicate operation to guide the establishment in novel directions.

Back to the Past

An immediate result of the cuts was sudden and unanticipated reduction in the numbers of new teachers being employed and likewise teacher training numbers. In consequence some of the home economics graduates were unable either to find jobs or complete their training at Jordanhill College. Twenty-two of them participated in a job creation scheme which was the brainchild of Jack Gisby, a lecturer in management studies. They were paid £49 per week, funded by the Manpower Services Commission, and their remit, as the *Scotsman* expressed it, was 'instructing underprivileged families in the preparation and presentation of food within limited budgets'.[4] It was a chilling echo of the original purposes of Grace Paterson and Margaret

---

[3]That these problems of adjustment were not confined to Queen's College is evident from the history of its counterpart institution in Edinburgh. According to its historian:

Notwithstanding the major progress which had been accomplished under Miss Morgan's leadership it is true to say that by the mid-1980s there were still areas of obvious weakness to be found in the College. When Mr Leach assumed office he experienced something akin to a culture shock at some of the attitudes which he encountered ... inefficiencies in the management structure, the lack of genuine debate in decision making, and the comparatively weak and underdeveloped academic culture were all areas of concern.

Tom Begg, *The Excellent Women: The Origins and History of Queen Margaret College*, John Donald, 1994.

[4]*Scotsman*, October 4, 1976.

Black, or rather for the continuing perceived necessity of such projects in late twentieth century Glasgow.

According to Jack Gisby:

> This is a service which should have been in existence for some time but never has. Previously the burden of educating people on how to eat well within limited budgets has been the responsibility of social workers and health visitors, But this scheme will now mean that old people, one-parent families and people with special dieting needs will have expert advice available to them.[5]

The students were to work under the direction of doctors, health visitors and district nursing sisters. As to their likely clients, Jack Gisby remarked:

> It might astonish you to find that among people most likely to benefit are the young newly-weds living in suburban housing plots and learning what married life is all about. They, too, are struggling. Many have to cope with heavy mortgages and other commitments in an effort to maintain their standard of life. A lot of them are anxious for help and, more important, likely to take it.
>
> Many elderly couples are too set in their ways for change. In many low-income families are wives struggling to cope while their husbands are more anxious to spend money on drink than listen to 'do-gooders'. Then there are the pensioners who live alone, depressed perhaps by illness or bereavement and drifting aimlessly through life uncaring about buying nutritional food.[6]

Planning

The scheme was a six-month emergency response to a particular crisis. So far as long-range strategy was concerned, it was believed that a more formal planning system would help to focus the attention of the College staff on stated objectives, achieve greater economy in day-to-day operations and establish a more efficient system of control.

---

[5] *Ibid.*
[6] *Daily Express*, October 7, 1976.

The line of development commenced, in late 1976, was a review of the whole operation of the College under the slogan 'Where are we now and where do we intend to be in five years' time?'

The College review was the first stage in a long, and at times, very difficult process of change affecting every part of the College's activities. The initial review period lasted for three months and staff, governors and student representatives took part.[7]

The outcome was the first College Plan, drawn up at the beginning of 1977, for a five-year period. It consisted of a statement of three broad aims and 29 objectives, each with an attached set of targets. Seven of the objectives were in the area of product market, 10 in organisation structure, five in organisation welfare and seven in resource allocation.

The plan was thoroughly ventilated and discussed, at least in principle. A whole-day staff conference was organised and it was discussed by the Academic Council before being endorsed by the Governing Body. However it is clear that the process, if relatively smooth, was not necessarily all that it appeared to be on the surface. Although the conference agreed the plan without major amendment, the mood was unenthusiastic and uninspired. Many members of staff, unfamiliar with a consultative process, used to an autocratic management tradition and inexperienced in open debate, withheld their honest expression of opinion and many showed themselves reluctant to voice widely-held doubts about the value of the planning and the feasibility of the objectives. On the part of the management, silence was taken as consent despite the vague nature of a number of the objectives and the staff's lack of awareness of the implications of implementing them.

Each January during the five years of the Plan a College conference was held to review progress with participation from staff, Governors and representatives of the student body. The aim of these conferences was to identify the priority areas from the plan to which resources of money and time were to be directed during the forthcoming year. Moreover the Principal personally interviewed every academic and member of the senior administrative staff annually during the initial five years. The aim was to

---

[7] *College Report, Academic Year 1984–85*, Appendix 1.

review each person's contribution to the College priorities for that year and to encourage the setting of personal objectives for the year ahead.'[8]

Certainly the CNAA appeared to be impressed upon its return visit in 1978. But again appearances may have been at least partially deceptive. It is worth quoting Andrew Greig's thesis at some length.

The college is currently one fifth of the way through the first formal planning cycle of five years. Some of the 123 sub objectives of the College Development Plan have been attained. Crucial ones, however, like the validation of degree courses still elude the college grasp. After three years of painful implementation process, the formal planning experiment is at a very vulnerable point. Very few benefits as yet have accrued to make the pangs of the change more bearable.

There are worrying signs:

1. apparently widespread disenchantment on the part of organisation personnel regarding the wisdom and competence of the college management;

2. widespread cynicism regarding the outcomes and values of activities like planning, participation in decision making, two-way appraisals, and student-centred learning. It has to be said however that disenchantment with management is not an uncommon feature of organisation personnel. Cynical attitudes and utterance are also part of daily life in educational institutions even more elevated than the college. ...

A number of difficulties could have been avoided by —

1. taking enough time to sift and evaluate the findings of the search groups;

2. endeavouring to identify and quantify relevant environmental factors at the initial stage, eg competition from other institutions, finance from SED;

---

[8] *Ibid.*

3. not putting together a bundle of objectives without considering such points as achievability, relative 'weight and balance' mutual interaction, resource implications;

4. planning the implementation process in advance, which would not have overloaded the Academic Council until such time as subordinate planning/decision making structure could be created....

Organisational stress is not reflected as yet in withdrawal symptoms, sickness rates or absenteeism. Resignations have been minimal. From casual inquiry the consumption of tranquillising drugs has increased, but this as yet has not been accurately measured....

It is therefore probably too early to judge whether formal planning in the college is or is not worthwhile. There has not been enough time to learn from the mistakes, and not all the mistakes have been identified and acknowledged.[9]

It is perfectly clear that the process of change was not an easy or unproblematic one and that many toes were trodden upon. The impression also comes across that Geoffrey Richardson was not a very diplomatic personality. Nevertheless, in the circumstances it is likely that no other way forward was viable given the changes which were occurring in higher education during the late '70s, the backwash of the Robbins Report and the 1960s revolution. It was impossible to continue in the old style. The pattern of student demand was changing and the College had to recognise the existence of competing institutions likely to absorb its market if it failed to develop. In late 1977 the three schools of physiotherapy based in city hospitals were amalgamated together into the College with the agreement of the Greater Glasgow Health Board. These same years saw a steadily expanding choice of advanced courses becoming available to its students.

Educational Patterns

As noted previously, the first College degree course, a BSc in Dietetics, was offered from 1976 in collaboration with Paisley College. The subjects

---

[9]Andrew Greig, *Planning and the Evolution of a Strategy in a Small College* (MBA Dissertation), 1990, pp.112–115.

studied included chemistry, biology, physics, biochemistry, microbiology, physiology, nutrition, dietetics, food studies, sociology, psychology and Social Administration. Following the amalgamation of the physiotherapy schools, involving about 220 students, a BSc in Physiotherapy was initiated in 1982.

A further ingestion of pre-existing hospital facilities occurred in 1984, when the Orthoptics School located in Glasgow Eye Infirmary (the only one in Scotland) was transferred into the College. Orthoptics is the investigation and treatment of strabismus (squint) and other anomalies of vision. A letter was received from Miss A S Hood, the Principal Teacher at the Infirmary, stating that she wished to negotiate formally with the College to bring the orthoptics course into a higher education establishment with the idea of upgrading it to degree status. Once the transfer was completed Miss Hood and her teachers joined the College staff. This was not the only discipline taken over from Glasgow hospitals. The same thing happened with radiography, which was transferred in January 1989 from the Royal Beatson Memorial Hospital. Its diploma course was validated externally by the College of Radiographers. Again the transfer was made possible by agreement with the Greater Glasgow Health Board and later, in 1992, a degree course was developed. In 1990 the Glasgow School of Chiropody and the Glasgow School of Occupational Therapy likewise joined the College, leading to degree courses in these subjects being approved shortly afterwards.

In 1987 further development of the BSc in Dietetics took place, when it became a BSc in Human Nutrition and Dietetics, no longer in collaboration with Paisley but the College's sole responsibility. Students on the new degree enrolled onto a common two-year programme, with some going on in subsequent years to become state registered dietitians, while others took on non-therapeutic options to qualify them for positions in industry and commerce. Later still the degree evolved into a BSc in Human Nutrition with options in dietetics, food science and community nutrition. Part-time provision was not neglected, for in 1988 a BSc in Health Studies came on stream as an evening programme for staff employed in professions allied to medicine. As a modular programme it could be completed in two to five years.

Home Economics
The area of work that had been the College's original purpose also moved to degree status — it had come a long way from the original School of Cookery. The first CNAA — authorised degree in Home Economics,

however, was started not in Glasgow, but in 1976 at Robert Gordon's Institute of Technology (as it then was) in Aberdeen, where the head of its School of Home Economics claimed that it represented a completely new approach to the teaching of home economics. Among other disciplines incorporated into this degree was consumer studies, which was its focus: 'The aim is to provide students with the knowledge and ability to understand and critically evaluate the living environment in a responsible way... concentrates on the social and technical aspects of the dwelling place and its contents, together with the physical characteristics of the human being'.[10] Contributing to the central discipline were applied sciences, textile studies, food studies, design studies and social sciences. The following year Queen Margaret College offered a BA in Home Economics. Queen's College initiated its own similar BA in 1982, and it was in fact the College's first individual degree, in view of the fact that the Dietetics one had been shared with Paisley. According to the prospectus:

> The course provides an interesting and challenging pattern of studies in Social Studies, Food Studies, Resource Management, Textile Studies and Inter-disciplinary Studies.... The course enables the Home Economist to relate the management of household resources to the management of resources in the national and international setting....
>
> Increasingly Home Economists are seeking employment as members of management teams in industry and commerce.... More posts are becoming available in testing, research and product development; textile and food retail management; textile, clothing and equipment manufacturing; in food commodities and food production; in demonstration and sales promotion work; consumer advice and liaison in the public and private sector. Home Economists also develop career opportunities in social work agencies and in community liaison.

In 1989 the degree was revised and in 1989 changed to a BA in Consumer and Management Studies. In 1985 the CNAA authorised a BA in Catering and Accommodation Management, in June 1991 one in Hospitality Management. Overall by the time that the merger was being discussed Queen's College was offering 10 full-time degrees, compared with three in 1984.

---

[10] Roderick Bennett, 'Designing a Degree in Home Economics', *Housecraft*, August-September 1976, pp.225–227.

In 1986 the Governors set up a company to market the staff's skills and expertise along with educational materials and products deriving from research and development work. It ran under the name of QCG Enterprises Limited and accorded with the pressures then developing from the Government of the day for the commercialisation of higher education. At that stage the Chair of the Governing Body was Mr Ian Hutchison, who held the office from 1981 to 1989. In 1988 the Secretary of State altered the composition of Governing Bodies of Scottish Central Institutions, requiring the majority of their members to be 'lay members with experience of industry, business, the professions or otherwise as employers'. It fitted in with the commercialisation strategy noted above.

Inspectors' Assessment

In December 1984 the SED decided to reactivate the practice of inspecting central institutions, beginning with Queen's College, and the inspection was held in May 1985. In general terms the eventual report was favourable, but it nevertheless incorporated a number of severe criticisms, sufficient to cause the Governors and Academic Council to complain, in their subsequent meeting with the inspectors, that it had been written in such a manner as to provide the press with the opportunity to take a negative approach towards the College:

The Board of Governors functioned in a commendable way...

Committees were organised and chaired effectively with relevant papers prepared in an exemplary manner by college and administrative staff. Debate was lively and well-informed...

The Principal who had been in post since 1976 had been responsible for implementing with energy and determination many of the changes which had been identified as necessary...

The Secretary/Treasurer ... had an excellent understanding of educational matters...

Course documentation ... was impressive in the formulation of precise learning objectives ...

The relatively low wastage rates were attributable, in part, to the calibre and dedication of the students.

The Principal and his staff are to be commended for their academic achievements.

But:

... excessive demands appeared to be made on the time of some academic staff by the frequency of attendance at committee meetings...

... in the Department of Home Economics and Management Studies the Head of Department has difficulty in coping with a diverse remit, a difficulty made worse by the absence of a recognised depute head of department.

... there was some feeling of resentment at the manner in which the system [of staff appraisal] had operated...

The College was committed to a policy of student-centred learning but it appeared that this had more to do with the management of resources than with an approach to the educational process...

The inadequate and unattractive communal areas did not meet student expectations. Student complaints about the cost of food in the refectory were, however, unjustified ...

Students appeared to have little inclination to be involved in college life. The general level of extra-curricular activity was very low.

At one time the Glasgow and West of Scotland College of Domestic Science was known nationally as a centre of excellence in home economics, catering, and dietetics. The role of the College was now less well known. [This must have been a particularly bitter pill — a suggestion of regression in reputation in spite of every material advance.]

Contact with the local business community had been developed ... Unfortunately the college had not yet effectively mobilised its own

resources ... and only one department was involved. Liaison with further
education colleges and other central institutions with similar interests
and expertise had been limited and not altogether successful.

The concluding paragraph noted:

The Principal had pursued the development of the College with vigour.
However the system of corporate management which had been established
had led to an over-emphasis on the importance of course committees and,
in addition, college departments had not changed sufficiently to match
other organisational developments and the expansion of course provision.
Subject and pedagogic developments had taken a secondary place to
course development and academic enhancement.

The Eldon Street Episode

One aspect of that vigorous pursuit of development had an unhappy
outcome. Eldon Street was not so much a street as a row of tenement houses
with a curved frontage, regarded as being of considerable architectural merit
and with a B grade listing. It backed on to the rear of the Park Drive site,
which stood on a higher level, the ground sloping down steeply from
Kelvingrove Park. The condition of the buildings however was much
decayed, and in 1972 Eldon Street was zoned for educational purposes,
whereupon the College began to buy up the properties as they fell vacant —
which it was able to do fairly easily as there was not much of a market for
such deteriorated dwellings and the zoning decision was a further deterrent
to purchasers. The intention, once all flats had been secured, was to
demolish the row and redevelop the site to accommodate expanded health
care courses. At the end of 1985 the College secured apparent encouragement
for its plans when the Scottish Office promised assistance with capital
funds. The courses would in any case initially be located partly at Jordanhill
College (which was finding itself with spare accommodation capacity) until
the new extension could be built. Queen's naturally wanted to avoid having
to run them permanently on a split site.

In the meantime public controversy had erupted. In 1983 an Eldon
Street Action Committee came into existence to campaign for the preservation
of the block for housing purposes and various local organisations added
their voices to the demand. Charing Cross and Kelvingrove Housing

Associations wanted to carry out the rehabilitation. Glasgow District Council, repudiating the acceptance of educational zoning by the old Corporation (which had disappeared in local government reorganisation), passed a Housing Action Area resolution, but the Scottish Secretary rescinded this. One correspondent in the press debate which blew up pointed out that the Secretary had conflicting interests in the matter as he funded the College and had enabled it to purchase the flats.[11]

Generally public opinion was very hostile to the College's point of view, both on the grounds that viable housing could ill afford to be lost and that aesthetic considerations were being overridden. The College was indicted for bricking up the flats and allowing them to fall into disrepair. 'More than ever the preservation of the West End's architecture is of paramount consequence. ... This fine building must be saved both for its elegant design, and for the increasingly chronic shortage of publicly owned housing stock.' [12] 'To throw away a significant element of such a remarkable asset in Glasgow, for the sake of an extension which could be built elsewhere, is an act of economic folly as well as of artistic vandalism.'[13] The action group collected 10,000 signatures on a petition to the Secretary of State demanding that the building be retained for family housing. At a local public meeting held in January 1987 at which representatives from the College attended to explain their case, they met with a very hostile reception. The local MP, Jim Craigen, also came out against the extension and in favour of rehabilitating the houses.

Queen's College was presumably embarrassed by the fact that on its Governing Body was a District Councillor, Jim McKechnie, who was also Convenor of the Maryhill constituency Labour Party and strongly opposed to the development. He tried to persuade his fellow Governors to save the building, and having failed, and seen the building demolished, commented, 'I am very sad and disappointed that what was an opportunity for providing much needed housing has now been lost. It looks as if the college will not be able even to build on the vacant site and that for years it will be used as a car park.'[14]

---

[11]Helen C Bovey, New Glasgow Society, *Glasgow Herald*, December 23, 1986.
[12]Alan Dougan, *ibid*.
[13]Dame Jennifer Jenkins, *Glasgow Herald*, January 9, 1986.
[14]*Glasgow Herald*, November 19, 1997.

There was nevertheless some support outside official channels for the College's position. A correspondent wrote:

> We have lived in the Woodlands area as a family for over 46 years. We look onto Eldon Street and find this building an ugly eyesore … I speak on behalf of a number of residents who wish to have this building demolished at Eldon Street and replaced with a modern extension to the Queen's College and give the area some dignity … 'Housing' is such an eye-catching subject and so often sheer sentimentality overshadows the making of sensible decisions.[15]

The Eldon Street flats prior to their demolition in November 1987.

Ironically, it was the District Council which summarily settled the issue in the immediate direction wanted by the College, for its Building Control Department judged the row of tenements to have become unsafe and had

---

[15]Cutting — date and source not indicated.

it demolished in November 1987. When the demolition order was issued the campaigners put out a leaflet declaring: 'An outstanding building is being sacrificed to provide … a car park.'

This reference here to the car park, like Jim McKechnie's, derived from the fact that the Scottish Office, anxious to save money wherever possible, was carrying out a feasibility study to 'consider to what extent the accommodation and services at Jordanhill College of Education could meet the needs … having regard to the cost and likely timetable of any development at Jordanhill, as compared with those expected at Eldon Street.'[16] The answer came in February 1988 when the Minister, Michael Forsyth, withdrew the Deparment's financial backing for the redevelopment of the now empty site, which does indeed remain as a car park. It was an episode from which neither the College nor the Scottish Office emerged with much credit.

Some rather happier events of the mid- and late '80s in which the College was involved included the Eighth International Home Economics Research Conference of 1986. It was the first time that it had been held in Scotland, and was hosted at Queen's, but significantly the College's own premises were inadequate to hold the Conference sessions, which had to go ahead elsewhere. The Glasgow Garden Festival of 1988 likewise involved College participation and a project was undertaken to produce undergraduate learning material from events at the festival. Video interviews were made of a variety of functions, including food and beverage operations, design and marketing, personnel and management. Finally, a footnote to the College enterprise of the inter-war years is worth mentioning, for in 1986 the Electrical Association for Women was wound up, being regarded as having fulfilled its purpose.

The New Principal

Principal Richardson left the College early in 1991 to take up the position of Director of Roffey Park Management College in Sussex. His drive, energy and undeviating commitment to the institution's development were appreciated by many, though some felt that his management style was a good deal too abrasive to produce the well-motivated collective that the College required in the exacting educational environment of the times.

---

[16]*College Report*,1986–87.

Professor John C Phillips, *BSc, CMath, FIMA, FRSA, MIMgt*, with Mrs Celia Urquhart, *RGN, DMS, MBA, FBIM*. Professor Phillips was Principal at The Queen's College, Glasgow from February 1991 until its merger with Glasgow Polytechnic on 1 April 1993. After the merger he became one of the Vice Principals of Glasgow Caledonian University. Mrs Urquhart was the Chairman of Queen's Board of Governors at the time of the merger and she went on to be the second Chair of the University Court, finishing on 31 July 1996.

The appointment as his successor of another male Principal underlined the College's break with its pre-1975 traditions. John Phillips was born in Dyfed, South Wales in 1943. He graduated in mathematics from the University of Wales (Aberystwyth College) and continued research in the Maths Department of Glasgow University from 1965 to 1967, and so was already familiar with the city. Thereafter he taught in the polytechnic sector, becoming Dean of the Engineering and Computing Faculty of Leeds Polytechnic, as a specialist in systems development, but from 1990 to 1991 was a freelance consultant in training needs analysis and institutional development.

As soon as he took up his appointment in February 1991 Professor Phillips circulated a letter to all staff members and the SRC Executive outlining his background, assuring them that he wanted to spend his first few weeks in the College engaged in a listening exercise and concluding:

> I view my appointment as a great privilege and a very challenging opportunity. I am looking forward to working closely with the Governing Body, staff and students to ensure a successful and expanding future for the Queen's College, Glasgow, as a source of high quality, relevant, higher education — respected throughout the West of Scotland and indeed nationally and internationally.

In September he initiated a remodelling of the College's academic structure, instituting a system of committees to give overall direction to areas such as research and staff development and academic and professional standards, together with a faculty structure guided by faculty boards. In his first Principal's Statement, dated September 1991, he declared:

> The Mission of Queen's College, Glasgow is to be a leading specialist provider of vocational Higher Education ... a centre of excellence in Health and Community Care, and Consumer and Hospitality Management.
>
> It is characterised by its quality of teaching, learning and working environment; its commitment to wider access to flexible course programmes; its responsiveness to student interests and employer and market needs; its concern to establish a network of educational ladders and bridges with other institutions; its determination to provide a cost-efficient and effective service within a maximised resource envelope.

> Planning is based on the phased achievement of five key objectives — a revised marketing strategy focusing on career and vocational opportunities, commitment to Total Quality Management, a fully operationalised policy on wider access with increased collaboration with other HE and FE providers, Efficient Resource Management Systems, and the development of a strong market-led growth path in course planning and resourcing.

It was a rather different style of address from that of the original Queen's College, let alone the College of Domestic Science in its early days, much less the Cookery Schools.

The College in Historical Perspective

Professor Phillips' Report also spoke of a Corporate Plan for the years 1991–95 and of a mission statement for the rest of the 1990s and the beginning of the next century. In actuality, however, the institution was nearing the end of its separate existence, and would within two years become part of a bigger establishment. How then ought its historical significance to be summed up?

The first point to make is that underneath the obvious discontinuities in the institution's functions during the period of its existence, a deeper level of continuity can be identified. In this the College and its predecessors were not unique, either in England or Scotland, but part of a steadily expanding system of social management, frequently ad hoc and improvised — and emerging from private and voluntary sources as well as local or national authority — aiming to cope with the proliferating contradictions of mass society as it evolved through a century of unprecedented social and political change.

In the 1860s urban Britain was beginning to emerge from the worst blights of the 'smoke and iron' industrialisation process. Significant improvements occurred overall in the average incomes of the working classes, though there were, needless to say, many who benefited minimally or not at all. That was also the decade in which basic public health issues — housing, sanitation, water supply, paving — began to be tackled seriously on the initiative of local authorities using Westminster legislation which was permissive rather than obligatory.

These processes continued into the 1880s and 1890s despite the onset of the 'Great Victorian Depression' (not that much of a depression by twentieth century standards) and further kinds of development were added: street lighting and urban transport systems, for example. It was the first age of scientific improvement, with a growing orientation towards social as well as physical science. The first social surveys using scientific methodology were carried out in the 1890s, revealing a huge accumulation of desperate poverty among low income groups — findings which stunned late-Victorian middle-class sensibilities. Simultaneously, an emergent labour movement and the newly-formed socialist groups were advancing, from different angles, demands to attack the contingent evils of modernity not by superficial palliatives, but, as they saw it, at their root by far-reaching social reconstruction.

In the late nineteenth century and well into the twentieth it was possible to recognise an individual's social class immediately by their dress and general appearance. Even without such markers it would have been possible to guess it from their height. Surveys revealed that the children of upper-class parents were consistently taller on average than ones of equivalent age from lower-class homes — who were in addition overwhelmingly more likely to show the signs of deficiency diseases such as rickets. The same correlation held for life expectancy (as it still continues to do, though in a much less extreme fashion). The differences were directly related to lifestyle, particularly nutrition. The disappearance of the more visually obvious of these phenomena[17] is to be attributed in the crudest sense to an improved calorie intake — the lower classes over the decades improved the absolute level of their incomes and were enabled to eat more — but it owed something as well to improvements in the preparation and handling of available foodstuffs, the quality as well as the quantity of the diet, in addition to advances in other areas of 'domestic science'.

It is here that the role of the teaching establishments must have been most influential. Although they did not begin on the basis of training teachers in the field to instil a knowledge of appropriate techniques into schoolgirls, that approach soon became the focus of their endeavours. To do so, however, meant moving beyond a purely private and charitable role, for the teachers had to be paid and the schools equipped. It was made possible only by becoming part of an expanding public education system, by operating in conjunction with school boards and the Scotch Education Department. At the same time the development of domestic science schools represented an element in the concurrent struggle to broaden educational and social opportunities for women beyond school-leaving age — though it has to be noted that many contemporary feminists were bitterly opposed to what they saw as any system of female education which accepted that women were to be directed into forms of 'tertiary' education marked off from those enjoyed by men.[18]

---

[17]Though in the late twentieth century rickets has returned to Britain.

[18]Tom Begg quotes Emily Davies: 'It makes me very unhappy to see the Ladies' Lectures, Ladies Education Association, etc. spreading. It is an evil principle becoming organised', *op. cit.*, p.13.

By the turn of the century the principle of state intervention and organisation to secure social objectives was coming to be accepted across the political spectrum. In the politcal centre New Liberalism, though committed as ever to international free trade, was starting to leave behind the free-market principles of its Gladstonian predecessor so far as they affected social relations. On the left the Fabian Society was the most articulate proponent of public intervention to tackle the deficiencies of unregulated capitalism, while from a more authoritarian position on the right the National Efficiency movement aimed to create a populace fitter for international competition and war. The conjunction of aim and bitter conflict over means was mirrored in the political crises of the new century's first decade; it produced considerable development in the educational field at all levels. The establishment of the Scottish central institutions was one outcome — and one which enabled the Glasgow cookery schools to advance from a lowly position on the edge of the system to a comparatively advanced status. As a central institution their successor college[19] stood, formally at least, on the same level as the mighty Royal College of Technology.

The elevation of the two original schools in this manner was part of the overall development in social policy occurring in Britain at the time, stretching from the control of sweatshop conditions to the beginnings of unemployment insurance. These developments can be viewed, according to one's judgement, as either a commendable response to identified public necessities or as an extension of social control and consolidation of the grip of the rulers upon the ruled. In any event it opened up vistas for the new College of participation in a process of social amelioration. That perspective was knocked awry by the onset of war in 1914 and subsequent chronic depression, but these events did not prevent the College from continuing as it had formerly done to train teachers of domestic science and to discover new roles in hard times, both in the course of the wartime emergency and the two decades which followed.

With the development of the second conflict and its aftermath the College's work (and those of others like it) became central to the fundamental underpinning of the war — the management of very scarce resources, particularly food. A prevision of this had come in the latter stages of the First

---

[19]Interestingly, the Edinburgh counterpart (from 1972 Queen Margaret College) which became a central institution at the same time, was not at first allowed to call itself a 'College' but had to continue with the designation of 'School' until 1930.

Students in model flat, c1960's.

Dressmaking and Design students, c1960's.

Students in the laundry, c1960's.   Setting the table, c1960's.

World War, when attempted U-boat blockade had led to a limited rationing system, but the universal rationing system imposed from 1940 was on an immensely different scale and the dominant reality of British civil life throughout the war years, and afterwards. In circumstances such as these the work of domestic science colleges came fully into its own, quite apart from their direct contribution to the war effort in instructing military personnel.

The birth in the '50s of the full-blown consumer society combined with the virtual disappearance since the war of a domestic servant class, opened up new avenues to the colleges for domestic instruction and development as new ranges of goods, technologies and facilities appeared upon the market, located in many instances in the new homes constructed by the housing drive, and it presented these institutions with the challenge of adapting their work to plenty in place of austerity. That line of advance certainly took place, but it was overtaken by and incorporated in the educational revolution of the '60s as it affected the tertiary sector. Domestic science, or home economics, as it was being redesignated, continued, but became a subordinate element within a sphere of higher education towards which the College was now reorientated.

As in the early years of the century the impetus came in the last instance from the state. Social management and the alleviation of social problems

Food and Nutrition students, c1960's.

provide the theme which links the developments of the post-Robbins era in institutions like the College of Domestic Science, though the impetus came in the form of encouragement rather than direction. In the 1975–76 session the prospectus still to a degree resembled those of earlier decades — home economics, institutional management, residential management, dietetics — though courses in social work made their appearance in that year. Over the next decade the momentum of change accelerated and the prospectus for the mid-'80s looked wholly different. To be sure, dietetics, institutional management and home economics still featured (and these of course were not without their own social connotations), but to them were now joined qualifications in consumer studies, home help organisation, health care (including a degree) and expanded provision for social work. Over the following five years the changes were equally striking. A raft of management studies, along with business administration, enterprise studies, marketing and communication, came on stream in those years, reflecting the growing commercial emphasis of the '80s. At the same time the health studies portfolio continued to expand. Home economics as such had shrunk to a remnant — a Higher National Certificate/Diploma of 1/2 year duration, the Home Economics BA having been revised and retitled as a degree in Consumer and Management Studies.

The position of Queen's College in the early 1990s represented the outcome of a complex interaction between three processes — the social evolution in Glasgow and Britain, pressure from the state in its remodelling of the tertiary education system and the internal potential for growth and change within the College itself as it responded to the demands emanating from outside. By the time John Phillips assumed the Principalship the basic transformation was largely complete; his reorganisation of the College structures was designed to bring them into a better relationship with its new role. The form which Queen's College had assumed was one which in England, where it would have been a local authority college, would have automatically meant its amalgamation into a polytechnic, but in Scotland, with the existence of central institution status, conditions were different.

At the beginning of the decade there was no presumption that Queen's College would do other than continue as an independent institution developing within the framework of its new identity and providing degrees and equivalent qualifications in vocational areas not covered by the other higher education establishments in the Glasgow area — at that point these were two universities and two polytechnic-type institutions. Undoubtedly that would have represented a viable future, and was in fact the option taken by Queen's Edinburgh equivalent, Queen Margaret College.[20] Possibly if, like Queen Margaret, Queen's had possessed an extensive, modern greenfield-site campus of its own on the edge of the city a similar course would have been adopted. In the event, however, as government policy in the early '90s yet again reorganised higher education on a national scale, the possibility of amalgamation emerged and quickly moved centre-stage.

---

[20]According to Tom Begg, 'Indeed it is a remarkable fact that of all the former domestic science institutions which were once to be found in towns and cities all over the UK, Queen Margaret College alone survives with its independence proudly intact.(Its last Scottish counterpart, the Queens College, was absorbed into Glasgow's Caledonian University in 1992)' — which is a slightly misleading way of putting the matter. *Op. cit.*, p.161.

Chapter Six

Glasgow College of Technology, 1971–1979

Following a lengthy gestation and a less than easy birth, Glasgow College of Technology finally opened its doors in 1971. In physical appearance it was striking. It stood on the brow of a hill rising from Glasgow's Cathedral Street, and at the time its two buildings were surrounded by a great deal of

Glasgow College of Technology.

open space. One of the authors recalls his first view of the complex as he walked up the hill, thinking that it gave the impression of a medieval fortress dominating its surroundings. Apart from some lesser structures such as the sports hall and the animal house of the Biology Department only the Main Block, the original college of technology, was in use at that point; the other principal building, the intended commercial college, termed the West Block, was still in the process of being completed internally.

There was a certain air of improvisation when the first full session commenced at the end of August that year. Hastily and temporarily converted classrooms were in some cases being used as staff accommodation prior to the West Block's opening. Even at that point there was some uncertainty regarding the establishment's ultimate future. A friend of one of the authors, who worked at Paisley College, remarked on the rumours that were circulating that the College might still be amalgamated with Jordanhill College and the Art School 'to make university number three'. A more immediate problem for large numbers of staff and students when the session opened derived from the fact that the currently operational building having been designed for technologists and with the assumption that technologists were invariably or nearly always male, there were scarcely any female toilets to be found in the Main Block.

The Academic Structure

Departments

An idea of the College's scope and future intentions can be read in the character of the 12 departments initially established. The flagship was unquestionably the Optics Department, the only one of its kind in Scotland and the only such department outside a university anywhere in Britain. It was also the only department within the College which had its own CNAA-authorised degree course at that time, though there was degree teaching elsewhere in the institution. These other instances however related to London University degrees. As might be expected of a college of technology, strong emphasis was placed upon engineering, and two departments were established in this discipline, one of Electrical, and the other of Mechanical and Civil Engineering, although civil engineering was a small component and something of a Cinderella. Biology has already been mentioned; it complemented optics. Again, given the character of the institution, computing was an essential component, while a Department of Mathematics and a joint one of Physics and Chemistry supplied an underpinning of pure science and theory.

On the non-technological side, a Department of Business Administration represented the centrepiece of the College's other component, and related disciplines included the Department of Law and Public Administration and Departments of Commerce, Management and Finance. The vocational stress of the College (which was of course to be expected) can be seen in these arrangements, as well as in the backgrounds of the individuals who were appointed to lead the institution. However the more traditional academic disciplines were not altogether overlooked. Five of these were grouped into a Department of Social Sciences, which incorporated economics, sociology, political science, psychology and history. The three historians were in fact the only grouping of historians in the Scottish non-university sector; all other such establishments had one at most. The thrust of teaching in this department was expected to be primarily vocational, however, with a lot of service teaching to widen the breadth of the courses taught in others — opticians for example were taught economics. Finally, a composite department, rather misleadingly termed Humanities, included communications, languages, nursing and geography, together with a single historian.

The comments each department made upon itself in the initial College prospectus for the year 1972–73 are informative. A selection is indicated below.

BIOLOGICAL SCIENCES
Although the biology department was conceived at a fairly late stage in the development of the college, it is housed in very well-equipped laboratories and has an excellent animal house.[1] Most of the department's courses are related to paramedical aspects of biology, an area of work which is expected to expand considerably in the next few years.

BUSINESS ADMINISTRATION
This department has a wide range of courses leading to recognised qualifications at degree level in the field of Business Administration.

---

[1] In the '80s the animal house had to be closed down because of fears of the attentions of animal rights activists.

Major initiatives, which should result in the commencement of new courses in 1972 include the development of an honours year for the Diploma in Commerce and of a sandwich course which, it is hoped, will be recognised as leading to the BA (CNAA) in Business Studies.

ELECTRICAL AND ELECTRONIC ENGINEERING

This department has one of the most modern and well-equipped suites of electrical and electronic engineering laboratories in Scotland.... The electronics group has specialised in the application of integrated circuits as system elements and offers specialist short courses on this branch of applied technology. Apart from its formal teaching, the department provides a service to industry in the form of collaborative research projects and investigations.

MANAGEMENT STUDIES

Mainly, this department caters for post-experience students, who, in addition to being academically or professionally qualified, have had a number of years experience in industry. Group and 'in company' individual projects, films, case studies, role playing situations, seminars and business games play an important part in its teaching approach. This is in close liaison with commercial and industrial companies and allied organisations in the area.

OPHTHALMIC OPTICS

The department has fifteen specialised ophthalmic laboratories, project and clinical rooms and uses other clinical facilities at local hospitals and at the Department of Ophthalmology of the University of Glasgow. Its basic course is the CNAA degree course in Ophthalmic Optics, which it is hoped will evolve into an Honours course in 1972, but the department also prepares students for professional examinations in ophthalmic dispensing and provides specialised and refresher courses for post-graduate students and qualified practitioners. Research facilities are excellent.

On the science and technology side of the College's work, apart from the one degree course in optics, the prospectus consisted of diplomas and certificates. From 1973 these were mostly validated by a body established by the Secretary of State. SCOTEC, the Scottish Technical Education

Council, was the equivalent of the English TEC and performed the same function as the CNAA for non-degree awards. A parallel body existed for business education, the Scottish Business Education Council (its English equivalent was BEC), which fulfilled similar functions in its own sphere, and was empowered not only to administer examinations, but also to devise and award diplomas and certificates within the area of business education in Scotland.

The Social Sciences Department had as its central field of work the London University BSc(Economics). This degree was rather misleadingly titled, for it was possible for a student to specialise in other disciplines such as sociology or politics, and consequently these were taught at advanced undergraduate level. On account of the different structures of Scottish and English degrees and because the entrance qualifications for the London BSc were A Levels, the initial year's teaching for entrants who did not possess them was devoted to A Level instruction. The Humanities Department was also concerned with degree work, though this was exclusively in the form of evening classes directed towards the London University BA in History.

College Government

The College had been established by Glasgow Corporation, which was its ultimate owner, but did not play any direct role in its government. In fact, though this was not a central institution, the Scottish Education Department, which after all financed the students and through them the institution, had a much more direct bearing on the College's academic life. The SED could determine, or at least veto, new courses which the College might consider introducing and shape the general direction of its academic development, since any proposals had to be cleared with the SED before they could even be submitted to the CNAA. The SED not unnaturally had its own broad brush ideas about the way it wanted higher education in Scotland to go, and could decide, for example, that certain types of development were more appropriate for the universities than the public sector.

The SED in 1972 had issued general guidelines for the government of central institutions, though of course the College was not bound by those. Its own statutes, however, corresponded fairly closely. At the level of resource allocation, overall staffing distribution and suchlike, authority was placed in the hands of a Board of Governors in which the local authority was the predominant element, though it was chaired by a local businessman of repute. Academic planning, implementation, quality control and academic

Dr Reginald beale, *BSc, PhD, Ceng, FIMechE,* first Director of Glasgow College of
Technology, November 1970 to 16 April 1982. (Prior to this he had been appointed
Principal of the new College of Science and Technology, before the decision to merge
with the proposed College of Commerce, as early as December 1968).

LEWIS BRODIE, *BSc (Econ), ASCC,*
Academic Registrar at Glasgow
College of Technology 1974–1985.

affairs in general were supervised by an Academic Board, chaired by the Director. Its members were the Directorial team, the Heads of Department and 11 elected members, elected on a first past the post system from the entire College without specific constituency. The structure also included a Chief Executive under the title of Registrar. The first of these was a Mr Ian Honeyman, but he departed at the end of 1973 to take up another appointment and was succeeded by Lewis Brodie.

The Heads of Department — there was no faculty system — were appointed as administrative managers rather than academic leaders (though the two roles were not of course incompatible). No formal structure of departmental committees then existed; meetings were on an improvised and ad hoc basis. The more important courses were supervised by course boards, usually composed of all staff members teaching on them — at the time they were small enough to make such an arrangement possible. In the case of CNAA degrees these boards were a statutory requirement.

Perspectives

The strategy of the College aimed at development — the portfolio of courses which it inherited was regarded as a starting point only and the strategic aim was to develop steadily towards higher-level work, with the focus on CNAA degrees. The complement of academic staff inherited from the existing Glasgow colleges was of course far too few in numbers to undertake this aim, or even to cover the initial range of courses, so very large numbers were appointed in the months before the College opened. At the beginning of the first full session there were roughly 250 in post. It should be noted that there was less than complete unanimity, even within the Directorate itself, regarding the College's strategic vision. While agreement existed certainly on the need to develop advanced courses and to make the institution credible and respected in the higher education sector, there was a body of opinion, reflected in the outlook of the Depute Director, Frank Ebbage, that it was important to maintain a strong portfolio of non-degree work in line with the nature of the college that the Corporation had intended to establish, and that undue emphasis on degree development would constitute a betrayal of that perspective.

The College in fact experienced from its earliest days the problem or dilemma that had affected all successful tertiary institutions since the nineteenth century, namely the aspiration to academic drift and the inevitable reality of its occurrence whenever popularity, reputation and resources provided the opportunity. Every academic success encouraged the ambition: the appetite invariably grew by what it fed upon. Nothing else could be expected in a very hierarchical system with university education at the apex of the pyramid in respect both of resources and public regard. The tendency to drift was greatly reinforced when it became clear that non-university status was not necessarily fixed in concrete, but that elevation could be attained by lesser institutions through a process of evolution. The notion that there were greater and lesser institutions (whether within or between sectors) might be officially deplored (the distinctions were supposed to be functional, catering for different needs, rather than hierarchical), but in reality the hierarchy was firmly fixed in both the academic and the public consciousness.

One drastic solution to the perceptual, if not the material, problem which was proposed in the '60s days of academic radicalism, was either to abolish the term 'university' and rename every tertiary institution from Oxbridge downwards a 'college' (so that Oxford University, for example, would have been retitled the 'Federation of Oxford Colleges'), or else, contrariwise, extend the title 'university' to every tertiary institution without exception, including the FE colleges. This interesting suggestion had little likelihood of acceptance. The newly-arrived polytechnics of the '60s would certainly have liked to have been granted the university title — the real grounds for refusing it were certainly not the officially propounded ones.

There *was* a case on academic and social grounds for keeping these establishments in a separate sector, eloquently developed by Eric Robinson in his paperback *The New Polytechnics*. Significantly, it was subtitled *The People's Universities*. The essence of this argument was that they should take advantage of their new creation by avoiding the bad habits of their predecessors — elitism, selectivity and the narrowness of vision which a university title would tempt them into; but instead be open to a wider range of intake and take advantage of the CNAA to ensure a regularity of standards which did not exist in the old universities. In reality, the prime motivations behind Anthony Crosland's decision to create a binary system were more likely to have been in the first place the objections of the local authorities to the loss of their institutions and secondly one of resources. The polytechnics could not be funded to the same level as the universities, nor their facilities brought up to equivalent standards, without unacceptable strain on the Exchequer. If they were in a separate sector with a different name their comparative poverty appeared less of an anomaly.

Nevertheless, even if they were not entirely committed to degree courses, they were emphatically part of *higher* rather than further education and extremely concerned to protect and develop the distinction. Academic drift had brought the modest colleges in which they had their origins to the relatively elevated situation they now enjoyed and inevitably, whatever official pronouncements might be, they began to drift further, laying increasing emphasis upon their academic role in contrast to their vocational one, chafing at the constraints of the CNAA and demanding autonomy in degree-granting powers and the institutional quality control that went with it.

The Glasgow College of Technology stood within this academic environment in a particularly anomalous situation. In institutional terms the Scottish scene differed dramatically from the English. In one aspect, the central institutions represented the level of tertiary education below that of the Scottish universities, yet they themselves were of drastically varying character. Once Strathclyde and Heriot Watt, university equivalents, had passed out of their circle, they were mostly monotechnic vocational institutions ranging from the Glasgow School of Art and the Colleges of Education to the Textile College in the borders. However Robert Gordon College in Aberdeen and Paisley College of Technology, the latter very much an aspirant university and a near counterpart of GCT or Napier College in Edinburgh, remained inside the category. To emphasise its ambitions it had ceased to use the 'of Technology' element in its title, preferring to be known simply as 'Paisley College'.

The Name
Glasgow College of Technology academics,when they reflected on the comparisons, thought of their institution as a polytechnic equivalent, or at least starting on the road to becoming one. As noted above, the term

'polytechnic-type institution' or similar had been frequently used in the documentation when the College was being established. The College's title could certainly be thought of as misleading or even perverse, given that technology constituted a minority part of its educational functions,[2] but it was difficult to envisage what a suitable one might be — 'Glasgow College of Technology and Commerce' might be more in line with its reality, but was still misleading to a degree. One early student publication declared, rather defiantly, that the College, being in reality a polytechnic, was therefore *ipso facto* the equivalent of a university. Much as there existed a strong aspiration on the part of many to use the name 'polytechnic', there were objections to this as well. It was thought of as distinctively English, and for that reason did not find favour with the SED, nor with a large number of Scottish academics.

In fact the question was formally considered early in the institution's career at a meeting of the Governing Council on December 16, 1971, which set up a working party to consider the question of the name. This reported on February 10 the following year, the report was adopted and the Council recommended that, since the existing name did not correctly reflect the standard of work undertaken, which was higher than that undertaken by other colleges of further education, the Education Committee be requested to approve a name change to 'City of Glasgow Polytechnic'.

The request was denied by the Education Committee, who noted that the SED

> had indicated that they could not consider such a proposal as it would give a wrong impression, especially to educationalists in England where Polytechnics were specially designated in view of the nature of the work done in them and as they felt the Glasgow College of Technology was not comparable with the English Polytechnics and as they were not convinced that the College was unique in Scotland and therefore deserving of special designation.[3]

Moreover in Glasgow there was an additional and peculiar difficulty, not mentioned in any of the official documentation. The big Lewis's department

---

[2] At its beginnings the College adopted a rather ugly logo made up of an arrangement of the letters GCT, but this was quickly dropped.

[3] Minute of Glasgow Corporation Education Committee, June 23, 1972.

store in Argyle Street had once been popularly known as 'The Glasgow Polytechnic' and though that name had long dropped out of circulation it was still remembered, giving rise to the rather implausible allegation that confusion or ridicule would result if the College adopted it.

The Governing Council was so at odds with the Education Committee's decision that it formally communicated its dissatisfaction, pointing out previous use of the term when the College was being planned, the comparability with the English institutions and the publicity benefits of having a polytechnic title. The Education Committee however remained unmoved and one of the Corporation representatives on the Governing Council denied that the local authority's position had been influenced by the SED, in plain contradiction of the Education Committee's own minute.[4]

The formal opening of the College did not take place until November 1972, and that too was attended by more than one element of disappointment. The first choice of the Corporation to perform the ceremony was the Duke of Edinburgh, but the only date on which he was available was in July, which was suitable neither for the Corporation nor the College. 'The Council felt strongly that every effort should be made to obtain the services of a member of the Royal Family to perform the ceremony as this would be appropriate to the status of the College and would obtain the maximum publicity advantage... especially in view of the possible re-naming of the College'.[5]

The Duke or any other royal family member being unavailable, the second choice fell upon Sir Alec Cairncross, the eminent economist, but he too was unable to fit the proposed timetable and eventually it was performed by Willie Ross, the Scottish Secretary in Harold Wilson's Government, who had therefore been in office when the final shape of the new institution was established. The Corporation proceeded to make a virtue out of necessity: 'Appropriately, the formal opening today is to be carried out by Mr William Ross MP who not only was once a teacher but is Shadow Secretary of State for Scotland and keeps a close eye on all educational matters in the country'.[6]

---

[4]Minutes of Governing Council, January 11, 1973.
[5]Minutes of Governing Council, February 10, 1972.
[6]Item in cuttings book, newspaper advertising feature, not sourced or dated.

In the Official Programme for the formal opening the term 'polytechnic organisation' was used once again. The programme noted a complement of 1,350 full-time and approximately 4,000 part-time students, of whom approximately 25 per cent of the former were reading for degrees, 25 per cent for degree-level awards and the remainder for higher national diplomas, final professional awards and similar qualifications. The Governing Council, or at least part of it, apparently felt that the local authority had monopolised the event, for it went so far as to record in its minute of January 11, 1973 that, 'A number of members of the Council expressed dissatisfaction at the failure of the Education Committee to involve Governing Council in the arrangements and organisation of the opening ceremony'.

White Paper
Soon after the College opened the Government, in 1972, published a White Paper on Education, and the Council discussed the sections relating to Scotland. This projected an expansion in student numbers within the higher education sector outwith the universities and colleges of education. The reaction in GCT was one of disappointment, for the paper appeared to emphasise the difference between central institutions and colleges such as GCT. Nor did it mention part-time students, for which the College was particularly well situated. The Director, at a Council meeting, pointed out that the difference would make it very difficult for potential students and for schools to understand 'the equivalence both in academic work and in character'.[7] He expressed the opinion too that the College was admirably fitted to fall in with the perspectives which the Government was announcing for higher education, namely a minimum critical size for institutions to obtain economies of scale, and the encouragement of home-based students to economise on maintenance.

Educational Developments
In any event the watchword throughout the '70s was development and, with some setbacks, expansion. Immediate and severe difficulties, however, faced any attempt to develop in the direction of engineering education. The essence of the problem was that the College was a new competitor with no

---

[7]Governing Council Minutes, January 11, 1973.

less than three nearby established institutions which had, in Glasgow's industrial heyday, themselves focused upon engineering. Glasgow University, Strathclyde University and Paisley College all possessed extremely high reputations in the field and were the likely first choices of the most able students, not to speak of staff.

GCT faced a choice: either to stick with the relatively low-level work which it had inherited from Stow College and accept a position of indefinite fourth-class status in the area from which it derived its name, or else to compete. Given the circumstances and the aspiration for recognition, it was inevitable that the second alternative would be the one adopted, but given the inequality of the competition the College could hardly hope to succeed. Moreover, the problem was compounded by market trends. Glasgow was ceasing to be an industrial centre, the demand for the courses which the College offered was dropping, engineering students became more difficult to attract from the local area and the College lacked the strength and background to attract large numbers from further afield or abroad. It would have made more sense in fact to concentrate on areas still in their relative infancy where big demand expansion could be anticipated, such as computing, and to build up a starting lead in them. Although there was some talk along these lines, such as proposals for the development of computer-aided engineering design, the opportunity was missed.

In 1972 the West Block was completed and the departments which had been allocated to it, the non-physical sciences, were able to move in. The building itself (now the Hamish Wood Building), was a lot less spacious than the Main Block (now the George Moore Building). The corridors are narrow and there was concern that the narrowness of the stairwells could constitute a hazard in the event of fire. Nonetheless the new occupants were mostly gratified by their new accommodation, now having proper offices for the first time, normally on the basis of two, three or four to a room depending on its size.

The College's second CNAA degree was approved at the beginning of 1973, a BA/BA Honours in Social Sciences,[8] which still continues to run, although much altered from its original format. Its location was in the department of the same name, which was however in the later '70s divided

---

[8]With the arrival of this degree the London BSc (Econ) was phased out.

into its component elements to create separate Departments of Sociology, Economics, Politics, and Psychology. Out of these a proposal emerged for a degree in industrial economics, but this did not gain CNAA approval and was dropped. History, being too small to warrant separate departmental status (and being proscribed in any case from such by the SED) had already been moved into the Humanities Department. The latter had also acquired a geography section in anticipation of presenting proposals for a BA in European Studies, though in the event this project was abandoned. By the end of the decade the College was admitting students to CNAA-authorised degrees. The last remnant of the London University connection was the BA in History (which used only a small part of the London syllabus), an evening-only course in the Humanities Department.

An area which was to have a significant future was that of nursing education. As noted, this began in a comparatively small way as a section of the Humanities and Complementary Studies Department. A health visitor training course was running from 1972 and soon afterwards the General Nursing Council for Scotland decided to bring nursing education into the higher education arena and the College was chosen to run a three-year experimental course. Edinburgh University already offered a degree in nursing training for teaching purposes. Dorothy Kilgour, who was the senior lecturer in nursing studies has given us an account of the development. The course introduced the students to an academic environment as opposed to lectures in the hospital where they were receiving training and the students had to cover the professional or clinical training and the practical experience as well. It was a block system of teaching which included practical experience on placement combined with attendance at the College. Miss Kilgour's first intake of students was 12, and these, while studying psychology, sociology and life sciences, did so separately from the other students in these disciplines. The training involved the lecturers going to the hospitals to visit their students on placement and the hospitals involved were in the west of the city — Western, Gartnavel, Yorkhill, and Miss Kilgour pays tribute to the support received from the Western Infirmary and Gartnavel.

By 1975, due to new intakes of students, three new members of staff were added. In 1977 a degree proposal was drawn up and accepted by the CNAA. It was the first degree of its kind in Scotland outside the university sector, preceding Queen Margaret's by a year. Miss Kilgour notes that in the '60s and '70s the nursing profession was overwhelmingly female and it was very challenging for the nursing staff to enter academia and have to prepare themselves for a mixed-gender environment. She believed this to be very healthy, especially as she had come from the all-female nursing department at Edinburgh University. The degree students also had the opportunity of mixing with the rest of the student community in their first year. Introducing nursing as an academic subject in the early years of GCT's history was a challenge, but successfully surmounted. In 1978, the paramedical commitment having expanded substantially, it was decided that a Department of Nursing Studies should be established, but this did not come to fruition until 1980. The first head was Miss Winifred Logan, who had taught at Edinburgh University, was involved in world health in Geneva, had worked in the Scottish Office and was the first woman Head of Department in GCT. The delay in finding a suitable head was due to the fact that the Department wanted someone who would be on a par with the other Departmental Heads; and somebody, preferably with governmental experience, who would be able to participate in the internal and external politics of College management, as well as willing to accept that the College was run by Strathclyde Region and was not a central institution, at least not yet.

Status Problems

The above concern was indicative of a wider problem. Throughout the years between 1971 and 1979 the College records make clear a constant undercurrent of tension running between the institution and its creator, the local authority. In 1975 the nature of the local authority changed substantially with the reorganisation of Scottish local government into a two-tier structure of regions and districts. The districts corresponded roughly to the old unitary authorities, the regions were superimposed upon them. By far the largest of the new bodies was Strathclyde Region, which incorporated around half the population of Scotland. Since education was allocated to the responsibility of the regions, the College, upon the institution of the new system, came under its authority.

The sources of the tension were both material and related to status. We have already noted the first attempt to change the name, rebuffed by the Corporation. All those working within the institution, as well as its Governing Council, were well aware that whatever the Corporation might assert, the name 'College of Technology' denoted both formally and informally a lower-level institution than 'Polytechnic' and in England was specifically associated with further rather than higher education. The problem had implications for the calibre of staff, for in consequence it was more difficult to attract recruits of the qualifications and experience demanded by the CNAA — potential applicants of this sort from any distance, who were unfamiliar with the College's role and position in the Scottish education system, were likely to be deterred by sight of an advertisement from an institution apparently below the level of their potential marketability.

A more concrete grievance was the differing level of salaries paid to tertiary staff of comparable grades in local authority establishments and central institutions. This, as the Council regularly pointed out, put the College at a severe disadvantage in relation to comparable institutions. In 1974 the maximum for a grade 1 lecturer in the College was £3,516, as against £4,173 in a CI; the maximum for a senior lecturer at GCT was £4,386, and in a CI £4,965. In fact the position was even worse than these figures suggested since the maximum figures for the College were reached only by lecturers with a Teacher Training Qualification worth £123 and 'increasingly our staff is being recruited from polytechnics, central institutions and universities, rather than from schools where the TTQ is obligatory'.[9] So far as Heads of Department were concerned, CIs provided a sliding scale according to the size of department, ranging at this point from £5,396 to £6,087, while the College maximum was £4,554 (including TTQ). The example of social sciences was cited in this minute, where the preferred candidates in sociology, psychology, economics and politics had all rejected the offer of appointment. Where departments were in competition with the professions and industry the situation was even worse. 'We experience many withdrawals in favour of the polytechnics.'[10]

The potential severity of the problem was exemplified by the threat it posed to the College's flagship course, the BSc in Ophthalmic Optics. At the April 1973 meeting of the Governing Council it was reported that the CNAA had agreed to permit its extension to honours level but only subject to a satisfactory report after two years demonstrating that staff/student ratios had been improved, along with improvements in the proportion of senior staff posts (a particularly important consideration) and research activity. Technical and administrative support was also judged to be currently inadequate and in need of enhancement.

---

[9]Governing Council Minutes, June 18, 1974.
[10]An additional grievance was that the College made no provision for removal expenses, whereas all its competitors did so.

The Council learned that a total of 17 separate advertisements had been placed for vacant academic posts, but many still remained unfilled. One member of the Council, a Mr Miller, with links to the profession told it that the latter was expressing 'profound concern' and that 'The comparative position of the course with every other course in Ophthalmic Optics in Britain in respect of staffing and salaries placed the College at a severe disadvantage'.[11] Worse, there was a rumour prevalent that the Secretary of State intended to make a teacher's certificate a compulsory qualification for further education (but not central institutions) as it already was in schools. Should this happen, 'recruitment to the academic staff would become almost impossible'. The council went so far as to minute its view that 'if the report on the course in two years time was unsatisfactory, then the responsibility for the course being withdrawn would lie elsewhere, and not with the Council which had repeatedly drawn attention to the difficulties of the situation'.[12]

The College suffered from being placed in an anomalous situation. Formally it remained part of the further education structure, with the academic salaries if not the conditions applying to other further education lecturers. But, as its spokespeople repeatedly pointed out, it was concerned wholly with higher-level work and what it was doing was in every sense comparable with those central institutions which operated in a polytechnic-style fashion. Consequently it was having to compete with them in the academic market for staff while being unable to offer equivalent salaries at any level. Naturally therefore its competitors got first choice of the best-qualified personnel. It is not surprising that both the College management, and in the main the staff as well, not only wanted to change the name but to get out of the local authority sector.

In 1974 therefore, the Council proposed to the soon-to-be-dissolved Corporation, rather than the imminent Strathclyde Region, that the College should be transferred to central institution status. Since the Corporation's Education Committee no longer had a material interest in the matter, its members were not wholly unsympathetic; contrary to their position a year earlier, when they had rather frivolously suggested as an alternative that all the central institutions be brought under local authority control — a hopeless idea if ever there was. However, the Education

---

[11]Governing Council Minutes, April 5, 1973.
[12]*Ibid.*

Committee was not willing to put the College's case directly to the Scottish Secretary nor to have a representative of the Council at the meeting it was seeking with him.[13]

In the event the Corporation relented on these points and in November the Director, Depute Directors and a Corporation representative met SED officials. The officials accepted that unit costs in the College were substantially lower than those in universities and CIs, and agreed with the principle of equal pay for equal work. 'No change was contemplated with regard to the central institutions but [the SED] recognised that institutions doing work of a similar level should be financed in similar ways and have similar administrative arrangements.'[14] The College was urged to await the outcome of the Houghton Report on salaries. Nothing came of the proposed change in status and GCT was duly transferred to the authority of Strathclyde Region.

The 1974 CNAA Visit

The first institutional visit by a CNAA panel to Glasgow College of Technology occurred in November 1974 and in general its perception was a favourable one, though reckoning that the College still had some way to go before attaining full academic maturity. The visit, in contrast to what was to come five years later, was an amiable and uncontroversial one, although the Report, received by the College in March 1975, did indicate that there were certain directions in which it expected improvements to be instituted. Principally it expected the College to develop a structure in which important policy decisions would be reached through a process of appropriate consultation and informed decision-making involving the Academic Board and a suitable structure of sub-committees which provided adequate representation of staff interests.

> Whilst it was recognised that many members of the Academic Board had not previously had experience of serving on such a body and had thus probably relied on strong leadership from the Directorate, it was nevertheless hoped that the Academic Board would now begin to enter

---

[13]Governing Council Minutes, March 26, 1974.
[14]Governing Council Minutes, November 26, 1974.

fully into its responsibilities and firmly take the initiative in reporting to and making recommendations to the Governing Council on all academic matters.[15]

Noting that estimates and resource matters were currently dealt with by the Directorate in consultation with Heads of Department, the panel were pleased to note the Director's assurance that the Academic Board would be increasingly expected to assume a major role in such discussions. The visiting party also observed that the Academic Planning Committee which had been instituted did not have a very high profile, but excused this meantime on the grounds that because spare accommodation and other resources still remained, it had not yet been required to take difficult decisions on the relative priority of different proposals.

It did however suggest that lack of clarity in the composition and terms of reference of standing committees could be a problem for the future and hinted that this was something which ought to be addressed. 'At present there seemed to be no way of really ensuring that the more junior staff could be active participants and that their views would penetrate and influence the direction of progress.' Strong recommendations were advanced that structures should be put in place to encourage the upward flow of ideas, that the Academic Board should be involved in resource allocation and that student representatives should become full members.

In consequence, a Working Party on Academic Structure was established, but its deliberations were slow and infrequent and still far from finalised five years later. In May 1977 the College Council established a Staffing Policy Committee 'to consider and make recommendations with regard to staffing provision in general, both academic and non-academic'. The committee never met, however, and the Director continued his practice of sitting on the appointment panel for *all* members of academic staff, no matter how junior. Another Council committee which was established but never met was a Policy Review Committee. Two which did meet regularly were the Chairman's Committee and the Finance Committee.

---

[15]Council for National Academic Awards, Committee for Institutions, 'Report of an Institutional Review Visit to Glasgow College of Technology on 18 November 1974'.

Internal and External Shocks

Added to the College's problems were unanticipated shocks of various sorts coming both from within and without. By the middle of the decade, whatever troubles may have been germinating for the future, the College had settled down as a functioning and forward-looking academic community which was steadily adding to its portfolio of higher-level programmes, providing for a growing student intake and acquiring sufficient academic reputation to attract teaching staff from distant parts of the UK and beyond. The position reached in 1975, however, proved to be only a prelude to an era of turmoil, difficulty and controversy. Some of this was occasioned by the decisions of public bodies in national or local government over which the College exercised no control and little influence; some of it to failures in the institution's own controlling machinery.

The Fire and the Bubble

There is an apocryphal legend that during the years of maximum student unruliness and dissident lifestyles in the late '60s and early '70s a male student President at Sussex University would dress in a leather mini-skirt while he rode around the campus on a motor-cycle which he would garage in his room in the university student residence. Nothing quite as bizarre took place at GCT, but a similar student carelessness with parking a motor-bike produced a much more disastrous outcome, which was extremely fortunate not to result in serious injury or even fatalities.

One of the student officials had been in the habit of parking his machine in a narrow space inside the back door of the West Block, fairly close to the then student union premises, with the aim of keeping it out of sight of would-be-thieves. One night in December 1976 during the holiday break the bike went on fire — for reasons unknown — and the fire quickly spread throughout the building, which was happily unoccupied at the time. The various floors of the building (it is eight stories high) suffered severe smoke damage, putting it wholly out of action for some time, but the student association premises and the refectory, adjacent to the ground floor, were gutted.

The teaching and office space above the ground floor were redecorated with maximum speed to allow teaching to recommence as soon as possible after January 1977, but damage to the refectory and the union premises was structural and required much lengthier repairs. To provide for alternative premises what came to be known as 'the Bubble' was erected in the car park. This was a low-cost large canvas-type building, measuring 34 by 15 metres, kept erect by compressed air, with assurances given that it was fireproof and burstproof. It was opened a year after the fire, in January 1978, and functioned well until the new permanent premises were ready.

It should be noted that a more satisfactory development for the GCT Student Association occurred in June 1979 when two of its representatives, the student President Peter Murray and a graduate student, Peter Kerr, won the Edmund Burke Memorial Debate, effectively the British championship. It took place at the Glasgow University Union and the motion was 'This House Regrets the European Parliament'. Five other establishments were represented and the judges were Ian MacCormack, ex-SNP MP, Teddy Taylor MP, and Robert Taylor of the Clydesdale Bank, which was one of the competition's sponsors.

Change of Ownership

With Scottish local government reorganisation in the mid-'70s GCT passed from the ownership of Glasgow Corporation to that of Strathclyde Region, which became responsible for education, though in practical terms that did not make a great deal of difference. The ambiguous relationship with the SED continued to cause occasional friction. Of more immediate impact was the sudden squeeze on government spending in 1976, the result of a financial crisis which appeared to compel the Chancellor to borrow from the IMF on highly restrictive conditions.

Education spending was cut alongside everything else; in GCT new appointments were frozen and projects with resource implications put on hold. There were even fears expressed that the institution might be shut down, but these were alarmist — such a prospect was never in contemplation. There was considerable discussion, however, over whether in view of the education cuts taking place it might become unavoidable to erode national standards as fixed by the CNAA if resources became too stretched to maintain existing staff/student ratios or teaching facilities. On the 1974 visit the Chair of the CNAA was asked at the Academic Board whether the Council would be prepared to tolerate such a deterioration, particularly in staff/student ratios, and he replied categorically that it would not. Following the events of 1976, however, it became increasingly doubtful whether such a principle could be maintained.

The Name Again

The College's relations with the new regional authority were not any easier than they had been with Glasgow Corporation, and for much the same reasons. Problems generated by the tendency towards academic drift and the anomalies of the institution's status remained sources of friction. Once more, in 1979, a proposal was advanced for renaming it; this time the suggested new name was 'Strathclyde Polytechnic'.

The document sent to the region incorporating the proposal began with the statement that 'The emphasis placed upon Technology in the title of the College is wholly inappropriate' and continued 'The balance of the Institution, both now and as planned, shows no particular preference for Technology'. The paper referred to the etymology of the word 'polytechnic' — 'many arts, many skills', noting that it exactly fitted the College's function, and reminded the Region of the original references to a 'polytechnic establishment'. It insisted nevertheless that the desired name change would not imply any alteration in academic level, range of work or resource needs but related solely to image and public standing, 'a factor of some significance to potential students'.[16]

There survives in the records detailed (though anonymous) notes taken at the meeting of the Region's Further Education Sub-Committee which considered the proposal, and these provide an instructive insight into the local authority's attitudes towards and suspicions of Glasgow College of Technology. The paper was introduced by Edward Miller, then the Director of Education. Explaining that he did not have a strong position either way, he referred to the successes which the College had achieved, describing it as 'one of the most successful in the whole of Scotland, including Central Institutions such as Paisley College of Technology'. The reason for wanting 'Strathclyde' rather than 'Glasgow' in the name was said to be that its catchment area extended to the entire West of Scotland, and indeed to Scotland itself. 'Glasgow College of Technology is a fine establishment; it gives us problems, of course', but 'if anything it has exceeded my original expectations which in themselves were high.' It is clear that he tended on the whole to favour the renaming proposal.

A councillor inquired about the SED's attitude if such a change were to be carried out. Mr Miller replied that such a decision lay with the regional

---

[16]It was pointed out that the term was not exclusive to England, being also used in Ulster.

authority alone, although he did not imagine that the SED would be very pleased about it. The subsequent discussion then revealed some of the councillors' worries and reservations: basically they feared that the College was doing its best to distance itself from local authority control, possibly to get rid of its lower-level courses, and in essence to be getting ideas above its station. Related to that, the discussion reveals a persistent history of uneasy relations with the Director.

The councillor who had raised the question regarding the SED then professed himself unhappy about the overall pattern of development and declared that he saw a number of worrying trends developing such as the establishment of professorial posts[17] and the 'establishment of autonomy', voicing his suspicion that the College wanted to demit its 'lower-grade courses'. 'It seems to me important that we maintain it as the only comprehensive institution of higher education.'

Councillor William Harley (after whom the library building is named) supported the College's proposal, arguing that to link the name change with alleged worrying trends inside the institution was a red herring, but he was answered by another who expressed very directly and straightforwardly the reservations felt:

> … this seems to me to be another step in the struggle between the Director and this authority to take, or force, the College outwith the control of the authority. I don't think there is any doubt in our minds that the Director has wanted the College removed from this authority's control; we go back to his appearing before this Committee with the 'insistence' that the College become a CI.[18]… The Articles were written to ensure that the College would become an educational bridge, not a CI, not a university,[19] and I see a more sinister side to the request.

The use of the term 'sinister' was deprecated by Cllr Harley, who pointed out that the request came from the College Council, which, beside regional councillors, included representatives of staff, students, industry and the STUC, 'a reasonably balanced group of people', and noted that the regional

---

[17]In fact these, although being proposed, were not instituted until much later.

[18]Evidently the pressure for CI status must have continued beyond the establishment of Strathclyde Region, but this is not clearly documented.

[19]In the end of course it became both, as well as a polytechnic.

councillors who opposed the proposal had not attended the College Council meeting at which it was agreed in order to try to persuade it otherwise. Another councillor, with a constituency which included 'a quite exceptional number of members of staff, opposed the request, partly on the grounds that pressures from the newly-elected Conservative Government in tertiary education were likely to be felt most severely in further education and that the renaming proposal was part of an ongoing attempt by the College to detach itself from that sector.

The councillor who had voiced the initial objections added that the proposal was driven by the Chairman's Committee of the College Council, that there had been an absence of formal consultation within the College, and suggested that the College Council (here described as 'the Board'), although unanimous, had been bounced into agreeing. Councillor Harley then proposed that the Committee should refrain from dividing but ought to go ahead and consult the SED, and this was agreed to.

In its reply,[20] the SED acknowledged that the question of a name for the College was indeed within the Region's competence, but made clear its negative view, claiming that the College was not 'completely polytechnic in character' because it was restricted to the provision of courses which did not conflict with courses offered in other colleges. The letter pointed out that central institutions of the same character as the College 'whose desires to be titled "Polytechnic" have been resisted so far' might well object and feel themselves being discriminated against. The letter went on to argue that the use of the term 'Strathclyde' was also inappropriate because, so it was claimed, 'most' English polytechnics had a city rather than a regional name and Paisley College might feel itself demeaned.

The Director responded with a letter to the Region[21] indicating that the College Council had requested him to write on its behalf pointing out that there were no particular courses which an institution had to run before it merited the name, and that the SED had specified nothing on that regard. Nor was there any type of course absent from GCT but offered in all the English polytechnics. Moreover, part-time courses were common to polytechnics and to the College. 'Clearly this College is already much more polytechnic in character than were most of the polytechnics at the date of

---

[20]R Naylor to G H S Bain, Depute Director of Education, July 3, 1979.
[21]R J Beale to D G Maguire, Assistant Director of Education, September 29, 1979.

their founding … There is no polytechnic stereotype.' And much more in a similar vein. But it made no difference, and the College had to wait another 12 years for the polytechnic title.

Chapter Seven

Glasgow College of Technology, 1979–1981: Internal Conflicts and Restructuring

Sources of Conflict

Students

G lasgow College of Technology opened at the tail-end of the student militancy wave which characterised the tertiary education scene of the '60s. This arrived rather later in Scotland than it did in England, though its more spectacular manifestations were dying away by then in Scotland as well. It may be remarked in passing however that GCT opened right in the midst of militancy of a different sort — the great Upper Clyde Shipbuilders' work-in was going on at the time. The Maoists from the beginning and for a few years afterwards had a presence among the students, holding meetings and issuing publications. The Communist Party too was organised in the College, and included members of staff as well as students. Both groups sold their literature quite extensively around the campus, often to the displeasure of the Director, who took a similarly unfavourable attitude to political material of any kind, including anti-apartheid publications. One member of staff who sold these regularly was made to stand outside rather than inside the building while he did so.

The Student Association, however, did not have a very marked profile. One sign of this was that it was never able, despite efforts on more than one occasion, to sustain a regular publication — a difficulty it has never succeeded in overcoming. One major reason for the rather anaemic character with which it began may have been the fact that the premises allocated to it were meagre and uninviting — no more than two medium-sized rooms separated by a corridor. In consequence there was no real student social life, and little scope for establishing any sort of corporate identity after hours. Admittedly after a few years better premises were allocated, but even these were far from salubrious. On the other hand, the sports hall was large and generously furnished. As the College increasingly acquired control over its courses, however, and became responsible for its own examining, the sports hall was required for lengthy periods as an examination hall.

During the course of the '70s there were a few student sit-ins in traditional militant style, spontaneous affairs, rather than organised by the Association, but they were low-key events, never lasted long, were not particularly aggressive and never required the police to be summoned. On one occasion, however, one of the ephemeral student publications scurrilously compared the Director to Idi Amin, with a vignette of him lecherously pursuing his secretary around his office, and also made extremely disparaging comments upon other lecturers, both male and female. It was to Dr Beale's credit in this case that he shrugged off the defamation and did not turn it into a major issue.

Staff Disputes

GCT and its successor institutions have probably had a more turbulent history than most others of this kind. The conflicts of the 1970s were eventually to build up to a climax that threatened the credibility of the institution's academic functioning with its Governors and the CNAA. It is more difficult to judge whether friction was endemic, inevitable in a new institution with inheritances from different sources and struggling to find its identity in a shifting and uncertain educational context, or the outcome of personality clashes and breakdowns in relations that could have been avoided. There were on occasion one-day strikes, not in these cases arising out of internal grievances but part of Scottish-wide actions called by the teachers' union, the EIS, over pay claims; but offence was caused among striking members of staff over what were regarded as unsympathetic and sometimes provocative actions on the part of the Directorate.

These occasions were not of long-term significance, aggravations rather than causes of an atmosphere of contention and antagonism. Press commentators at the time attributed much of the trouble to a clash of cultures. On the one side were said to stand the staff members who were brought into the College at its foundation and were steeped in the rather authoritarian outlook and values of old-style further education. Contrasted with these, so it was suggested, was the fresh generation of academics who had been recruited to make up the staff complement of the new institution, who had been mostly undergraduates during the radical '60s, and were similar in their outlook to lecturers in the English polytechnics. These, it was claimed, had ideas regarding academic democracy and staff participation in policy making which clashed with those of their more traditional colleagues. Since, on this interpretation, the Director himself and nearly all the Departmental Heads were adherents of the old school, conflict was all too likely to ensue.

"Does every technical college have staff meetings like this?"

Cartoon taken from the *Times Education Supplement*, 13 February 1981. *Courtesy of the Times Education Supplement.*

However, since in its first few years of existence the College was still finding its feet, the tensions took some time to accumulate. Changes occurred in the Directorate. The two initial Depute Directors, Frank Ebbage and Harry Law, did not remain long, the former retiring and the latter going on to appointment as Director of Preston Polytechnic. They were replaced first by Norman Meadows, an engineer by profession but with wide cultural interests, and Bernard McManus, likewise an engineer. The latter was viewed by many as a very abrasive personality, a judgement which appeared to be confirmed by his later career when he was obliged to resign as Principal of Bournemouth University on account of a too authoritarian style of management. There were grumbles from some sections of the staff that all the members of the Directorate were non-Scottish, but this was not a significant issue and was never cited in the subsequent disputes — after all, many of the new younger staff members themselves originated from England.

Dr Beale's own style was not the best calculated to mollify resentments and win over potential opponents. He came over as a rather remote figure who did not readily engage in small talk or mingle with ordinary staff members. In general he did appear to find it difficult to communicate. The main criticisms, however, were that he was not prepared to direct the College on the basis of discussion and dialogue but expected his own ideas of what was best to be accepted without question and that he compounded this fault with brusque dismissal of any criticism and refusal to engage in discussion.

Dissatisfaction and mutual mistrust simmered for some years before it emerged unmistakably in 1979. When the Social Science Department was broken up into its separate disciplines, appointment committees for the four new headships contained no specialists in any of the disciplines. As a result the external examiner in economics wrote letters of concern, as did the President of the British Sociological Association, while 23 of the 35 staff in social sciences sent a letter of protest to Strathclyde Region. Another issue arose around the College's flagship degree, the BSc Ophthalmic Optics. The Region was considering whether it would be most appropriate for this to continue being validated by the CNAA or instead by Glasgow University. Naturally the staff in the department had a point of view which they wished to express, but this they were prevented from doing by the Departmental Head. So great was their indignation that they tried to remove him as Chair of the board of studies for the degree. He ruled that resolution out of order despite Lewis Brodie's advice that to do so was *ultra vires* and the academics complained to the College Council demanding 'more open and democratic procedures for taking important decisions'.[1]

The Academic Board

The detonator for the ultimate explosion was supplied by the elections for the Academic Board which fell due in 1979 and in which a complete turnover[2] took place in the 11 members who filled the allocated places — nine men and two women were elected. They came from a wide range of departments and held extremely varied political views in general terms, but they were all committed to achieving what they and their electors regarded

---

[1] *Times Educational Supplement Scotland*, March 7, 1980.
[2] It was remarked upon that none of the 11 sitting members offered themselves for re-election.

as a more accountable structure of government in the College with the Directorate obliged to take more notice of sentiment among the rank-and-file staff.

New sources of irritation were added to those already in existence at the time the new members took their seats. As noted, whatever reservations individual Heads of Department might have about the manner in which the Director conducted affairs, in practice they all gave him public support. They were seen as acting as a caucus who all followed the Director rather than exercising independent judgement, and who agreed their joint position in an extra-constitutional fashion, usually at their weekly meetings over coffee. Since the appointed members (there were 25 in all) outnumbered the elected ones on the Academic Board, they could always be sure of carrying their point of view. A particularly striking example of this occurred on one occasion when an agreed decision was reached which elected members pointed out had implications which favoured the latter's views but not the Director's. Immediately a vote was called to reverse the decision, and was of course carried by the votes of Heads of Department.

In response to the Heads' dominance the elected members formed a caucus of their own which they openly referred to as 'the caucus' and held regular meetings with a permanent Chair. When challenged on this practice they replied, accurately if a little disingenuously, that these meetings were merely for discussion and exchange of views on the agenda and that the meetings had no power to bind the members who participated in them. A Head of Department then suggested that in that case heads be allowed to attend as well, but desisted when it was pointed out that this would amount to the caucus Chair summoning meetings of the Academic Board, which would scarcely be acceptable to the Director.

A second major point of friction was the Director's claim that a clause in the College's Instrument of Government (clause 17) concentrated all executive authority in his own hands and enabled him to override at his discretion decisions reached anywhere else, including those of the Academic Board if he disagreed with them. It was disputed whether the clause actually meant what the Director said it meant, but it was also pointed out that if the clause really did confer such power, the Director could in a self-denying fashion refrain from operating it if he wished to be regarded as a practitioner of academic democracy. On one occasion after he had again asserted the comprehensive powers which the clause entitled him to, an elected member asked loudly 'Then what's the point of us being here?' causing considerable embarrassment. Naturally, however, Dr Beale denied that he ran the College in an authoritarian fashion:

> It is very difficult to have much authority in higher education these days, I prefer the word 'responsibility' and, yes, I do consider that I have the final responsibility for the way this college is run. But there is no question of dictatorship or anything like that … there has been a lot of consultation.[3]

A third point of contention was the alleged reluctance of the Directorate to act upon the Report of the CNAA's 1974 Quinquennial visit, which had recommended the establishment of a more coherent and rational committee structure with clearer lines of responsibility than currently existed, and for the Academic Board and its sub-committees to assume a role in determining estimates and allocating resources. The Director at the time had given an assurance that this would be done and the CNAA report included the statement that it 'was pleased to note the Director's assurance that the Academic Board would increasingly be expected to take a major part in future discussions of such matters.' Up to 1979 nothing had been done to implement this. The report had also expressed dissatisfaction that student representatives were not full voting members of the Board or the College Council. Again by 1979 this had not been rectified for the Academic Board, although such rights had been conceded for the Council.

The Director's support was weakened in some degree by turnover in the Headships, resulting in at least one new incumbent very much in the mould of the innovative and radical academic, who from time to time was willing to give support to the elected members. This was Dr Tony Dickson, appointed to head the Sociology Department. At the same time, in a contested election for a vacancy on the Academic Planning Committee, an elected member defeated a Head, which could only mean that not only had the Board not divided along elected/ex-officio lines but several Heads must have voted against one of their own number in a secret ballot.

The elected members were further offended by the Director's insistence that they had no representative function but sat on the Board in a purely individual capacity. Attempts to resolve the friction by meetings between

---

[3] *Times Educational Supplement Scotland*, March 7, 1980.

Dr McManus and a delegation appointed from the elected members got nowhere. The position of Lewis Brodie in these developments was an important and difficult one. As the College Registrar he had no policy-making responsibilities, but he did in a number of ways act as a mediator between the two opposed groups on the Academic Board, not least in respect of the fact that he had to compile the minutes of increasingly disputatious meetings. More importantly he was responsible for interpreting procedures, which he was able to do the more effectively because he was always completely in command of regulations and paperwork as well as remaining calm and 'unflappable' while turbulent argument was raging around the Board.

He was intensely committed to the vision of an expanded and improved higher education system as represented by Robbins and the developments of the '60s, and had deliberately chosen a career in educational administration as the most effective means of promoting this vision. However, because of the position of studied neutrality he assumed between the two sides in the dispute, he was regarded with disfavour by the Director, who felt he ought to have been identified with the management, and was even suspected of orchestrating the elected members' campaign — which was wholly inaccurate.

A number of extraneous events contributed to the growing sense of crisis, including, by academic standards, lurid press reports of the dispute. The two academic staff unions in the College intervened as well (the elected members were of course attending their union branch meetings and some had positions in the branch). The College Council had agreed in 1977 that a joint union committee should meet the Director twice a year, but only three meetings had been held between then and 1980, and two of these had merely discussed holidays.

The Pat Wilkie Case
A series of events which occasioned the Director the utmost embarrassment arose from the outcome of two industrial tribunals, relating to the case of a temporary lecturer, Pat Wilkie. She was an extremely well qualified person. Having become a registered general nurse with an additional qualification in neuro-surgery she went on to full-time study at Edinburgh University some years later. There she first obtained a certificate in social studies and then an honours degree in sociology with social and economic history, as part of which she studied social administration and law, proceeding from that to register for a part-time PhD, researching in social

administration while working as a tutor in the Department of Social Administration. During that time she published widely and 'became widely recognised as an authority in her particular field'.[4]

In 1977 she was invited to take an appointment as a temporary part-time lecturer in social policy within the Department of Social Sciences, this later being renewed from year to year and extended in scope, so that she became involved in the formation of courses and became a full examiner in some of the subjects which she taught. Her teaching responsibilities were not confined to the Social Sciences Department's degree but involved nursing studies, health visiting and public administration.

With the reorganisation of the Social Sciences Department in 1979 it was widely expected that a permanent post in social policy would be created in the summer, probably within the envisaged Department of Sociology, and that Pat Wilkie would be a strong candidate to fill it. But a further round of government cuts combined with administrative confusion delayed the establishment of the permanent post and in July the acting Head of the soon-to-be-divided Social Sciences arranged for renewal of her temporary post on a monthly basis pending resolution of the issue.

In September, apparently on the instructions of Dr Beale, another person was appointed to take over Pat Wilkie's teaching. She questioned this action, along with her senior lecturer — the same person who had incurred the Director's displeasure on a previous occasion by selling anti-apartheid newspapers within the College premises. The Director however refused to discuss the matter, and when the aggrieved parties went public on the issue he responded by moving responsibility for teaching social policy away from Sociology to the Department of Law and Public Administration (another of the new Departments). Pat Wilkie took advice from ACAS and discovered that under the Employment Protection Act she had been unfairly dismissed. ACAS took up the matter with Strathclyde Regional Council, the employer of all College staff, but this did not produce a resolution and in January the case went to an industrial tribunal.

Meantime the permanent social policy appointment had been authorised and advertised. Pat Wilkie applied for it and was placed on a short-list of four by the Head of Department. The Director who, as noted, scrutinised

---

[4]Industrial Tribunals (Scotland) Case N. S/128/80, held August 13–14, 1980, decided August 27, 1980.

all appointments, struck her name off and one of the other applicants, a man, was offered the post, whereupon she initiated a complaint of sex discrimination under the Sex Discrimination Act of 1975. The first of these industrial tribunal cases, that unfair dismissal in relation to the part-time appointment, came up for hearing in January 1980, with the tribunal finding in favour of Pat Wilkie and awarding her damages of £2,300. It was not a very favourable piece of publicity for the College management just over a month before the institution was due to receive a visiting panel from the CNAA to assess its fitness to offer CNAA-validated qualifications.

The CNAA 1980 Visit

This visit in early March marked the initial climax of the dispute. So bad had relations become that the elected members and other staff organisations were determined to bring what they conceived to be the staff's grievances out into the open before the CNAA panel, disregarding the unified institutional fronts that are usually put up on such occasions. That they should act in this way raised the stakes, because not so long before in 1978 the CNAA had threatened to withdraw accreditation from Teesside Polytechnic owing to its institutional deficiencies. The January 1980 meeting of the Academic Board, with the CNAA visit imminent, had very belatedly set up discussion groups on the College's structure and functioning and also approved standing orders for the Board's sub-committees (though not the Board itself). Only at that point was a role in resource allocation specified for the sub-committees, though the relationship between sub-committees and Board remained without clear definition.

The two union branches and the elected members made submissions ahead of the visit, 'uniformly critical of the management in general and Dr Beale in particular'.[5] The action was motivated by the hope that the CNAA if nothing else would compel change to be initiated. At the beginning of March, anticipating the CNAA visit a few days later, the *Times Educational Supplement Scotland* ran a splash headline on its front page, 'Staff launch protest over running of Glasgow Tech', followed by a lengthy article which began:

A party of 20 from the Council for National Academic Awards will pay their five-yearly visit to Glasgow College of Technology next Wednesday

---

[5] *Ibid.*

and Thursday amid growing dissatisfaction among the staff with the allegedly authoritarian manner in which the College is run. The College director, Dr Reginald Beale, says this dissatisfaction has come as a complete surprise to him.[6]

Dr Beale had in fact muddied the waters by claiming to the College Council at the end of February that 'The CNAA is primarily concerned with the standards and content of courses and with the way they are run. It is not so much concerned with the way a management runs a college' — a claim that was immediately contradicted by the CNAA's Registrar for institutional reviews, who affirmed that the purpose of the Quinquennial visits was to 'look at everything that could affect the academic standards of their approved courses, which includes staff-management relationships'.[7]

The submission to the CNAA by one of the unions spoke of 'widespread feelings of disappointment and disillusion among staff'. The other included the comment:

Achieving the right balance between line management and committee structure is a problem which faces all institutions, and there is probably no uniquely correct solution. In our opinion, however, there must be a balance, not a subjection of one to the other, and the rights, responsibility and authority of each must be as clearly defined as possible

In this College it is clear that the line management system is accorded the greatest importance and is the mechanism through which a style of policy making has been developed in which participation of the staff is ineffective ... [it went on to observe that formally constituted committees of the College Council had failed to hold any meetings].[8]

The elected members' submission spelled out their grievances in detail:

... we have serious misgivings about aspects of management within the College which at present both affect the general morale of the staff and inhibit academic developments...

---

[6] *Ibid.*
[7] *Ibid.*
[8] EIS Glasgow College of Technology Branch, 'Report of subcommittee on college Administration for discussion at a branch meeting on Wednesday 23 January, 1980', forwarded to CNAA, February 8, 1980.

Many of the recommendations contained in the report of the last CNAA quinquennial visit to GCT … have not been implemented or even discussed … Where attempts by the College management have been made to deal with some of the recommendations they often date from December 1979/January 1980. Furthermore, as of February 1980 there has been no discussion on the Academic Board about the coming quinquennial visit …

…although [the 1974 CNAA Report] comments about the need for an upward flow of ideas, the Director has made it quite plain that he alone makes the final decisions in the College and that the College is managed through meetings of the Directorate and Heads of Departments …

In spite of [the 1974 CNAA Report] the Academic Board has up till now played no role in the formulation of estimates or the allocation of resources. Decisions on these matters are taken by the Directorate and Heads of Departments. Moreover these decisions are taken in secret and are not generally properly communicated to staff… Furthermore, in the absence of any power to make recommendations on allocations of resources and estimates of expenditure, the Academic Board is severely restricted in the role it can play in establishing realistic priorities relating to academic policy …

A proposal that a working party be set up to look at the composition of the Academic Board was rejected by the Academic Board on January 23 1980, at which occasion the Directorate and Heads of Department outvoted the elected members on this matter…

…the elected members are unhappy about the powers given to the chairmen of the standing committees … ie the chairman has essentially two deliberative votes and his rulings cannot be challenged in any way …

… As recently as September 18 1979 the College Council requested that discussions between the Working Party on Academic Structure and Academic Staff should take place. No such discussions have occurred…

The operation and lack of standing orders of Course Development Boards and Boards of Study has at times given cause for concern … as also has the lack of clear guidelines for the constitutional composition of Boards of Study. For example, certain inconsistencies exist in the chairmanship of Boards of Study … There have been occasions when members of some Boards have wished to censure the Chairman or call special meetings. However in some cases the Chairman has over-ruled or ignored such motions. As a consequence of such problems, at least one Board of Study has almost ceased to function…

It must be stated that Strathclyde Region has a very difficult job, with many demands on its limited resources. However, it would seem that the relationship between the College and the Region could be better, and that the College Directorate should see it as a priority to improve this relationship. One of the major difficulties is that the College, in terms of its teaching and research aspirations, would seem to be similar to the English polytechnics or the Scottish Central Institutions. This has implications for the appropriate resource funding of backup facilities …

It is realised that research activities should have a major role in an institution like Glasgow College of Technology. Many academic members of staff are actively engaged in research, though often this is achieved through great personal endeavour rather than through any help provided by the College [and] in spite of obstacles that have been placed in their way … there are, for example, at least two instances in which the College has failed to honour cost sharing arrangements which it entered into with external research funding organisations … Although an ad hoc study leave scheme has been put into effect … not all academic staff were given the opportunity to apply …

It is considered that adequate resource and backup facilities within the College are a prerequisite for achieving a high standard of academic quality both at the undergraduate and postgraduate levels. Consequently the poor state of these central resources in the College has had an adverse effect on student learning, staff teaching and staff research. [The document went on to list Library facilities, computing, administrative clerical and technical staff and overcrowded staffrooms.][9]

[9] *Report of the Elected Members of the Academic Board to the CNAA Quinquennial Visiting Party to Glasgow College of Technology*, February 4, 1980.

One thing which both sides to the dispute did at least agree upon was that in terms of administrative resources the College was severely underfunded by the regional authority. Popularly, however, the Region's unsympathetic attitude towards what should have been its flagship tertiary institution was reputed to be due to the Director's abrasive attitudes towards the regional officials as well, and the bad terms he was on with its Director of Education and the Further Education Sub-committee.

The Student Submission

The document which the Student Association submitted to the visiting party supplies an interesting insight into the worries and concerns of the student body as they existed at that point. The section on the management of the College, which so exercised the academic staff bodies, is comparatively short, though severely critical. It disclaims any wish to engage in 'the now familiar debate about the conflict of line management with the Committee System', but goes on to list seven sources of concern. These comprise the irregularity with which committees, particularly the Joint Committee for Student Affairs, were convened; unhappiness regarding interviewing procedures, such as the notorious failure to have discipline experts on the appointment panels for the new Social Science Department Heads; the failure on the first occasion to appoint a Sociology Head and the action of Dr McManus, the Depute Director, to take over as temporary Acting Head; general failure to communicate the division of responsibilities between members of the Directorate team; antagonism towards the campus trade unions; failure to meet new students for a welcoming session; and failure to involve members of the Academic Board and College Council in decision making.

However, the main headings in the document were under the philosophy and status of the College, resourcing, academic and non-academic staffing levels, facilities and accommodation, student services, student accommodation, sports facilities, nursery provision, academic development and student representation.

The Association deprecated any strategy that sought to turn the College into a purely degree-awarding institution and the dropping of diploma courses: 'we would also wish to emphasise that we feel the College should offer a comprehensive type of education which encompasses a broad range of subjects and qualifications'. It regretted the refusal of the Region to allow the title to be changed to 'Glasgow Polytechnic' (the proposal had been raised again in 1979) and stressed that it felt the existing one to be unsuitable. Any alteration in title, it suggested, must however be accompanied by resource enhancement 'sufficient to compare favourably with Polytechnic Institutions of a comparable size in England and Wales'. Any such comparison did indeed show the College to be under-resourced, and the same was true for similar measurements against comparable central institutions such as Robert Gordon's or Paisley. All points of view within the institution agreed at least upon one thing: that they were being compelled to supply higher education, of equivalent quality to universities, polytechnics and central institutions, on the cheap.

In developing its concerns about resources the Association singled out first the library, where the actual staffing complement was only just over half of what it should have been (18 as against 32) and there was a seven-month cataloguing backlog. It foresaw the new library under construction as likely to exacerbate the problem rather than help to solve it, on account of the difficulties involved in moving the library stock. Academic staffing levels in general were likewise criticised, noting that the average ratio had deteriorated to 11:1 and mentioning specific instances such as a mathematics lecturer having to teach a class of 95 students and a part-time secretarial studies lecturer having to supervise a class of 38 typists.

So far as non-academic staffing was concerned the students again referred to and elaborated upon the complaints made by the College in its submission document regarding regional underfunding. They noted that the Institutional Review of 1974 had already drawn attention to this but little had been done to rectify the deficiencies, and again went on to cite examples: 'The provision for the Matriculation of students for this session, especially the issuing of their matriculation cards was frankly a shambles' (due to shortage of appropriate staff).

The student document, while welcoming the College commitment to improve student welfare services, argued that performance fell well short of intentions, noting that while the College possessed only one overstretched full-time welfare advisor without secretarial backup, Paisley College, with fewer students, had two. A particularly bitter complaint appeared over student accommodation for the 10 per cent of students who did not live at home: 'The College's Student Accommodation Officer has bravely striven to house students, despite a contracting housing stock in the Glasgow area and the crippling handicap of having NO HALLS OF RESIDENCE OF OUR OWN.' No such halls were projected in any financial plan, nor given the state of the Region's finances were they likely to be. Instead, a plan was in hand to refurbish certain very high tower blocks, known as the Red Road Flats, on the edge of the city to provide accommodation for up to 50 students as well as other residents. This scheme was conceived to be a less than ideal solution to the problem.[10]

Only a part-time Careers Guidance Advisor, employed directly by the Region, was available and had to service other colleges in addition. Sports facilities lacked storage space, playing fields, squash courts and swimming pool, and the sports hall was unavailable during the third term, when it was required for examinations: 'College sporting successes have been despite rather than because of the facilities available.' Catering, 'a service dear to the heart of most students', was both inadequate — a new refectory was six months late in opening and understaffed — and expensive, with a recent 20 per cent price increase. Foreseeing an increase in the number of mature students, the Association declared the lack of even a perspective on nursery provision to be particularly short-sighted.

A long section of the document was headed 'Academic Development of the College', but showed little coherence or clear perspective. Noting that 'it would seem that the priority for the next 5 years will be survival rather than expansion' it refused to accept the logic of the education cuts but, not surprisingly, could not suggest how they might be reversed. Non-degree work should be maintained and developed, but comments by the Academic Planning Committee that there would be little scope for the development of 'less vocationally orientated courses' were deplored, particularly since social sciences had been cited as an example of such. Rather surprisingly there is no reference in the document, among the deficiencies in student services, to student union facilities which were certainly not comparable to those enjoyed in other higher education establishments. The absence in the document of any reference to the science and engineering side of the College's work was owed most likely to the fact that the officials of the Association tended to be drawn from among students of other disciplines, particularly social sciences.

Conclusions of the Visit

When the visiting party arrived and set to work the spectacle was presented of elected members of the Academic Board openly criticising, at meetings

---

[10]It was however eventually adopted.

with the panel, the institutional documentation that had been prepared for the occasion, drawing attention to its inadequacies and the contradictions contained in it. They had made the request in their submission for a discussion between themselves and the CNAA visiting team, but this was not granted. Meantime they were also writing to the Chair of the College Council putting their case. On the part of some there were rather extravagant hopes that Lewis Brodie would openly commit himself to their point of view during the visit, but this he quite properly declined to do.

At the final meeting of the visit, between the panel and the full Academic Board, the argument raged uninhibitedly. The panel Chair, who was also the CNAA Chief Officer, Edwin Kerr, opened the meeting by exploring the way in which the Academic Board viewed its role and function, stressing that the roles of Council, Academic Board and Director were 'inextricably interwoven'. An elected member then responded that the view of most of his colleagues was that the line from the Regional Director of Education to Dr Beale bypassed the Academic Board, rendering it a merely advisory body. Dr Beale's response to the Chair however was that the Academic Board's remit was restricted to matters such as course monitoring, patterns of student choice and rationalisation of course provision, and that the Director of Education had never intervened in such matters.

Another elected member affirmed that while the Academic Board should be at the apex of the College's committee structure it was inhibited from playing this role because of the dispute over the interpretation of the constitution and because the Academic Board could not discuss resources. When it had tried to do so it had been prevented. 'Furthermore voting characteristics clearly indicated divisions between Heads of Departments and the elected members which led to considerable mistrust in the Institution'. The first workshop to discuss academic growth and progress had been held a week prior to the visit. A strong impression existed that attempts to address the College's problems had been triggered by the visit and would not have been made otherwise. Two of the newly-appointed Heads of Department however suggested that new structures would help the system to work efficiently and encourage participation, one of them noting that he didn't view himself as a line manager but an academic leader.

The panel took up a stance of impartiality and severely rebuked both sides for undermining the credibility of the College by prolonging the dispute and allowing it to dominate academic affairs. These criticisms, later to be read in the published report, were expressed even more sharply in the verbal comments at the end of the meeting. The College in effect was told to get its act together — or else. This was no idle threat, for should the Council withdraw institutional recognition the degree courses conducted under its authorisation would necessarily have to be terminated. Although they did not escape criticism the elected members felt their stand to be vindicated in the visiting party's recognition that there were serious weaknesses in the way the College was being run and that these would have to be addressed. The most pertinent points of the eventual Report were the following:

> ... The 1980 visiting party found that until recently the College had not attempted to seriously respond to the major recommendations set out in the Council's 1974 Report ...

> Against the range and levels of advanced work of the College, its constitutional position appeared inappropriate to an institution of higher education and inconsistent with the recognition by the Regional Authority of its premier position ... the line management of the College has been strengthened as a form of decision-making, at the expense of the operation of the formal academic structure, thereby diminishing the Academic Board as a major policy-forming and monitoring body ...

> The Council does not believe that the Director has distinguished sufficiently his executive responsibilities from his involvement in formal academic decision-making ... as a result of which there exists a serious lack of confidence and morale across the College ...

> The College, as suggested both by its current provision and by its Quinquennial Plans, aspires to a role as a major institution of higher education. However, prima facie it was doubtful if sufficient progress was being made in developing the internal structures and attitudes in ways appropriate to such a role...

> The visiting party was disappointed that the Director, in his interactions with the local authority, had not sought to strengthen his authority in representing the College by engaging and drawing more upon the considered deliberations of the Academic Board. Indeed it was not

obvious that the special academic needs of the College (within the total administrative responsibility of the Region) had been made clearly apparent to the Authority by either the Directorate or the College Council…

… it was not clear that … the Academic Board was in receipt of the kind of resource data that would enable it to pass an informed judgement upon those plans…

… The visiting party formed the view that, in the general climate of mistrust that it detected, members of the Academic Board (especially those other than ex-officio members) were often reluctant to speak openly, given their perceptions that significant de facto decision-making took place outside of the formal academic structure…

… it was observed that no standing committee possessed obvious responsibility for overseeing matters such as academic structure, staffing appointments and promotion procedure, staff development and the approval and validation of new courses nor was there explicit provision or mechanism … for the consideration of matters affecting courses conducted jointly with local colleges…

The visiting party was disappointed to note that no report, as requested in 1974, had been received from the College detailing the progress made by the former Research Board, and it was appreciated that the recently established Research Committee had not yet been in existence a sufficient length of time to be effective. Consequently, the Council has still to be convinced that the College is implementing, under the direction of the Academic Board, a coherent research policy known to all members of the teaching staff…

An Appendix underlined the last point in even stronger terms, declaring the absence of a report to be 'a cause of concern and disappointment'.

The Report, which reached the College in October 1980, reiterated the Council's demand for student representation on the Academic Board, and while disclaiming any intention of prescribing the College structures of government and organisation stated that 'the APC [Academic Planning Committee] should take on all the terms of reference specified in the documentation' and 'strongly encouraged' it to take responsibility for advising the Academic Board on the allocation of staffing and resources. At the top of its recommendations was the following:

> The review of the Constitution, as recommended by the Working Party of the Academic Board, be conducted forthwith, with specific recommendations being made thereupon through the College Council to the Regional Authority; that review to embrace the role of the Director vis-a-vis the Regional Authority and the Academic Board (especially in terms of the preparation of budget estimates), and the inclusion of students on the composition of the Academic Board.

The Report stated that the Council was of the opinion that the College had the potential to overcome its problems and proposed to return in the autumn of 1981 to see what progress had been made. Until then it 'reserved its position'.

Organisational Reform

Following the CNNA's Report and its consideration by the Governors, the atmosphere in the College and on the Academic Board did not undergo any immediate change — in fact if anything the confrontation intensified. It would have been too much to have expected Dr Beale suddenly to reverse his approach to running the College or drastically modify his ideas of what he felt was in its best interests. On the other hand the 11 elected members (there had been a small degree of turnover since 1979) now felt they had official (if coded) endorsement for their criticisms and redoubled their efforts to secure a change. More than once the elected members' caucus seriously considered going to the Board with a motion of no confidence in the Director, but never resorted to this extreme measure since there was uncertainty that enough Heads could be persuaded to support it. A piece of doggerel unofficially circulated at the time began:

> It's Wednesday the Board convenes,
> And there you see such dreadful scenes,
> Of hate, backstabbing, rows and blether,
> That members feel at end of tether.

The deterioration in relations can be measured by the fact that in the course of these events the College Communist Club convened a public meeting under its own auspices to discuss the College's academic situation and future, doing so, it was claimed, because no other open forum could be found for the purpose and the Director refused to convene a general meeting of the staff. The meeting was packed, and among those attending was the Depute Director, Norman Meadows, who in the course of the discussion openly criticised the Director.

That strife was likely to continue was signalled in the document which the Director circulated in the aftermath of the visit, a memorandum dated March 17. Paradoxically, the document itself was generally bland and anodyne, and for those who opposed the Director's approach, that was precisely the difficulty. His interpretation of the panel Chair's remarks scouted the bad press publicity which the College had latterly received: 'The involvement of the press in the affairs of the College is unfortunate; it does not influence the CNAA, nor make friends, and is not the best way to effect improvement'. This, however, was the only hint in the document that there was serious contention taking place in the institution's affairs: for the rest his summary of the discussion at the joint meeting presented an entirely positive picture which merely required enhancement, and only mentioned as an afterthought the return visit planned for 1981.

Dr Beale's opponents read this as an indication that he had little intention of taking seriously the need for far-reaching changes in decision-making structures and management style, and intended to regard as an endorsement of his approach remarks from the panel which they saw as intending precisely the opposite. Accordingly the elected members, through a letter signed by two of their number and claiming to be speaking on behalf of academic staff in general, requested a meeting with him in his capacity as Chairman of the Academic Board to discuss arrangements for a general meeting:

Following the CNAA visitation a considerable number of members of staff have expressed a desire to have an open meeting of staff to discuss the visitation.

The elected members have agreed that we should ask on their behalf for an opportunity to meet with yourself prior to the weekend to discuss a possible format for such a meeting.

Dr Beale's reply was not encouraging:

> Firstly, I must be quite blunt in saying that I consider it quite wrong for 'Elected Members of the Academic Board' to identify themselves as a representative group whom I could meet or correspond with. As Chairman of the Board I must regard the Board as a whole, and would consider it improper in any way to encourage fragmentation of the Board…
>
> Replying to you, therefore, as individual members of the Academic Board, I do not consider that it would be proper for me to take Chairman's action on a matter involving the Academic Board in an 'open meeting of staff' without this being discussed and agreed by the Board itself.…
>
> On the question of discussing the CNAA Institutional Review Visit, in my opinion it would not be meaningful, and indeed it could be most unwise, to have any such general discussion before we receive the Report of the Visit from the CNAA. I could not support any such premature discussion.
>
> …As Chairman, I cannot take the stance of differentiating between elected, ex-officio and any other form of membership. Again the members who are elected to the Board are regarded as members in an individual capacity, and are in no way 'mandated delegates' nor spokesmen for any particular group of staff.…
>
> I would appeal to you to make every effort to support the workings of the Board in a fashion which does not create or emphasise any division of the Board into Groups.

The elected members held a caucus meeting to agree the response, which they forwarded on March 26 and which was signed by all of them. While expressing appreciation of the prompt reply, willingness to avoid emphasising divisions in the Board and consciousness of the CNAA's injunction to 'stop the infighting and start pulling together', they reasserted the legitimacy of their actions.

> … While we do not take up the position that we are 'mandated delegates' and while none of us has ever used such a term, we feel most strongly that

we have a responsibility to consult and seek the opinion of our colleagues who have elected us and take the generality of their views into consideration. Such a responsibility includes meeting staff for the purpose of conveying information on Academic Board discussions, particularly in view of the fact that in some Departments this is the only medium staff have got for receiving such information.

We feel that the regrettable division of Academic Board members into specific interest groups can be more readily avoided by the widest possible consultation and participation of all members of staff in the taking of significant decisions. We hope that the projected discussions on the Visiting Party report will be the beginnings of such a process....

Despite the proclaimed eagerness of both sides to work together in collective harmony in order to sort out the problems identified at the visit, the stage was undoubtedly being set for a further round of conflict, the rival perceptions of what was required being so much at odds. The main arena for the continuing struggle remained the Academic Board and its committees, but representations were now also made to the College Council, upon which sat two members of the academic staff. That body, in the wake of the CNAA visit, had set up an ad hoc Committee with the remit of examining 'the responsibilities and relationships of the various bodies within the College to each other and to the Regional Authority'.[11] The Council too was in some degree of disorganisation, as demonstrated by the fact that the election for one of the staff members, which fell due in June, had to be cancelled and re-run on account of the muddle: 'I am aware of the considerable dissatisfaction felt by many colleagues, caused by delay in circulation of papers, the extended nomination date, the uncertainty surrounding the nomination of one of the candidates, the withdrawal of one candidate in mid-election and the inevitable disfranchisement of any colleagues who may have voted for him'.[12]

The Chair of the Committee, Mr Alastair Denholm, put out a general circular inviting staff within the College to comment upon developments, and both collective and individual representations were received. One of the

---

[11]Ad hoc Committee Report, November 1980. It prefaced with a quote from Edmund Burke: 'An event has happened upon which it is difficult to speak and impossible to be silent'.

[12]K S Reader, Acting Clerk to the College Council, June 19, 1980.

latter referred to a collapse in morale among very large numbers of the teaching staff and went on to claim that the College's advantages were being irresponsibly dissipated and its academic credibility put at risk: 'The impression at large is that the College leadership — in the person of the Directorate and Heads of Department — is addicted to arbitrary, perverse and incompetent behaviour and absolutely refuses to listen to or consider a reasoned case or contrary viewpoint.'

The writer went on to claim that the flurry of activity initiated by the Directorate prior to the CNAA visit had now entirely died away and that the Director now appeared to behave as if no problem existed (the letter was written at the end of June). He also wrote that a group of staff teaching nursing courses and making representations about their dissatisfactions were told, 'in so many words, that they must assume that any decision, no matter how inexplicable, irrational or perverse it appeared to be, was taken in their own best interests'.

The Director endeavoured to stand out against the demands for radical restructuring, to the extent that the elected members were again in August formally requesting that he be required to report on developments since the CNAA visit and what initiatives were being taken arising from its verbal report.[13] But three developments in the summer and autumn of the year undermined his position. The first of these was the second industrial tribunal decision on the Pat Wilkie case, the second the long-awaited CNNA Report, and the third the Report of the Council's ad hoc Committee.

The Three Reports

The tribunal was held on August 13 and 14 and its report emerged two weeks later and found unanimously that the applicant had been subjected to sex discrimination because of the failure to interview her for the permanent social policy appointment, and awarded her compensation of £1,000. That in itself would have been embarrassing enough for the College management, but the comments which the tribunal made on the Director's behaviour were utterly damning:

> Mr Finch [the acting Head of Law and Public Administration] quite specifically stated that the matter of the removal of the applicant's name

---

[13]G Dunlop and W Thompson to the Clerk to the Academic Board, August 29, 1980.

from the short leet was not discussed with him. He was simply told that it was being removed and he in his position had no right to go against that decision. … Doctor Beale in his evidence claimed he had discussed the removal of the applicant's name… The Tribunal preferred the evidence of Mr Finch on this point….

Before discussing Doctor Beale's evidence in detail it is right to say that the Tribunal found [his] evidence to be so self-contradictory and so changeable that they found it difficult to place any credence on any part of his evidence. … He was so evasive in answering straightforward questions … that it was difficult to avoid the conclusion that he was being deliberately evasive. There was no way in which his evidence could be looked at as a whole because so much of it was inconsistent.[14]

In fact the Director and his solicitor were prepared to concede that an act of discrimination had indeed been perpetrated, but now claimed, though this defence had not been previously advanced, that the discrimination was motivated, not on grounds of gender, but by Pat Wilkie's successful action in January for unfair dismissal, since he felt that that was not the way in which academics should behave. The tribunal found this unconvincing, noting that his previous defence had rested purely on the claim that the other applicants were better qualified and remarking acidly that Dr Beale's own qualifications were in engineering.

The CNAA Report, whose conclusions have been noted above, appeared at the beginning of October, with a copy sent to the Strathclyde Director of Education. With the Director now evidently on the defensive, the various advocates of change within the College stepped up their activities. A communication from the elected members was forwarded to the Council's ad hoc Committee claiming that the worries of the academic staff had been confirmed by the CNAA Report and declaring 'A satisfactory resolution of existing difficulties and the healthy academic development of the institution can only be attained by the recognition that serious problems do exist and by application of the will to resolve them.' The elected members went on to summarise the changes they wanted to see instituted:

---

[14]Industrial Tribunals (Scotland) Case N. S/128/80, held August 13–14, 1980, decided August 27, 1980.

The satisfactory progress of academic affairs requires that the Academic Board should be clearly and unambiguously responsible for the formulation and monitoring of academic policy within the institution. It follows from that that the Academic Board — within the framework established by the College Council — must have control over the allocation of resources, otherwise it is unable to fulfil responsibly the function of guiding academic policy. The structure of committees now established within the College must operate more effectively in integrating academic development and in assisting the upward flow of ideas within the College. It is essential to the development of a mature Academic Board that the Directorate and Heads of Departments' influence on academic policy should occur within Academic Board and there should be no attempt to use the Directorate-Head of Department management chain as an instrument for formulating academic policy.[15]

Emboldened likewise by the CNAA Report the Depute Director, Dr Meadows, who was not greatly in accord with his superior, issued a document fiercely critical of the management style, including the following points:

> Staff/student ratios are not used as a basis of allocation and there are no agreed norms or bands ... Repeated up-dating of figures occurs due to certain variables .... When available it is not clear how derived figures are used for control purposes and allocations have a high degree of arbitrariness about them.

> ... Full-time equivalents are calculated, a delegated function within the Directorate. These are presented to a meeting of Heads, at one of the monthly formal Heads' meetings or at an internal meeting ... At various times some Heads present their personal views on appropriate staffing levels to the Director. Some Heads make much more use of this technique than others, and are often more successful than their colleagues. The Director then decides who shall get which staff and informs a meeting of Heads accordingly. Then the haggling starts and various special pleas are made. The resolution of any disagreements resides

---

[15]Comments to the ad hoc Committee of the College Council from elected members of the Academic Board of Glasgow College of Technology, October 1980.

almost exclusively with the Director, who does not actually consult with other members of the Directorate.... Claims for academic staffing in Central Service Units, such as the Library and Computer and for Student Services are very difficult to present or sustain.

He went on to describe further confusion and lobbying, then produced his most acerbic criticisms:

> Such a system lends itself to the exercise of personal patronage, staff allocation as a reward for support or 'good behaviour' and to the exigencies of special pleading. Decisions do not necessarily map need, and there is no informed decision-making. Academic Board is nowhere in this process, nor its committees. Regional policy and the College reaction to it, or a positive lead from the College to the Region are not matters of common knowledge within the College. Correspondence on these matters is not presented to Heads or all members of the Directorate. There are no meetings of the Directorate as a body to discuss staffing levels or policies so the senior management of the College is no better informed than, for example, individual Heads. Negotiations with the Region on staffing levels are conducted by the Director.[16]

The report of the Council's ad hoc Committee, emerging in November, though expressed in less robust terms than the CNAA's, tended in the same direction. Its preamble noted that it had met 10 times since being instituted in May, had taken both written and oral evidence, and not having had the services of any member of the College staff had thereby maintained the confidentiality of all the submissions it had received. It summarised its view as being that the Principal should be responsible to the Council for internal organisation, management and discipline and that subject to the overall responsibility of the Council the Academic Board should be responsible for the planning, co-ordination, development and oversight of the academic work.

The Committee, though its language was discreet, made clear its attitude to the Director's erstwhile claims:

---

[16]Dr N G Meadows, Academic Board and its Involvement in Resources, October 15, 1980.

The Committee are confident that the Director will not interpret [Clause 17] as over-riding the policy forming responsibilities of the Academic Board and Council and that he will involve his staff and the Council in the decisions relating to:—

a) the opportunity to submit budget proposals;
b) the receipt of the allocation of finance taking account of his proposals;
c) the provision of staff complement based on agreed course programmes;
d) his responsibility for input of course plans for the College.

The Committee expressed its view that while the 'Region rightly wishes to maintain final control ... a change in the constitution is required so that the Director [is] responsible to the College Council [ie not to the Region] for the internal organisation management and discipline of the College.' It also noted that one of the Council's own committees was unsatisfactorily constituted:

The purpose and concept of the Chairman's Committee is not easily defined and the committee views with some disquiet the apparent authority which it wielded in the past. If it is desired to continue the remit then it should be redefined with clarity, in that it is an Advisory Committee for the Chairman and has no executive powers.

The Committee also noted that, 'We believe that there should be additional students as full members of the Academic Board' and the peroration to the Report concluded that to release energies and secure all-round improvement 'is not by recrimination or exhortation but by putting the relationship between the region, staff and students on to a new basis which will involve not just the management but the whole College in sharing responsibility for the success of Glasgow College of Technology.'[17]

Another Report
A further report deserves to be noted, that of a Special Review Group on the College, which was set up by the Region itself and reported in January 1981. Some of its phraseology left the reader in no doubt of the Region's dissatisfaction with the management of the College hitherto: 'internal

---

[17]Ad hoc Committee Report, November 1980, *op. cit.*

management leaves much to be desired … There have been problems of management virtually since the inception of the College'. 'Clause 17 … clearly has not worked.' 'Criticism must also be made of the College Council. It seems to us to have been … a remarkably passive body … In our view the College Council has been ineffective … an atmosphere of suspicion and mistrust prevails… there must be a change in attitude among Directorate and Heads of Department towards greater responsiveness to the views of members of staff as put by their elected representatives. Within the Directorate there is no cohesion … It is through this mechanism of strict line management that rigid control is exercised over academic policy within the College, whereas in our view the proper forum for determining and controlling academic policy is the Academic Board … subject always to control as necessary by the College Council … we consider that greater leadership is required in executive from the Directorate of the College. By "leadership" we do not mean "dictatorship". There has been too much of a tendency to this in the past' — with much more to the same effect.[18]

Reformulation

By the time this Report appeared, however, the reconstitution of the planning and management structures was already in hand, pushed by the CNAA and Council reports. The Director's opposition was overborne, and he submitted to a reformulation of the decision-making processes which greatly circumscribed his powers to determine academic policy. The two key bodies in the reorganisation were the Academic Policy Committee (which replaced the old Academic Planning Committee) and the rather clumsily titled Committee on Committees and Procedure. This was established jointly by the Academic Board and College Council in October (and also contained a representative from the Region's Education Department). It reported on the College constitution in December and on the committee system in March the following year. It was a fairly elaborate process, and during this period the Academic Board was meeting monthly or even more often.

It was during this period that Lewis Brodie's influence on the College's development was at its most pronounced. He was the person who was

---

[18]Strathclyde Regional Council, *Report of Special Review Group on Glasgow College of Technology*, January 15, 1981.

principally responsible for drafting the details of the new structures, their composition, remits and relationships with each other. These drafts became the basis for the academic structure which emerged. Three faculties were established: Business and Administrative Studies, Life and Social Sciences, and Science and Engineering. Underlining the Board's involvement in resource allocation an Estimates and Resources Committee came into being:

> The Academic Board shall make arrangements for ... draft estimates which have a direct bearing on the responsibilities of Course Boards, Boards of Studies and Faculty Boards to be considered by those bodies which shall have the right to comment on the draft Estimates; Course Boards and Boards of Study to Faculty Boards and Faculty Boards to the Academic Board or to such of its Standing Committees as the Academic Board may nominate. This process shall be completed by late May each year.[19]

The process of reorganisation was rounded off when the Regional Council's Special Review Group Report recommended a new constitution for the College embodying the changes. The composition of the Academic Board itself was altered significantly. All Heads of Department would of course continue to sit on it, but in future elected members would be drawn partly from the separate faculties and partly from a constituency of the whole College, and these elections were to be held on a proportional representation basis with transferable votes. At the base of the committee system were to be instituted Subject Area Boards. In single-discipline departments these were equivalent to a departmental board, but not in multi-discipline ones. The idea was to stress that the academic policies and plans of individual disciplines/departments would, within the overall perspectives and rules of the College, be made by the members collectively and that the role of the Head was an executive one, taking responsibility for resources and implementing decisions — but not making them of his/her own accord. A longstanding grievance was remedied, namely the lack of any input by ordinary members of staff in appointments. According to the new rules

---

[19]Report by the Committee on Committees and Procedure (Augmented) on the College's Academic Structure, March 1981.

drawn up, staff in the department would henceforth appoint a representative to sit on appointment panels from Head of Department downwards.

Although Dr Beale chaired the Committee on Committees and lent his agreement to the changes, sometimes allowing his viewpoint to be overruled by a vote, it would have been very surprising indeed if his heart had really been in the developments. In the course of 1981 he announced his resignation, which came into effect from April 1982. The appointment of the College Director remained in the hands of the Strathclyde Regional Authority. The candidates to succeed Dr Beale included the two Depute Directors, and rather surprisingly the appointment went to one of them, since there was a general feeling that the authority would probably go for an outsider who had not been involved in the preceding imbroglio and would therefore come to the institution with an unclouded perspective. The new Director was Dr Norman Meadows. The same year Bernard McManus left to become Head of the then Bournemouth College. His successor was Professor Neil Buxton, an economist previously employed at Heriot Watt University.

Norman Meadows, Head of Electrical and Electronic Engineering at Portsmouth Polytechnic, had been selected in 1974, aged 56, as Deputy Director out of 44 applicants. On leaving school at the age of 15 he worked at Vickers Aviation for several years, later spending six years with the Admiralty in their engineering laboratories and then at their Bath headquarters as a design draughtsman working on electronic and computer control of gunnery systems. During this time he completed Ordinary and Higher National Certificates by night school study. From there he went to Garnett College as a mature student, gaining a FE Teachers' Certificate with distinction, followed by FE teaching for three years.

Returning to industry for another year as a patent engineer of flight simulators with Redifon Ltd, he returned to teaching as a lecturer at Wimbledon Technical College.

There he discovered that there was a qualification called a degree which everyone else seemed to have and which guaranteed them the promotion he was not getting, so he acquired one in Mathematics, Physics, Psychology from the University of London after three years of private study preceded by O and A levels.... He went to Battersea CAT during the final year of his studies.... During this period he was publishing regularly on engineering subjects and continued this at Battersea. There he discovered that a mystical qualification called a PhD elevated people into more senior posts and that they were rather quaintly addressed as Doctor, so he decided to acquire one of these and as the private study route had been alright so far, he studied for his PhD on the same basis. When this was nearing completion he was appointed to the University of Sussex as Reader in Control Engineering ...

At this time the Polytechnics were emerging and, with this rag-bag of experience, Dr Meadows decided that his future lay in that sector. He went as Head of Department and then as chairman of a large Engineering Faculty at Portsmouth. ...He spent four months in Nigeria as Visiting Professor at Amhadu Bello University.[20]

The Chair of the Council also changed during this period of turmoil, though in this instance for reasons quite unconnected. As mentioned above, the first Chair of the Governing Council — after 1975 the College Council — George Moore retired in 1980 on account of ill health. His successor, who was elected at the September meeting, was Charles Drury, a nominee of the STUC and a member of the Council since 1976. Mr Drury had been born in London during the First World War, but the family later moved to Manchester. Much of his career was spent in the labour movement, initially through the Clerical and Administrative Workers' Union. During the Second World War working in an electrical factory, he also served in a bomb disposal unit. In 1948 he became a full-time trade union official in Glasgow, transferring two years later to the National and Local Government Officers' Association (NALGO) Scottish District Office.

Elected to the General Council of the STUC in 1970 he was Chair of its Education Committee for 7 years. He served on the General Council for 10 years, being President of the Congress in 1978–7. After retirement he continued with strenuous activity, serving on the Central Arbitration Committee, the Scottish Business Education Council, the Scottish Arts Council, the Cinematography Film Council, the Advisory Council for Social Work, as well as the GCT Council.[21]

---

[20]Glasgow College of Technology, *Contact*, Issue 12, December 1981, presumably written by Dr Meadows himself. A considerable sense of mission must have been required to move from a Readership at Sussex University to head a polytechnic department.

[21]GCT, *Contact*, No 10, December 1980.

Assessment: Culture Clash

Undoubtedly the events of 1979–81 reflected both the general features prevailing in higher education at that period and the particular circumstances of Glasgow College of Technology. A conflict that as well as being academic was partly cultural and partly generational (the elected members of the Academic Board tended to be younger than the ex-officio ones) was exacerbated by the tightening resource constraints being experienced across the sector, frustrating hopes and expectations and causing the control of such as were available to become a matter for contention.

If resources had been plentiful and sufficient to meet material expectations of what a higher education establishment ought to be, constitutional grievances might well have been moderated, though not altogether absent. Paradoxically, the area in which the frustration was most keenly felt, in the shortage of non-academic staff for administrative and backup functions, was one in which the Director himself did not have any control. Appointments here were wholly at the discretion of the Region (formally the same was true for academic staff but in practice the College was allowed to determine their allocation within a resource envelope) and the report of January 1981 emphasised that whatever else might change, this state of affairs would not be modified.

So far as the culture clash was concerned, although the Director along with most of the Directorate and Heads of Department were accused by their opponents, at least implicitly, of authoritarianism combined with bad faith, that was probably not how they themselves perceived matters. No doubt they saw themselves merely as running the College and exercising their particular responsibilities in the manner to which they had been accustomed from their previous experiences, as well as doing their best to grapple with difficulties of establishing a new institution on a solid foundation and coping with sudden and unexpected contractions in funding.

What they saw as institutional leadership their critics, aspiring to more open styles of management, were likely to interpret as autocracy, but there was a personal element as well which helped to inflame the situation. Had the Director been willing to engage in give and take with his critics, submit to questioning and seek for compromises when points were strongly at issue, then he could probably have got most of what he wanted in any case without exciting strong antagonisms. He appears, however, to have been familiar with habits of command which he was unable to alter (possibly his background in nuclear engineering may have had something to do with that), to snatch at decisions and then if challenged to justify them after the event in ways which tended to be incoherent and ill-thought out and which, as with the Pat Wilkie case, laid him open to charges of prevarication. When he retired the Assistant Director, K S Reader, who wrote the farewell notice in the College bulletin, amidst his commendations was constrained to note that 'Dr Beale had his own style of management which did not please all who worked with him, but it is a poor leader who courts popularity for its own sake'.[22]

---

[22]*Contact*, No 13, June 1982.

Chapter Eight

Glasgow College of Technology, 1981–1992

The Early Eighties

The reformation which the College had undertaken of its structures and its ambience averted the threat of de-recognition by the CNAA, and the intended full institutional visit in autumn 1981 was replaced by a more informal visit from a smaller CNAA group to conduct an interim assessment. One reason for the alteration was that continuing shortage of administrative staff (over which the College had no control) had impeded the full implementation of the revised academic structure — faculty boards for example became operational only in March 1982. This visit, however, approved on a provisional basis what had been done so far, and the full institutional visit was postponed until November 1983.

Although that institutional visit pronounced itself generally satisfied, the satisfaction was severely qualified. The Academic Policy Committee came under particular scrutiny, the panel expressing itself as being unclear about whether it was supposed to be a clearing house for departmental initiatives or a directive agency. The meeting at the end of the visit between the visiting party and the full Academic Board was, in the words of one participant, a disaster. The contributions from Academic Board members who spoke were, to quote the same participant, nearly all 'sycophantic votes of thanks' which thoroughly displeased the panel members. A panel member responded with a sharp reminder that the College had to work out its own destiny, 'not ask us what it's necessary to do to become good boys'. The panel Chair was said to be furious and resolved to make the same point in the Report of the review.

The Report emerged at the beginning of March 1984. The covering letter to Dr Meadows noted that while it was agreed that the direction of developments had been encouraging 'It did not however share the College's satisfaction at the extent of the progress that had been made'. It was acknowledged that 'a new spirit of harmony and unity of purpose had been generated in the College' but 'The visiting party was not, however, convinced, particularly on the evidence of the comments made by members of the Academic Board during the final formal session of the visit, that all members of the Board were yet fully aware of the extent of the work still needed to be accomplished'.

DR NORMAN MEADOWS, *BSc, PhD, MIEE, FBIM, MinstEnvSc* (pictured left), Director of Glasgow College of Technology, 17 April 1982 to 31 December 1988, having previously held the post of Depute Director (from 1974).

The visiting party was also convinced that the College was not playing the part it might in the overall progress of higher education upon a national scale:

A further clear impression received by the visiting party was that the College was unduly parochial, and that it at present lacked the self-confidence, perhaps understandable in the light of the recent history of the relationship between the College and the CNAA, to make a full and positive contribution to the debate about the future development of the public sector of higher education outside the Region.[1]

However the report did refer to the satisfactory relationship now existing between GCT and the College of Building and Printing.

The College's eternal complaints regarding underfunding were not endorsed, for 'Members concluded on the basis of their experience with comparable institutions that the College's overall budget was not demonstrably less favourable than elsewhere'. While commending the self-critical awareness of some of the papers presented for the visit, the panel was 'very disappointed not to find evidence of a similar level of critical self-awareness in its meeting with the Academic Board'. The meeting had evidently made a significant — and bad — impression.

Nevertheless, having announced at the beginning of that same meeting that the intention was to approve the College, the CNAA could hardly renege on it, and so the approval of the College as a suitable institution for conducting courses leading to CNAA awards was confirmed although 'The visiting party was not however convinced that all staff ... had successfully distinguished satisfaction from complacency [and] the College still has much hard work to undertake before it reached the level of development achieved by many of its peers in public sector higher education'. Consequently, further progress would be kept under close review.

In spite of these qualifications an academic structure now existed which was generally regarded as satisfactory within the institution, and further disputes were within this framework rather than about its basic justification. Moreover Lewis Brodie's alterations to the electoral system for the Academic Board, now with a steady biennial turnover of members rather than a dozen elected simultaneously en bloc, diluted the elected members' cohesiveness. Their caucus meetings were maintained for a short while longer but then faded out on account of poor attendances. Essentially the caucus had been the product of a crisis and disappeared along with it.

[1]Council for National Academic Awards, Committee for Institutions, *Report of an Institutional Review Visit to Glasgow College of Technology on November 29–30 1983*, February 28, 1984.

In the light of the reorganisation the Board, with its locus on resourcing now constitutionally entrenched, began to direct its attention to financial matters as they affected academic development. This was something of a mixed blessing, however, for it meant that the Board now had to plan and take responsibility for the severe cuts that were imposed as public spending on higher education was fiercely reined back in the early '80s. The Academic Policy Committee indeed set up a sub-committee to allocate the cuts across the board and decide how each department's estimates would be reduced.

Academic Growth

The College continued to grow both in student numbers and the range of courses which it offered. In the early '80s serious concern came to the fore regarding its position in the engineering field. The deep economic recession of those years still further tightened the market for entrants and intensified competition with its academic rivals. Suggestions were advanced in informal discussion that it was not worthwhile trying to sustain a convincing Engineering Department within the College and that it would make more sense to close it down and redeploy elsewhere the resources thus released. But such ideas never got to the stage of serious consideration since, apart from practical difficulties, engineering was regarded as being much too central to the College's vocational identity.

Instead it was decided to embark upon a drive to improve the standard of engineering education which the institution offered. A BSc Engineering was already in place by this time, but the decision was taken to embark upon a more ambitious project, namely to develop a Bachelor of Engineering degree. In time the undertaking was brought to successful conclusion and the new degree received CNAA approval, even though the College remained handicapped by the paucity of its facilities compared with the other three institutions.

The College regarded evening teaching as an important part of its remit, and these courses continued to expand. The BA Social Sciences degree became available in an evening study mode (the evening study London University BA in History now being phased out) with precisely the same courses as were available for the full-time degree, although students could progress only so far as the unclassified degree by this method and had to switch to the full-time mode if they wished to pursue it to honours level.

Demand was high and many more applications were received than there were places. Both the departments involved and the College regarded this initiative as fulfilling its remit of bringing higher education closer to the local community.

The nursing studies commitment continued to develop following the introduction of the degree. Winifred Logan brought with her her international contacts and strongly developed the department in the field of research, in which she pushed and encouraged her staff. She also encouraged them to become external examiners throughout the UK and beyond. Dorothy Kilgour was an external examiner in Botswana. Following her retirement in 1986 she was succeeded by Dr Margaret Alexander, who became one of the College's first professors under the scheme described below. She had previously worked for the Welsh Office and continued her predecessor's commitment to research. By the end of the decade an honours degree was in place.

Another principle which the College had committed itself to was the development of joint courses with neighbouring further education establishments, and development in this area had begun as early as the mid-'70s with the College of Building and Printing. In 1974 a collaborative degree in Quantity Surveying had been approved for a period of six years. As the renewal date approached, however, its future became entangled with the institutional problems affecting the College of Technology. The College of Building and Printing itself received an institutional visit in May 1980, which concluded that:

> ... the model of association between the College of Building and Printing and the College of Technology had not been at all effective in underpinning the academic standard of the degree-level work conducted jointly by the two Colleges, and that further attention needed to be given to the model of association ... to the provision of resources appropriate to degree work, and to an improved perception on the part of the College of Building and Printing of the climate appropriate to degree studies.[2]

In the light of this Report the Quantity Surveying degree was approved only for a further two years and a proposed additional collaborative degree in Building was rejected.

---

[2] Council for National Academic Awards, Committee for Institutions, *Report on Discussions with staff from Glasgow College of Technology and Glasgow College of Building and Printing on May 14 1981*, October 5, 1981.

A year later, however, a visit to consider the joint courses reached a very different conclusion and, though noting that certain difficulties still remained, expressed itself satisfied with the efforts made to address the previous criticisms. The Building degree was now approved to start if possible in the 1981–82 session.

Lewis Brodie

Lewis Brodie's activities were not confined to his work as the College Registrar. He was also active in charitable organisations and became one of the founders in Scotland of the Social Democratic Party when it was established in 1981, though of course his educational role precluded him from assuming a high profile within it. In the course of 1984 he began to suffer from severe internal pains, which he self-medicated with a growing intake of pain-killers, eating them, in the words of one of his staff, 'like smarties'.

Repeated medical investigation of suspected liver trouble failed to detect the source of the problem, until at the beginning of 1985 tuberculosis of the bone was diagnosed and he was told that he would be hospitalised for some time. The diagnosis, however, was soon shown to be mistaken and further investigation at the beginning of May, involving surgical procedures, revealed that he was suffering from advanced cancer, with primaries in both lungs and secondary growths in his spine, the source of the excruciating pain. He was a very heavy smoker, and unquestionably this was the cause of his illness; he even smoked at Academic Board meetings, these being days before no-smoking provisions became routine.

Released from hospital in what was unmistakably terminal condition, Lewis Brodie refused to abandon hope but, receiving radium treatment which reduced the cancer in his spine and alleviated the pain he was suffering, preserved an attitude of determination to recover and even attended the Academic Board meeting in August. He was compelled, however, to return to hospital shortly afterwards and died in the late summer. He left his body to medical research and consequently had no funeral. His death represented a grievous loss to the institution, for without his work and influence it might well not have succeeded in recovering its credibility with the CNAA. Had he survived and continued in his office the institution might have avoided some of the debacles which subsequently overtook it.

Central Institution Status

The mid-'80s saw the consolidation of Thatcherism in British public life. Following exploratory measures in her first Parliament between 1979 and 1983, including a dramatic financial squeeze upon higher education, sweeping electoral victory in the latter year led on to the programme of large-scale privatisation, trade union attack and government centralisation associated with the name of this premier. The years 1984–85 were the years of her epic victory against the miners and equally comprehensive defeat of recalcitrant local governments. The extension of centralised control applied also to education at every level. So far as higher education was concerned this was mainly exercised by means of financial allocation and control of funding, but could be strikingly direct when opportunity offered, as in the case of one central institution, Paisley College, where in 1983 the Scottish Office minister responsible for education, Alex Fletcher, forced the discontinuance of a course because, reflecting government perceptions, he didn't like the term 'Social Sciences' in its title.[3] Paisley simply re-established the course under a different name, but the non-university higher education sector was left in no doubt of the direction of the Government's thinking.

Glasgow College of Technology suffered no such infliction, although in this same period it came at last under SED control. During 1983 and 1984 a Council for Tertiary Education in Scotland had been sitting, aiming to rationalise the situation that had grown up through the evolutionary processes of development during the previous century, and doubtless to further central control at the same time. In 1984 it announced its findings, and recommended that colleges where the bulk of work was at advanced level should be centrally rather than locally funded. At first glance only two institutions appeared likely to be affected, namely Napier College and Glasgow College of Technology; but such perception was misleading, for what was envisaged was that some colleges should be downgraded and transferred to local authority control, while their advanced courses were hived off to the centrally funded institutions. Since the Report did not specify which institutions should necessarily be promoted, some of the more ambitious local authority colleges, such as Bell College in Hamilton, also had hopes of joining the favoured group. Their disappointment when they failed to achieve promotion however was as nothing to the angst affecting the one

---

[3]The government attitude was probably not improved by the fact that the Head of the Department in question was a well-known communist.

which was unlucky enough to be relegated, Leith Nautical College. In the end only Napier and Glasgow College of Technology improved their status.

The Secretary of State, George Younger, announced on July 19, 1984 acceptance in principle of the Council's recommendation in relation to GCT and proposed a Steering Group to oversee the transition. Even prior to this announcement the College had set up a Central Institution Working Party which produced a substantive report for the ad hoc Interim Steering Group, composed of representatives of the Region, SED, the College Council and College staff. The most immediate and pressing concern of the Council and the Steering Group was the question of finance — for not only was the College historically underfunded compared with other central institutions, but additional costs would necessarily be incurred from the change in status — for example payroll administration, computer and other maintenance would pass from the Region to the College.

For these and other reasons the transfer did not proceed without friction. A well-informed and perceptive article in the *Glasgow Herald* of October 4, 1984 indicated what some of them were. The reporter wrote that staff at both Colleges were strongly in favour of the change, for reasons which varied from 'high-minded desires for academic freedom' to 'the less enlightened but no less potent, appeal of academic snobbery which would come from pulling out of the low-brow further education sector and sharing the CI sector with others of a more "advanced" bent.' In fact the reporter, Stewart McIntosh, was wrong in this respect so far as GCT was concerned, or at least over-generalising, for not all the staff supported the move and opposition was expressed on the Academic Board.

Among those who opposed there were two main considerations. The first did indeed relate to the issue of academic snobbery — those against reckoned that this was one of the motivations and should be opposed for precisely that reason. They urged that the College would better fulfil its intended educational mission of keeping close to the community by remaining with the local authority, for transfer to CI status would strengthen an elitism that would reinforce the trend to abandoning sub-degree qualifications.

The other principal argument was that academic freedom, far from being enhanced, would be more likely to be jeopardised by CI status as the SED, given its political complexion, would be likely to exercise a more restrictive and intrusive authority over how the institution's funding was applied. The reporter noted this point, commenting that 'it could be that losing the local authority "buffer" which cushioned GCT and Napier from direct Government control might lead to even tighter controls as the Government continues to sharply consider the value for money which it believes it is getting for its expenditure'. However within the College the reluctance undoubtedly represented a minority viewpoint and the *Glasgow Herald* was right in essence if not detail regarding staff attitudes.

The article was punningly entitled 'Cash is the Central Issue' and it noted that both Colleges were hoping for extra funding following on from their change in status, but might not get it. Should that be the case, the author speculated, additional costs would force them to cut back somewhere, perhaps severely. He also speculated that such might be precisely the SED's intention, to use the new recruits as object lessons to their better funded traditional counterparts, Robert Gordon's, Paisley and Dundee, to demonstrate that these latter could well manage with less and 'produce their graduates more cheaply than they do at present'. Commenting on the particular position at GCT, the article correctly noted, in rather picturesque language, that 'Staff at the college would argue that it is an overworked carthorse, almost broken through lack of nourishment', and that the institution 'does not want to be used as a rod for others' backs'.

Financial considerations were not the only point at issue, the other principal one being the composition of the Governing Body for the new CI, and in this respect the objections of both the College and the Region were identical. SED proposals envisaged a reduction in representation from the College staff, trade unions and local authorities (the district Council was to be excluded entirely) and increase in nominees from business and commerce. Moreover they stipulated that the Chair of the new body would be appointed directly by the Secretary of State rather than elected from among the Governors. It may be noted in passing that even the Conservative-controlled Lothian Regional Council was unhappy with the composition proposed for Napier, but since it was not, unlike Strathclyde, prepared to challenge it, the Scottish Secretary was able to go ahead in early April 1985 with laying regulations before Parliament changing Napier's status and appointing its Governing Body.

Because Strathclyde, the College Council and the College trade unions (not to mention the Students' Association) held out longer, the process was delayed in the case of GCT. The College Council complained that the SED had produced no stated justification for its attitude and produced an alternative proposal more in line with the existing composition. The Scottish Office made some minor concessions[4] (though not on the question of election as against appointment of Chair) and on May 2, 1985 George Younger was able to lay the appropriate regulations before Parliament, to come into effect on September 1. The press release which accompanied his action defined central institutions (there were now 13 in Scotland) as follows:

> They provide most of the full-time courses of education of degree standard in Scotland outside the universities and colleges of education in subjects which include science and paramedical studies, engineering and technology, business studies and management, art, architecture, home economics, music and textiles. Facilities are also available for postgraduate study.

The definition failed, however, to distinguish between the five CI's of an unmistakable polytechnic character and the other largely monotechnic ones, including Queen's College or Queen Margaret College — though they too were moving towards a broader range of provision.

The first Chair of the new Governing Body was Mr John Wotherspoon, the Vice-Chair of the existing College Council. He was a Fellow of the British Institute of Management and had formerly been the Managing Director of the big Singer's sewing-machine factory in Clydebank (it had been closed down by that time: following its closure he was appointed Chair of Singer's UK company). Born in Glasgow, his family background was predominantly an engineering one, his paternal grandfather being an ironmaster and his father a marine engineer, who eventually became Chief Engineer to the Egyptian State Railways. John Wotherspoon's original ambition was to be a vet, but this fell by the way when he became a toolmaker at Kelvin, Bottomley and Bairds. From there, promotion through middle and senior management at various firms was combined with further study and recognition by business and civic bodies, as well as the award of the CBE in 1977.[5]

---

[4]*Inter alia*, a representative from the District Council was conceded.
[5]GCT *Contact*, No 8, December 1979.

College Name

Prior to the changeover the question of the institution's name had been raised once more and suggestions invited by the new Governing Body, though nothing more came of it at this point. The matter was taken up again in May the following year, when it was claimed that 'The change to CI status as an institution of higher education had not been understood or recognised by the general public', and that a clearer identity was required. The Finance Policy and General Purposes Committee of the Governing Body therefore proposed a bold innovation: that the College should become 'Kelvin College, Glasgow' in recognition of Lord Kelvin, whom it described as 'an outstanding son of the city'. It was recognised that this name reflected science and engineering rather than the other disciplines pursued within the College, but was felt that no single name could be fully comprehensive.[6]

The full Governing Body, however, rejected the proposed title and decided instead on 'The Glasgow Institute of Technology and Business'[7] — provoking jokes among the staff about comparisons with the Massachusetts Institute of Technology or Harvard Business School. The proposition having been put to the SED, a rather negligent and offhand acceptance was returned, declaring that 'the Department does not consider the arguments for a change of name to be quite as persuasive as the Governors, but if it is the view of the latter that the benefits justify the costs … so be it'.[8] However, the letter intimated that the change could not occur before the following summer when Designation Regulations were to be amended to remove Leith Nautical College from the CI list.

This proposal never came to fruition because the Academic Board did not support the new title and on November 28 requested the Governing Body to reconsider its decision. One member described that particular meeting as an afternoon of fear and loathing. There were a number of reasons for this (dealt with below) but in relation to the name change strife erupted because the Director, Norman Meadows, declared that the proposal to ask the Governing Body to reconsider was out of order because the Academic Board had previously expressed its agreement. A Head of Department objected that this was inaccurate, for the Academic Board had

---

[6]Governing Body meeting, May 26, 1986, paper submitted by Finance Policy and General Purposes Committee.

[7]Minute of Governing Body, May 27, 1986.

[8]E W Frizzell, Scottish Education Department to Alan Irons, Secretary, Glasgow College of Technology, July 7, 1986.

merely heard a report and expressed no opinion. The appropriate minute was sent for, and contradicted the Director's interpretation. He was obliged to back down and the meeting went on to ask the Governors to reconsider, despite an impassioned plea from the Assistant Director not to do so. The suggestion adopted came from the Faculty of Life and Social Sciences, that the existing title should be retained for official purposes but shortened to Glasgow College for general and advertising ones.

On February 24, 1987 the Governing Body acceded to the Academic Board's request, but this was not quite the end of that chapter of the story. A corporate identity launch was scheduled for January 1988 and the Governing Body agreed in the October beforehand to add the phrase 'a Scottish Polytechnic' to the shortened title. All legal and contractual documents naturally had to continue with the old name. However, the ambition which had been pressed since 1971 to use the word 'polytechnic' was at least halfway towards realisation.

Not long before Lewis Brodie died the College had decided to appoint a Secretary to exercise a range of administrative functions and act as a link between the Directorate and external bodies. The person engaged was Alan Irons, previously an official of the Scottish Education Department — Dr Meadows, announcing the appointment at the Academic Board, described Mr Irons' position as that of a gamekeeper turned poacher, such was the Director's style. The experiment does not appear to have been an unqualified success (see below) and after his departure a few years later the appointment was not renewed. Following Lewis Brodie's death the position of Registrar was continued but changed in nature, for the actual functions of the post were divided between different individuals.

Academic Developments in the later 1980s

At the point at which the College was designated as a central institution the full-time courses on offer included 14 degrees and 12 Higher Diplomas and Higher National Diplomas. There were in addition seven other diplomas and professional courses, such as certificates in various fields of nursing. Over 50 part-time courses were taught, only two of these being degrees, the BSc in Mechanical Engineering and the BA in Social Sciences.[9]

---

[9] At that point the London External BA in History was in the process of being phased out.

The CNAA institutional visit following the College's change of status occurred on February 6, 1987. In academic terms the visit was a success from the College's point of view, for it ended with an agreement that the Council and the College should enter into a new relationship giving the College enhanced responsibility for course validation and review, which might be followed, if successful, by application for full institutional accreditation status (which Napier already possessed). The CNAA Report summary stated:

> Since the last institutional review visit in November 1983, the College has made substantial progress in several areas. The College has acquired Central Institution status, which in turn has provided a new level of resources. There is also evidence of a strengthening of the College's validation processes, and of its determination to keep those processes under review and to improve their effectiveness.

The College management however also used the review as a pretext for beginning to reinforce the line management structure and start dismantling or weakening the elaborate structure of representational committees that had been established under Lewis Brodie's guidance. The Directorate claimed that they were adopting this view under CNAA urging. When the Academic Board was assembled on the afternoon of the visit, it received first of all a briefing from the Directors at which it was claimed that the CNAA was most unhappy with the College's committee structure, which, they alleged, failed to give a sufficient leadership role to line management, which ought to have more emphasis. It would be essential for the College to take into account the visiting party's comments regardless of internal feeling. The Assistant Director declared that in the '60s and '70s the emphasis had been all upon democracy and committee systems, but in the '80s line management was coming back into its own. A member commented that it sounded as though the visiting party had received a communication from Downing Street.

In fact when the briefing was over and the Board met the visiting party all the latter had to say about the committee structure was that it was one of the things the College ought to look at. Nevertheless the Directorate went ahead with a proposal to alter the character of the system's base, the Subject Area Boards. The significance of these was that, comprising all the academics within a specific discipline, they did not necessarily have to be Chaired by a Head of Department (though they most often were) and their purpose was policy-making, which the Head was then responsible for executing. Under the proposals advanced by a working party established for the purpose they were to be replaced by Departmental Boards, which the Head would Chair ex-officio, thereby strengthening his/her control over policy. Moreover in multi-discipline departments the individual disciplines would lose the official collective identity which the SABs conferred upon them.

The proposal was brought to the Academic Board meeting on May 1. Following formal business the Director began his verbal report by announcing the name of the new Chair whom the SED had appointed for the Board of Governors. This was Hamish Wood, the Professor of Chemistry at Strathclyde University, a more significant appointment than was appreciated by most around the table at the time. Professor Wood was born in Hawick in

PROFESSOR HAMISH C S WOOD, *CBE, BSc, PhD, Duniv, Cchem, FRSC, Fscotvec, FRSE* was the Chairman of the Governing Body of Glasgow Polytechnic at the time of the merger in 1993 (being appointed in May 1987), and he went on to become the first Chair of the University Court. The University named a building after him.

1926 and graduated from St Andrews University in 1947 with a first-class degree in Chemistry, gaining his PhD three years later. He spent most of his academic career at Strathclyde University, serving as Vice-Principal from 1984–86 and retiring as Professor Emeritus in 1991. His research interests were mainly concerned with the inter-relationship of chemistry and biology, the mode of action and design of pharmaceutical agents, and the development of what came to be known as biotechnology. He was made a Fellow of the Royal Society of Edinburgh and a member of its Council.

The proposal on SABs was introduced by the Depute Director, Professor Neil Buxton, who was obliged to acknowledge that the working party (which he had Chaired) consulted nobody and took no evidence before writing its report, but claimed that it had before it evidence from a previous report of the Committee on Committees, even though that had reached an opposite conclusion. However, the three Faculty Chairs all reported overwhelming acceptance from their SABs (unanimous in the case of

Science and Engineering) and the proposal was duly endorsed. The return towards a line management-dominated system commenced.

In June 1989 the CNAA carried out a further institutional review which conferred the coveted institutional accreditation, to apply from September 1. By then however the CNAA's own future was very much in question and its inspections were probably less rigorous than they had been in the early days — which is not to say that the College would not have passed in any case. The *Glasgow Herald* reported on July 20:

> Glasgow College has been granted full accredited status by the Council for National Academic Awards, Britain's largest degree awarding body. The CNAA yesterday praised the College, and said it would be given wider powers to operate and develop its portfolio of degree and diploma courses.

Professorships

In the wake of becoming a central institution the College authorities moved to institute professorial titles. The matter had been raised in a speculative way as far back as the early '70s, when it had stimulated some press correspondence: a sneer that the College was getting ambitious beyond its station was countered with the reply that Strathclyde University had used the title long before it was a university, as central institutions like Paisley College were also currently doing.

When it was resuscitated in the '80s, this time seriously, it went through committee procedures and came before the Academic Board on December 20, 1985. Some opposition was expressed, again on the grounds that the title would not be taken seriously by universities and that Paisley in fact did itself no good by pretending to it and that the general introduction of the title in CIs had done more to devalue it than to raise the status of the institutions. Even setting that point aside, it was argued that the College was not yet sufficiently established and matured. From the other side of the argument came the claim that students needed this to convince potential employers of the credibility of their institution:

> Attracting candidates at this level, capable of displaying academic leadership, is dependent upon several factors. These include status, salary, the 'image' of the institution, the desire to promote academic development in a particular area and so on. Experience elsewhere has

shown, however, that the advertised status of Professor has helped significantly in attracting high calibre applicants. In particular, the ability to appoint at this level is crucially important in certain areas of academic activity. In such areas, market shortages mean that Central Institutions are not only competing strongly with each other but also with Universities and industry. To attract personnel of the requisite quality, this College must be able to offer the same portfolio of 'inducements' — status recognition and career fulfilment, as well as appropriate financial incentives.

There is little doubt that Professorial status commands a measure of respect in academic, business, commercial etc circles outside the College.[10]

The issue was actually pushed to a vote and one member, who opposed the idea strongly, had dissent minuted.[11]

Not surprisingly the Governing Body at its meeting on February 25, 1986 formally approved an Academic Board recommendation that such appointments should be introduced in four categories. The first of these was that future Head of Department appointments might be made at professional level (though they would not necessarily be); the second that existing heads could be considered for receiving the title; the third that all other academic staff could apply for consideration for a personal professorship; and finally externally funded professorships where appropriate.

Information Technology and the WANG Affair

Since the beginning of its existence the College had possessed a mainframe computer and a Computing Department. The '80s, however, saw the appearance of the personal desktop computer, a new dimension in information technology and one which no educational establishment could ignore. The new Director was to the forefront in advocating that the College should be turned into a computer-friendly environment with a

[10]Paper to Academic Board meeting of December 20, 1985.

[11]This meeting also discussed the question of honorary degrees, with an assertion from the Director that CNAA regulations effectively put such awards within his gift.

workstation on every desk linked to a College-wide network.[12] In this, it has to be acknowledged he showed imagination and foresight. Unfortunately his judgement did not match his vision and the actual network he opted for installing did not measure up to the hopes which were placed in it. That might well be excusable at a time when various firms were in hot competition for the personal computer market and it was far from clear which systems were going to emerge as the most popular and effective; however the Director's actions were ill-judged, not taken in line with proper procedures and in the end were largely instrumental in bringing about his downfall.

He concluded, with what advice we do not know, that the WANG company was best equipped to provide the network. The decision was certainly questioned on at least one occasion at an Academic Board meeting, it being pointed out that some press reports on this company, particularly one in *Computer Weekly*, were not particularly favourable. But the WANGNET was installed, at considerable expense and trouble, and linked to the WANG desktop computers which had already been supplied to the administrative staff, though few if any academics used them. Before long it became apparent that the system was not up to the demands which were placed upon it, and eventually the ambitious developments which were envisaged were abandoned, although not until after WANG had delivered a lot of very expensive equipment which was never utilised. Thereafter desktop computers were introduced on an ad hoc departmental basis, some choosing Applemacs and others preferring IBM machines. Some use, however, continued to be made of the WANGNET, and a degree of collaboration with the WANG company continued into the '90s.

In the words of a report into the way matters had been handled:

The only common theme throughout the project was Dr Meadow's [sic] determination to have WANG computer system and communications network implemented at the College.

---

[12]His personal aim was 'to create an environment within the College which is at the leading edge of information management and computing'. Touche Ross International, *Report on the Acquisition of Wang Equipment*, June 1988.

Without this force behind the project, it is unlikely that it would ever have become reality, since detection of some of the problems by existing College systems and procedures would have halted the acquisition process.[13]

To summarise the financial complexities of the developments which occurred: in essence the Director and the College Secretary between them committed funding which the College did not have and so in the event were unable to pay for large quantities of equipment delivered and were threatened with having it repossessed in consequence. Eventually, to save embarrassment the SED unwillingly made the funds available, amounting to c.£100,000. A second, though still highly significant, problem was that the project was entered into hastily and at half-cock so that 'The College's requirements were not properly identified prior to inviting suppliers to tender'. No detailed technical consideration had been given to the College's needs in relation to an administrative computing system; the requirements were conveyed verbally to the chosen suppliers by the Director and Secretary, neither of whom could claim specialised computing expertise; and the Computer Policy Committee, which should have exercised supervision, was bypassed by the Director. In the words of the Touche Ross Report 'we do not believe that proper use was made of the considerable "in-house" experience available to the College'.

To get his way initially Dr Meadows employed a stratagem which enabled him to bypass the College committee system. This was to claim that as Director he had sole responsibility for administrative as distinct from academic matters and since the commitment to WANG was for administrative work there was no obligation on him to consult academic bodies. Once the administrative network was in place it then appeared to be an irresistible argument that it should be extended for academic purposes, and the necessary committees were induced to agree. WANG conducted a prestigious launch in September 1986 and partially funded two WANG professorships within the institution.

The funds which the Director, his Administrative Assistant (who was heavily involved in the events) and the College Secretary imagined were

---

[13]Touche Ross International, *Abstract of Report on the Acquisition of Wang Equipment*, June 1988.

available derived from a rates rebate due once the College, on becoming a central institution, received charitable status; student fees over which the Director was in dispute with the College of Building and Printing; and £100,000 of anticipated SED capital funding. The Touche Ross Report pointed out that the project had been embarked upon with no certainty that any of this money was actually secure. 'Revenue funding identified as being available to fund the initial project was not properly determined and did not in fact exist.' [14]

The allocation of the £100,000 capital grant to the project was disputed within the College, for there were urgent areas of maintenance needing attention — repair of roofs and lifts, and the replacement of the Biological Sciences centrifuge, a piece of equipment vital to the department's honours degree course. At the relevant Academic Board meeting of November 28, 1998, one member, after listening to the Director's rhetoric, commented that there wouldn't be much use in having a developed computer network if the rain was running into the workstations. The Board nevertheless approved the allocation, but in January the SED withdrew the grant.

This move triggered a crisis, for the WANG equipment had already been ordered — though the ordering mechanism was extremely ill-organised and sloppy and the Director claimed that the equipment had been delivered 'by mistake'.[15] The SED now intervened in the form of HMI inspectors and conducted an inspection of the relevant accounts (arriving, apparently, in April 1986, when the Director was holidaying in Cyprus) and motivating the Governors — whose Chair was changed by the SED, with Professor Hamish Wood appointed — to commission the Touche Ross Report. The Director and the College Secretary blamed each other in a most unseemly fashion: 'The Director expresses personal concern over this and is of the view that he may well have been misled by advice given by the College Secretary.'[16]

This last comment reflected the fact that while the WANG project was in process the Director and the Secretary were engaged in the most venomous and bitter dispute with each other — a dispute which evidently,

---

[14]*Ibid.*
[15]*Ibid.*
[16]Director to SED, March 9, 1987.

from the voluminous correspondence associated with it, consumed an inordinate amount of the time of these two top managers of the College. A stream of imperious memos issued from the Director's office criticising the

PROFESSOR J STANLEY MASON, *BSc, PhD, Ceng, FIMechE, FIMarE, MIMinE,* Principal of Glasgow College/Glasgow Polytechnic from 1 January 1989 to merger (1993), having previously held the post of Depute Director (from 1 October 1987), and thereafter he was the first Principal and Vice Chancellor of Glagow Caledonian University, remaining in that position until 16 May 1997.

Secretary for alleged failings in his administrative capacity. Mr Irons was evidently of the opinion that the Director was determined to downgrade both his status and his responsibilities and remained determined to assert his right to a role in responsible administrative decision-making against what he felt was an attempt to reduce him to clerical status.

The Touche Ross Report came out in June 1988 (circulation was highly restricted). Even before that, however, the Director's position had become unsustainable and, following a visit to his office by the Chair and other leading Governors one Saturday morning towards the end of April, he requested immediate early retirement.[17] Dr Meadows' successor was Dr Stan Mason, formerly of Woolwich Polytechnic where he had headed a research unit in bulk solids handling. He had been encouraged by Dr Meadows to apply for the vacant post of Depute Director in Glasgow College (following Prof Buxton taking up the position of Director of Hatfield Polytechnic) and on his appointment to establish the unit there.

John Stanley Mason (always referred to as Stan) was born in Wigan in 1934. Educated at Wigan Grammar School he worked from 1950 to 1954 for the National Coal Board as an apprentice and underground employee. He gained a first class Honours degree in Mining Engineering from the University of Nottingham on a Coal Board Scholarship between 1954 and 1958, and then returned to the NCB. However as the large-scale closure of coal mines was beginning to get under way he looked for alternatives, was employed as a mathematics teacher at Leeds Grammar School and in 1963 saw service as a Lieutenant in the Royal Navy. In 1966 he became principal lecturer in mechanical engineering at Liverpool Polytechnic. During that time he gained a PhD for research into gas-solid suspensions flowing through pipelines and was Senior Research Fellow at the University of Nottingham, leading a project on the effect of climatic transients on the thermal response of buildings. He was appointed Head of the School of Mechanical Engineering at Thames Polytechnic in 1973, subsequently Dean of the Engineering Faculty and in 1985 Dean of the Technology Faculty. The distinction of his work in bulk solids handling had been recognised by the Institution of Mechanical Engineers and, as noted, the unit he formed was transferred to Glasgow College.

A minor irony in relation to the turbulent developments at the College was that at almost exactly the same time as Dr Meadows' resignation, there took place the retirement, in his case full of honours and acclaim, of Mr Edward Miller, the Strathclyde Director of Education, who as senior Depute Director in the old Corporation had been among the guiding lights in the establishment of Glasgow College of Technology. Of that he said:

I rate my most worthy achievement in Glasgow days to be the creation of Glasgow College of Technology as Scotland's first polytechnic-type

---

[17]It was claimed that he wished to concentrate more on his research into the great international exhibitions of the 19th century. He later also claimed to be translating the Koran.

institute of higher education in 1970, very much a personal brainchild in the face of opposition from the Scottish Education Department, Strathclyde University, key councillors and officials in the City Chambers.[18]

To put these events in perspective it is necessary to focus on Edward Miller's comment. The dramatic happenings at the top of the institution did not alter the fact that throughout all this time it was functioning effectively as a centre of higher education and equipping thousands of students to enter the employment market with excellent qualifications. The average student or the ordinary member of academic staff would have noticed no impact on their day-to-day lives. The nature of higher education institutions as disaggregated collectives in which the function of leadership or management is — as a rule — enabling rather than directive, means that problems at the controlling centre need not have any *immediate* effect upon what goes on at the grassroots, where, within available resources, activities and programmes are constructed to fulfil the institution's purposes. In the longer term of course, incompetence, lack of vision or foresight will eventually produce detrimental effects.

The problems which Glasgow College experienced in the mid-'80s cannot be viewed as either accidental or inevitable. The personalities of the individuals involved — and there were others apart from the Director and the Secretary — undoubtedly played a part, but they could do so only within the context of the pressures being applied to higher education in the 1980s, the nature of management cultures and the situation of Glasgow College in particular. Government policy was to push higher education by a variety of devices towards a more managerial style of operation in contrast to the collegiality which was the prevailing tradition in the universities; to measure 'output' and 'productivity' more rigorously and to extract more; and to raise the proportion of funding derived from business and private sources. The model of the polytechnics provided an initial sketch of the favoured outcome — while at the same time the academics in polytechnics and equivalent institutions were aspiring themselves to imitate, in terms of governance if not style, the older universities.

A culture was therefore being generated in which 'robust' and decisive managerial action was being encouraged and applauded as a public virtue and consequently clashing with ingrained traditions or, in the case of the non-university sector, expectations of how academic institutions should

---

[18] *Glasgow Herald*, April 22, 1988.

operate. A situation of straightened resources was an additional and most important factor in pushing institutions towards greater emphasis upon directive leadership — it is easier to employ a relaxed style when funds are plentiful. Frequent changes in the implementation if not the thrust of government policy — towards more students or fewer, or alterations in funding formulae — might also be seen to require stronger and more interventionist leadership and particularly to affect central institutions as these were directly funded from the Scottish Office.

In the particular case of Glasgow College all these considerations were at work. The underlying tensions which had been manifested in the early '80s had not, despite restructuring of the institution's governance, been resolved. The tension was a generational one between the more authoritarian FE tradition, from which a majority of Departmental Heads, as well as many lecturers, senior lecturers, and administrators had been drawn, and the more collegiate approach expected by others. Frictions arising from this state of affairs were exacerbated by the mood of uncertainty hanging over higher education during this period and the particular uncertainties around the College's own standing then and in the future. All that was required to cause these problems to erupt into crisis were strong personalities pursuing courses regarded as unacceptable by significant numbers of their colleagues.

Polytechnic at Last

At the end of the decade the Scottish Education Department at last gave the green light for the College to assume the name it had coveted since its foundation, and the institution soon moved to take advantage of the opportunity. The proposal was placed before the Academic Board on April 27, 1990. An accompanying paper prepared by Professor Peter Bush, a Depute Director, noted that 'Dissatisfaction with the College's name has been a recurrent theme in Academic Board discussions, practically since the Institution was established'. After briefly summarising the history of argument over the name and noting Napier's adoption of the title, the paper went on:

Notwithstanding the improvement of Glasgow College, confusion remains. Some overseas students have recently indicated that their sponsors will support them only at approved 'Universities and Polytechnics'; industrialists visiting the College for the first time are not clear regarding the level and the range of work until they are assured that we are 'like the Polytechnics'; enquirers often ask 'Glasgow College of what?' Many of the Region's FE Colleges use a location + College for designation, eg Springburn and Anniesland Colleges. ... The arguments in favour of Polytechnic designation have not diminished.'

The Academic Board is invited to consider recommending to the Governing Body that Government approval be sought to change the name of the Institution formally to 'Glasgow Polytechnic' as soon as the time required for legislative procedures and the preparation of an appropriate launch allow.

In the debate that followed there was general enthusiastic and overwhelming support for the recommendation, with the feeling expressed that the College's existing title disadvantaged it in the market place. Polytechnic designation would clarify its position and enhance public perception of the nature of its work. The Board resolved to recommend to the Governing Body that it seek the necessary approval, that the Principal's Management Group submit a range of costed options for the launch and that a clear and cogent mission statement accompany the launch.

On June 25 the Governing Body endorsed the Academic Board recommendation and resolved to take the necessary measures. Consequently application was made through the SOED (as the SED had been retitled) to Parliament and final approval was notified to the College on January 7, 1991. A logo — not a very impressive one it has to be acknowledged — was approved by the Governors later in the month. A public launch was held on May 1.

The *Glasgow Herald* reported the name change on January 12:

> Glasgow College has agreed to its third name change since it was established nearly 20 years ago. The Scottish Education Department, which funds it, has approved the title Glasgow Polytechnic. It will remain as Glasgow College until the new name is given a public launch this year.

Following the launch, under the headline 'College turns into Polytechnic', it reported on May 2:

> With a glitzy launch which lacked only a trumpet fanfare and a fire-eater, Glasgow College yesterday became Glasgow Polytechnic.
>
> Its new corporate image, achieved at a cost of about £70,000, was unveiled as the institution celebrated its 20th anniversary with the

announcement of a new graduates' association, and increased sponsorship for the Scottish karate team.

The Cowcaddens campus, originally Glasgow College of Technology, is now one of Scotland's biggest central institutions, although Napier in Edinburgh beat it in the race to become the country's first polytechnic three years ago.

The Principal, Professor Stan Mason said yesterday there would be no change to its approach to teaching, or its interaction with industry and commerce, but the new name reflected more accurately the work of the institution and its 7,300 students. He pointed out that hundreds of students from the Far East — whose fees are a lucrative source of income — had been prevented from taking their chosen courses at Glasgow College because their governments funded study only at officially designated universities and polytechnics.

Glasgow Polytechnic, launched 1 May 1991.

Another Dispute

Scarcely was the Polytechnic established than the *Glasgow Herald* — and other newspapers — were voicing much less congenial sentiments, thanks to an embarrassing dispute which broke out between the Principal and three members of staff, including the Secretary Alan Irons.

Professor Roger Willey, who had been in the institution since 1974, was an internationally renowned expert on the use and handling of asbestos and a most successful entrepreneur in asbestos consultancy — he maintained an office in New York — and on his earnings from consultancy was able to afford a Rolls Royce, in which he regularly drove to work, where, in addition to his duties as Head of the environmental division within the College company, he ran his own Asbestos Consultancy Services Ltd. In the *Glasgow Herald* of May 24 appeared an article in which he was reported as alleging clashes with officials amounting to persecution and harassment, and that 'the last straw came when summoned to a disciplinary hearing on return to lecturing from full-time secondment as chief executive to the polytechnic's business arm'. He was scathing about relations within the Polytechnic, claiming that staff morale was worse than it had been at the point of Norman Meadows' departure and that the situation amounted to 'a management shambles'. He went on to claim that the institution 'only seemed interested in making money and not the educational philosophy'. Professor Mason was reported as dismissing the allegations as 'absolute rubbish'.

As though that were not sufficient the paper the very next day printed a report under the title 'Unprofessional, says polytechnic secretary' containing an attack from Alan Irons (who at that point was on sick leave pending early retirement)[19] on the management style within the institution, claiming that 'little has changed since Dr Norman Meadows resigned as director in 1988'. It also cited Dr Chris Woodcock, a former Chief Executive of the Polytechnic commercial arm who had accompanied Professor Mason from Thames Polytechnic, as alleging that his abrupt departure the previous year was due to stress-related illness brought on by bad management and because 'my face did not fit'.

Further unwelcome publicity followed, with claims being made that one Head of Department had summoned his staff to a 'loyalty meeting' during which he had demanded that they put their names to a prepared statement supporting the management and denying that staff morale was low. The staff, however, had declined to express any opinion one way or the other.[20]

The same issue contained a further scurrilous attack on the institution's reputation from the paper's diarist, Tom Shields, not referring specifically

---

[19]Following his retirement the position of Secretary was discontinued.
[20]*Glasgow Herald*, May 29, 1991.

to the incident, but recycling his perpetual complaint that, in the item's own words, 'the upstart educational establishment had delusions of grandeur and kept changing its name in attempts to go upmarket'. Now 'life has overtaken fiction' and it was only a matter of time, Shields predicted, before university status would be sought, and 'we are told that entrance requirements for the new yooni will remain as strict as those for the polytechnic. You will have to be able to do joined-up writing as well as quoting your mum's co-op number'. The remarks are evidence not merely of an individual journalist's bile but expressive of one of the less attractive aspects of Scottish popular culture, the identification of individuals or bodies getting above themselves and requiring to be ridiculed into a more conforming posture. Shields followed up with further denigration two days later: 'Two set books must be completed — one fully coloured in (without going over the lines) and the other with all the dots joined up'.

On May 29 the Polytechnic issued a press release in which the Principal expressed disappointment that Mr Irons and Professor Willey should seek to discredit the institution and risk jeopardising the employment prospects of even one student. It noted that 'Mr Irons retires on Friday after the independent medical adviser considered him "permanently incapable of discharging his duties" and Professor Willey [intends] to accept a post at Paisley College'. At the same time the Chair of the Governing Body, Professor H C S Wood and the Vice-Chair Mr A K Denholm wrote to the *Herald* unreservedly supporting the Principal and his management team, rejecting all the allegations made in the articles. They declared that 'Glasgow Polytechnic, a mature, highly respected academic institution has earned the deserved praise of Government Ministers, academic bodies and industrial organisations worldwide'. The letter referred to the Polytechnic's graduate employment record and increases in government funding. The episode did not have any further consequences, and was in any case overtaken by the beginnings of the process which was to lead to the merger with Queen's College.

Afterword — Eminent Employees

It is worth recording that two members of the College's academic staff were later to become nationally famous. The first of these was James Boyle, who had been a member of the Humanities Department at the time of the College's opening, and whose work was concerned with media studies. He was to go on to work for Radio Scotland, eventually becoming its Controller, before passing on to become the Controller of Radio 4, which continues to be his position at the time of writing.

Gordon Brown was to enjoy even greater national eminence. He was, as a student, elected as Rector of Edinburgh University, and went on from there to become a leading figure in Labour Party politics in Scotland. Prior to being elected as an MP he taught politics at GCT. He is at the time of writing Chancellor of the Exchequer.

Chapter Nine

The Merger and After

The merger of existing higher education institutions in and around
Glasgow — and even further afield — was something which had been
discussed tentatively for many years. We have noted that it was being
mentioned even as early as GCT's foundation. Later on, Paisley College and
Stirling University held discussions with the idea of amalgamation in view,
though nothing came of these. One apparently obvious amalgamation
which might have suggested itself, but which does not appear to have ever
been considered, was that between GCT/Glasgow Polytechnic and Paisley
College. The reasoning against it (apart from geographical separation) may
possibly have been that Paisley, since the arrival of the '60s universities,
regarded itself as worthy of being included in their ranks and never
abandoned its ambition to gain the title, spurning that of polytechnic.
Consequently it may have felt that association with the newer and less
prestigious institution might have been to its disadvantage.

The eventual union which did take place, between Queen's College and
Glasgow Polytechnic, was not the most natural of marriages. It was
stimulated by the publication in May 1991 of the Government White Paper
Higher Education: A New Framework. In his foreword the then Prime
Minister John Major stated:

> In higher education our key reform will be to end the increasingly
> artificial distinction between universities on the one hand and colleges
> and polytechnics on the other. This will build on our plans to transform
> education and training for 16–19 year-olds by removing barriers between
> the academic and vocational streams.

And in the words of the Secretaries of State involved:

> The Government's policies have helped to secure record numbers and participation in higher education. We need to build on this success.... The distinction between universities on the one hand and polytechnics and colleges on the other, known as the binary line, has become an obstacle to further progress. The Government therefore proposes to abolish it and establish a single framework for higher education.

> The title of polytechnic has never been widely understood. The British academic world realises that polytechnics are higher education institutions achieving the same academic standards and giving the same quality of education as most universities. Many able school leavers and their parents tend, however, to regard the title as a reason for making them a second choice to a university when seeking a place in higher education. In their international contacts polytechnics still find that they have to explain that they are not further education or sixth form or technical colleges.[1]

Cynics might have perceived behind the Government's intentions other motives than to stimulate progress or even rationalise the system. There could of course be no question of the universities losing their titles, and if the binary line were to be abolished it could therefore only mean that the university name would be extended to the institutions doing work of a comparable kind. In view of the drive to cut costs in higher education therefore, this initiative could be interpreted as a means of demonstrating to the existing universities that higher education could be carried on at lower unit costs, since there would then be a set of universities doing exactly that. Extension of the university title could also be viewed as a cost-free way of rewarding the polytechnics for not complaining as student numbers were raised (with favourable impact on the unemployment figures) without corresponding funding increases.

The Polytechnic

The Vice-Principal, Professor Peter Bush, prepared a paper, dated June 12, 1991, for the Academic Board reviewing the White Paper's implications for

---

[1] *Higher Education: A New Framework*, HMSO 1991, Chapter 6, para. 90.

the Polytechnic. The paper laid special emphasis on quality assurance and the mechanisms for securing it. Professor Bush recommended that 'Glasgow Polytechnic should address at an early stage, the opportunities heralded in the White Paper', and invited the Academic Board to commend *inter alia* to the Governing Body the statement that:

> The Polytechnic welcomes the acknowledgment of the erosion of the binary line and, in view of its existing range and quality of courses, its imminent powers to award its own degrees and the establishment of a single funding mechanism for higher education, believes that the title 'university' reflects the range and level of its activities and that its adoption is in the best interests of its students and staff.

Although there was no compulsion on polytechnics to adopt the university title — or more accurately to apply to be renamed — none felt that they could stand aside. Both material considerations (principally attractiveness to students and high-calibre academics) and the matter of status prescribed that if one sought the title, all must do so. At Glasgow Polytechnic, where the likelihood of university designation was the subject of informal discussion during the autumn term, there were a few academics who thought otherwise, and argued that if all were rushing to change it would be more distinctive to stand out by remaining as a polytechnic and building up the institution's reputation on that basis. Not surprisingly, that was very much a minority viewpoint. A somewhat larger number, once the merger idea became public, supported the application for university title but saw little merit in the proposed unification — in principle there was no reason why Glasgow Polytechnic should not have applied alone for transfer to the university sector. The arguments for the agreement with Queen's were far from evident, they argued. Others, while approving of the merger and university status, were reluctant simply to adopt Queen's name.

General opinion, however, favoured merger and the name; the attractions of having a larger rather than a smaller university and a high-profile title were seen to outweigh any possible inconveniences. On December 2 (less than a year since the College had formally assumed its Polytechnic title), the Academic Board convened to consider the proposal, departments having been asked to consult their staff during the previous week and feed opinions to the Academic Board meeting. Divided views were reflected in the fact that the proposal was put to a vote, but the majority was clear enough, 24 to nine.

The following day the Governing Body, with the Academic Board decision referred to it, met to deliberate and decide on the proposal. The paper placed before it opened with the statement:

> Glasgow Polytechnic has always welcomed collaborative activities with neighbouring and more distant institutions when such arrangements enhance opportunities for students in terms of access to higher education, extension of programmes of study and greater resource availability.

It then went on to list examples of such co-operation: with Strathclyde University in Industrial Mathematics and Journalism, Glasgow College of Building and Printing in Built Environment, Jordanhill College in Media Studies, Dumfries and Galloway and Lanarkshire Colleges of Nursing and Midwifery, and with various FE colleges in franchised HND courses and 'top-up' access courses. It noted that in the 1991 Corporate Plan the Polytechnic had reaffirmed its policy of establishing links with a range of other bodies wherever these were feasible and in the interests of students, and referred to the fact that even earlier considerable advantage had been seen in establishing academic relationships with Queen's College, the 1991 Plan observing that 'This view remains unchanged'.

The paper went on to outline the elements of commonality between the two institutions:

> There is considerable commonality of purpose displayed in the Institutional Plans of both GP and QC. In its Mission Statement QC emphasises 'its commitment to wider access and to flexible course programmes; its responsiveness to student interests and employer and market needs; its concern to establish a network of educational ladders and bridges with other institutions; its determination to provide cost-effective and efficient service within a maximised resource envelope'...

> Both Corporate Plans emphasise a wide range of levels of courses, widened and increased access, credit accumulation and transfer, mature students, applied research and consultancy and the enhancement of the quality of learning and teaching. Both institutions are committed to an ethos of course quality assurance underpinned by commitments to self-evaluation and peer review and to the general enhancement of the quality

of provision in all services offered by Departments and Sections throughout GP and QC.

The student complement of the combined institution was estimated at 7,500 (full-time education), approximately 10,000 students in all. Emphasis was placed upon the undertaking to avoid job losses — though economies of scale were nevertheless projected — together with the statement of an objective to enhance staff opportunities. Commitment to Credit Accumulation and Transfer on the part of both institutions was also stressed, noting that Queen's scheme was the first to be validated in Scotland. It was asserted that opportunities for research and scholarly activity would be enhanced and that the new institution would provide a major UK centre for group research in the health-related area. A number of non-teaching departments or units would be expected to combine operations at an early stage — these included Continuing Education/CATS, the libraries, finance offices, international offices, and computing.

The Principal presented an oral report on the state of developments to date. He explained that, in response to an invitation from Queen's the Polytechnic had been assisting the College with an option appraisal which included merger with the former as one of the possibilities. Involvement with the appraisal had been kept confidential to the Principal's Management Group in order to 'avoid unnecessary speculation'.[2] Discussion in the Polytechnic, following the decision of Queen's Academic Council on November 27, had involved trade union representatives and student representatives as well as departmental meetings of academic staff. Thirty-one of the 34 staff groups had been in favour of the proposal and the other three were neutral rather than opposed.

The Chair of the Board, Professor Wood, also presented an oral report on the result of discussions in Queen's Governing Body and went on to say that Mrs Urquhart-Logie, its Chair, had conveyed to him the appreciation of the Governors and senior staff at the manner in which the Polytechnic management team had co-operated with Queen's during the preparation of its option appraisal. Following extensive discussion the proposal, as with the Academic Board, was put to the vote and in this case the majority was even clearer. No negative votes were recorded, and only one abstention, that of the Student Association President — though general belief outside the

---

[2]Minute of Governing Body Meeting, December 3, 1991.

meeting was that there had been one vote against and two abstentions. In any event, approval was overwhelming.

A number of riders were added to the basic resolution. One of these was that the draft mission statement should be made more concise and include a clearer vision of the distinctive role of the new university; 'Appropriate reference should be made to revenue earning activities.' Also included was reference to the transitional arrangements which would be required, including the centrally important 'Shadow Court'. This was to consist of seven Governors from each institution, to be Chaired by Professor Wood with Mrs Urquhart-Logie as Vice-Chair. The staff member elected by the Academic Board, Mr Jim Leahy, was also to be a member. The two Principals were not members, although they were of course to play a central role.

Queen's College

The problems which the White Paper created for Queen's were more immediate and pressing. The point of crisis was the proposed abolition of the CNAA, for the distinctive attribute of a British university was that it alone had responsibility for validating its degrees, whereas other institutions of higher education did not — such authority as they had was delegated either by the CNAA or a recognised university. However the White Paper postulated the accreditation of non-university institutions, and so in principle Queen's was not formally obliged to change its character — Queen Margaret College continued and continues as a stand-alone institution, and that choice was one of those presented in an option appraisal which the College undertook in November 1991.

When Professor Phillips was interviewed by one of the authors he was asked if he had come to Queen's College knowing that a merger might be on the cards. His reply was 'Absolutely not. I came as Principal of a stand-alone college. In fact the governors had voted for no amalgamation prior to my appointment' (February 1991). The college's initial response to the White Paper therefore had been to adopt the same stance as Queen Margaret and aim to uphold its existing identity. The Governors on June 7, 1991, shortly following the White Paper's publication, had resolved that:

> The Governing Body of Queen's College, Glasgow reaffirms its commitment to the College remaining as an 'autonomous national institution' as referred to in the Mission Statement.

The option appraisal paper acknowledged that meeting the criteria for a separate university title was not a realistic prospect and noted that 'realpolitik dictates that these criteria are more a rationalisation of a desired outcome in terms of numbers of new universities than an attempt to set logical threshold levels'. The author of the paper noted that without the university title the College was likely to lose standing with potential students as well as the public. Should the title be achieved against the odds however, then problems would be created around the site-share agreement the College had with Jordanhill College, which, once it amalgamated as foreseen with Strathclyde University, was unlikely to be very willing to continue to share facilities with a rival university. The impression given is that the stand-alone option was not being very seriously considered and was being raised only to be dismissed.

Three other possibilities were canvassed. What was in fact the original preferred outcome was a three-way association or amalgamation between QCG, Paisley College and Jordanhill College of Education. Discussions on this had begun following an exchange of letters between the three Principals in May 1991. At first the prospects had appeared good, for there was 'a clear synergy and a remarkable degree of complementarity in course provision and discipline coverage'. The proposed association would have also realised the optimum use of the Jordanhill site. However in September Jordanhill withdrew from the discussions and announced that it was pursuing an amalgamation project with Strathclyde University (which was eventually realised). The continuing dialogue with Paisley now became less viable, for both institutions had similar accommodation pressures, with relatively restricted urban sites. Discussions continued amicably, but in the end, the document suggests, Paisley became focused on its intention to attain on its own the university status it had long felt itself entitled to, so that 'I am not therefore now in a position to put before you a substantive proposal in respect of PC and QCG'.

The next alternative was linkage with Strathclyde University, and the historic associations between the two institutions were noted, as well as joint course developments and research projects. Accordingly discussions were initiated, but it soon became apparent that the kind of semi-detached union that was envisaged between Strathclyde and Jordanhill would not be appropriate, for there was too great commonality and overlap in the management and health areas, requiring 'structural and attitudinal movements by both institutions'. Queen's would 'not wish to merely "buy into" the existing value systems and mission statement of SU even if the structural problem can be overcome. This option would therefore not enable the College to take advantage of the White Paper's challenges and opportunities.'

'Proposal B' was entitled 'The establishment of: *The Queen's University of Glasgow* through an association of two current institutions: The Queen's College, Glasgow and Glasgow Polytechnic'. The situation of the two institutions in relation to each other was evaluated soberly (there are some incidental inaccuracies in the presentation of the Polytechnic's background) and this was presented as the favoured option:

> The following scenario for a new University represents the degree of commonality established after a series of detailed meetings between staff teams of both institutions. The validity of this information base and common position has been confirmed by both Principals.

The scenario envisaged a period of initial preparation stretching from September to December 1991, the announcement of merger in December and the following year spent laying the necessary groundwork. In approving the intention to merge, one of the things upon which the Secretary of State was particularly insistent was that the project should be a full merger and not two continuing separate institutions loosely bolted together. Consequently planning for the amalgamation was lengthy and intense and the initial timetable slipped slightly, though not significantly.

From the Glasgow Polytechnic side considerations relating to initial acceptance of the merger idea were somewhat different from those affecting Queen's. As part of the Further and Higher Education (Scotland) Act 1992, the Privy Council granted degree-awarding powers to qualifying institutions to replace the CNAA procedures. The Polytechnic, like Napier, Dundee, Paisley and Robert Gordon, but unlike Queen's College, was adequately situated to apply for university designation on its own account. This it embarked upon as the merger preparations proceeded. The first stage in the process was to seek the degree-awarding powers specified in the Act, and this the Polytechnic did on May 1, 1992. The application was based upon:

> 1. its receipt of accredited status for taught courses from the CNAA in September 1989; and

2. the notification, on October 31, 1991, of the acceptance by the Secretary of State for Scotland of the advice of the CNAA that the Polytechnic met the criteria for the award of research degrees.[3]

The letter included a mention of the proposed merger to form a new university, which was at the time being considered by the Scottish Secretary and it included the intended name of the new institution. The Privy Council order was laid before Parliament on June 2 and from September 1992 the Polytechnic was able to award undergraduate and research degrees. There was some feeling in the Polytechnic, though it was never publicly articulated, that the merger was a diversion and that the Polytechnic should proceed to seek university status on its own account, inviting Queen's College to merge later on if the latter still felt inclined. However from the Polytechnic's viewpoint the attractions of the proposed merger were much greater, in the first place one of size, creating a bigger institution to stand comparison not merely with the other new universities but even the old ones, and secondly extending the range of courses which the merged institution could offer.

From Queen's point of view on the other hand, undoubtedly one of the principal attractions for the merger was not only the material ones discussed above, but a symbolic consideration. It had been agreed between the institutions that the new university, if approved, should take on the name of Queen's University, Glasgow. Since the College, as was acknowledged, had no chance of becoming a university on its own, a merger on these terms would nevertheless enable its name to be perpetuated in that form — although the decision did not rest with the partners alone, for other universities were convinced that they had a legitimate interest in whatever name was assumed by the university-to-be.

Queen's College — the Crucial Meeting
The Queen's College Governors met on December 2, 1991, Chaired by Mrs Celia Urquhart-Logie and joined by representatives of teaching and support staff unions, Academic Council and senior management. They had before them a recommendation from the Academic Council that 'The Traditions of The Queen's College, Glasgow are best preserved and the

[3]Prof J S Mason to Mr G I de Deney, Privy Council Office, May 1, 1992.

future of the College's work is best assured, by the formation of the Queen's University, Glasgow in conjunction with Glasgow Polytechnic'. The Chair advised the Governors that the meeting marked a historic turn in the College's history, which was certainly the case, for merging with another institution to create a university would mean, even if it preserved traditions, a final transformation of the identity which had marked the College's existence since its beginning and indeed its two predecessors as well.

The discussion which followed was lengthy and comprehensive. The Chair began by outlining events over the 18 months since the proposal of linking with Jordanhill College had fallen through. The White Paper and legislative proposals had changed the educational climate and led the College to actively pursue links with other institutions, ending with the recommendation from the Principal and the Academic Council to pursue Option B, the unification with Glasgow Polytechnic. That preference, it was reported, arose from the unique opportunity and challenge offered by the creation of a new university, which it was felt outweighed the disadvantages of a merged identity. It would also mean that the Faculty of Health Studies would be able to occupy a building on a city centre site, a consideration which was felt to be important.

A lot of concern had been felt about equality of representation in the transitional stage between two objectively unequal institutions, but detailed discussions about management had satisfied Queen's staff that Queen's would be well represented. Areas which the discussion had covered had included modes of operation, structures, course developments and articulation of the mission/vision statements of the two establishments. Future items for discussion included academic drift versus diversity (ie concentration on high level courses), seamless programmes unifying teaching between the two in cognate areas, wider access, and networking with FE colleges.

The EIS representatives professed themselves satisfied with assurances that there would be no job losses, that staff would be kept fully involved in discussions and there would be little immediate change in the basic teaching job. The support staff unions however were less happy, foreseeing threats because library and computing facilities, estates and other functions would be replicated. These concerns were general rather than specific, but it is common observation that mergers between relatively equivalent institutions in the commercial world tend to be followed by rationalisation and there were fears that the same principle might well apply in an educational sector increasingly responding to commercial pressures.

College students (understandably) would have liked to become part of a university if the opportunity was offered, but did not want impersonality to replace the high standards and good staff/student working relationships which were currently in existence at Queen's. Moreover they insisted that they did not want the standard of student facilities, particularly sports, to be lowered beneath the level of the two established universities —— a rather vain hope it might be thought, given the huge advantages enjoyed by Glasgow and Strathclyde and quite outside the control of the Polytechnic, Queen's or their putative successor.

After hearing these various inputs the Governors were briefed by the Principal on recent developments. He explained that the Scottish Office Education Department had been kept fully informed and he had constant meetings with SOED senior officials. As a result the Department was now satisfied that the Governors would be able to make a realistic decision based on the Option Appraisal document and that the proposed timescale was also realistic. According to the record of the meeting,

> Governors were impressed by the unanimity of the staff and were gratified at the way in which the Principal had encouraged openness. It was important that such a culture was carried forward into a new institution and it was quite essential that the Principal's position was very clearly enshrined in the new institution.

In the discussion which followed some concern was expressed, not unnaturally, that it would not be realistically possible to carry forward the College's ethos into a much bigger institution, and regret that Jordanhill, which might have appeared a more natural potential partner, had sought its links instead with Strathclyde. However 'The Governors recognised that there was tremendous staff and student enthusiasm, that the Faculties were in a position of strength, and that Option B offered the best scenario for the College in the current climate of threats and opportunities.' Accordingly, the Governors resolved unanimously to go forward with Option B and establish the Queen's University, Glasgow through an association (as it was named) of the two institutions.

Mrs Urquhart-Logie was thanked for steering the meeting through such a historic decision and Principal Phillips declared optimistically that this was not the end but the beginning of a period of opportunity. It is interesting to speculate what the founding Principals of the Schools and the College would have made of it if they had been able to be present.

Announcement and Reactions

The two institutions announced their intention to merge on December 4, 1991, with Professors Mason and Phillips attending a news conference seated on either side of Stewart McFarlane, the President of Glasgow Chamber of Commerce, an indication of the ambience that was sought for the new institution. The 'Joint Statement of Mission and Purpose' is quoted below in full:

> The new University will create an identity for itself based on the principles it regards as fundamental to its philosophy of education. It will seek to position itself in the minds of students, employers and the wider community as distinct from the current Higher Education provision in Scotland.
>
> The new University will be a provider of non-elitist high quality education and training to as wide and diverse a range of students and clients as possible.
>
> The programmes of study will be designed to offer the maximum degree of flexibility in order to provide greater opportunities for study and to widen access to the whole of society.
>
> In pursuing its mission, the new University will collaborate with commercial and industrial organisations and other educational providers both in the UK and abroad in order to ensure that all its students, whether full time, part time or mixed attendance receive a vocational education which is highly relevant to the world of work.
>
> The new University will be founded on the conviction that Higher Education in the 21st century must seek to extend its provision to meet the changing needs of a wider group of students and clients, industry, commerce and the professions in order that, through its innovative teaching and learning and applied research and consultancy, it should be able to make a full contribution to the prosperity and regeneration of Scotland's economy.
>
> In particular, the new University will be a leading specialist provider in the areas of engineering, technology and the built environment; health care, life

sciences and optometry; the physical sciences; risk, financial and accountancy services; commerce, business, consumer and hospitality management; social sciences,media studies, and legal and professional studies.

Across its specialist degrees the new University will offer Post Graduate courses, Honours Degrees, Degrees, Higher National Diplomas and Diplomas of Higher Education, Higher National Certificates and Certificates of Higher Education, the awards of professional bodies, and any additional awards that are appropriate to the needs of the community. It will be committed to the concept of credit accumulation and transfer and the recognition, where appropriate, of prior learning including employment and life experience. The new University will reflect in its provision the importance of lifelong and continuous learning.

The new University will be characterised by its strong student and client focus; the high quality of its learning, teaching and research, and by the opportunities it will provide for a wide range of students with diverse entry backgrounds and varying entry qualifications. It will be characterised by its emphasis on personal self fulfilment; by its development of teamwork, interpersonal skills, and initiative; and by its commitment to the understanding of European culture and language.

The culture of the new University will be recognised by its creativity and by its encouragement of innovation. It will be an open and caring institution, welcoming staff and student debate and so contributing to a vigorous exchange of views and ideas which will support and encourage the individual's progress to extended learning and scholarship.

Press comment was not confined to the Scottish media. The *Daily Telegraph* of December 6 reported, under the heading 'College and Poly plan Glasgow's third university':

Proposals to create Glasgow's third university unveiled yesterday would mean the city's Queen's College and Glasgow Polytechnic forming a single institution to be called the Queen's University. Professor John Phillips, Principal of Queen's College, said of the new institution which would have about 10,000 students and an income of £29 million: 'This will be a totally new type of 21st century university with no barriers between vocational, professional and academic qualifications — as strong in part-time return to study and credit accumulation courses as full-time education.'

Glasgow is already home to two of Scotland's eight universities: Glasgow which was founded in 1451 and Strathclyde University, formerly the Royal College of Science and Technology, founded in 1964.

The initial report in the *Glasgow Herald* laid more emphasis upon the politics of the merger. The *Scotsman's* report on December 5 was fuller, and also quoted Professor Phillips as remarking that, 'There is a real sense of excitement. What we have agreed is that we are not merging, not bolting things together but working to create something new.' It also drew comparisons with the situation in Edinburgh and the likely fate of Queen Margaret College.

The broadcast media also took an interest and the two Principals were interviewed both on Radio Scotland and Radio Clyde. Speaking on the former, Professor Mason explained:

> If you look at healthcare, which is a huge area and will continue to expand throughout the country ... the extension of paramedical work at Queen's College and ... the health and nursing studies, the optometry, the orthoptics at Queen's College and the bio-medical areas at Glasgow Polytechnic, the two are just so natural to come together to form what we believe [will be] the most impressive Institute of Health Studies in the United Kingdom not just Scotland.

Scottish Television News also interviewed two students, one of whom commented, 'I think Glasgow Polytechnic certainly deserves to be a university at the moment ... there are plenty of courses here that are more than equal to university standards', and the second, 'It can only be good for the city and good for the student that it's got access to funds. It's good for everybody all round, it gives Glasgow a bigger image'. The reporter, Jackie Marshland, concluded by saying that, 'in the meantime prospective students will have to apply to Queen's College and Glasgow Polytechnic separately but come September they'll find themselves at University'.

Reaction, as it happened, was nevertheless not universally favourable, the source of unease being the imminent disappearance of Queen's as a separate entity and the wider implications of this. On December 5 the report from the *Glasgow Herald's* education correspondent was headlined 'Mergers decried as a university is born'. The objector was Principal Donald Leach of Queen Margaret College, who declared, according to the report, that

'"Merger Mania" in higher education would lead to the demise of Scotland's vocational, centrally funded institutions', as he launched a paper entitled *Scottish Education in the 21st Century*.

The paper postulated that Scotland would require 15 universities (including a University of the Highlands) by the year 2000 to accommodate the number of students the Scottish Office estimated would be in higher education by then, but was emphatic that these new establishments should maintain the values of the existing central institutions and not 'genuflect to the mission and values of the [existing] universities' after spending the previous 30 years building up their distinctive activities: 'In the hour of greatest achievement the polytechnics and colleges are in the greatest danger.' He objected to the criteria Scottish colleges must meet to become universities, which he considered had been based upon the English higher education system: 'What the centrally funded colleges in Scotland ought to bring to the feast of higher education is an alternative menu.'[4]

Denigration of the concept of the new university also came from less elevated sources, notably the local press, some of whose columnists had displayed a consistent animus against the Polytechnic and its predecessors, regularly mocking the recurrent alterations in the institution's title. One of these columnists, Tom Shields, had made a habit of referring to it, since its early days, as the University of Coocaddens. The target of attack was nearly always the same — that the institution was exhibiting pretensions beyond its station. Another of them, Jack McLean, now expressed his prejudices thus:

Glasgow College of Technology, now Glasgow Poly, first took to naming itself simply Glasgow College. Later it subsumed every college it could get its hands on…. It took over the old Dough School, a once splendid establishment for the pretty but thick daughters of the middle classes. …Today the poor lassies don't know what they are about and are made to read all the time instead of finding out how to make a decent dumpling. Glasgow Poly now wants to call the two merged entities 'Queen's University', impervious to the fact that one already exists in Belfast and is a proper one at that…. Anybody who can confuse Belfast with Coocaddens shouldn't be in a Yooni in the first place.[5]

---

[4]*Scotsman*, December 5, 1991.
[5]*Glasgow Herald*, January 24, 1992.

Neither Principal Leach's strictures nor the effusions of the would-be-humorists were likely to deter the Glasgow institutions from proceeding with their merger and preparations for its implementation went ahead. On February 10, 1992 the two through their Governing Bodies submitted a joint proposal to the Secretary of State for Scotland, Ian Lang. The justification for the merger was summarised as:

> In particular, the institutions believe they can, jointly, better meet the aspirations of their students, the development needs of their staff and the educational requirements of their client groups by harnessing their complementary provision and common institutional objectives in the establishment of a new University with a distinctive mission.

The Scottish Secretary requested advice on the proposal from the Mergers Committee of the Scottish Committee of the Universities' Funding Council. Supportive recommendations were obtained from Professor Jack Shaw, the Chairman-Designate of the soon to be created Scottish Higher Education Funding Council. Pending formal approval from the Scottish Secretary a Task Force was established in January 1992 by Queen's and the Polytechnic to plan the merger, and by October had put in place 'shadow' structures at Court, Senate and Faculty level to enable the institution to function as if it were already merged.

What's in a Name?

But in the meantime a major problem had emerged. It was foreshadowed as early as the announcement of merger in December 1991, when in its report the *Glasgow Herald* had mentioned that the views were not known of Queen's University in Belfast on the Glasgow proposal. The *Scotsman* report of December 5 noted that Queen's in Belfast had reacted cautiously, and reported its information director as commenting that 'For many years we have been known throughout the United Kingdom as Queen's University and clearly we will have to consider this seriously.' On Radio Scotland the Principals had been asked whether the preferred name might not cause confusion with Queen's University in Belfast and Professor Mason had responded:

> I think … 95 per cent of our students at the present time come from Scotland and it's hard for me to believe that these Scottish students are going to get confused whether they are in Glasgow or Belfast.

The Radio Clyde news item on the merger had concluded by noting that the title proposal must meet the approval of the Secretary of State and the Queen herself.

Very shortly Queen's, Belfast began to lobby strenuously against approval of the desired title, feeling that its identity would be infringed. Glasgow University was likewise unhappy, objecting to the appearance in the city of another university with what was regarded as a very distinguished title that might disparage Glasgow University's seniority. At first however this was taking place behind the scenes and it was unclear to the Polytechnic and College why acceptance of their applications for both merger and title were being held up. Time passed, and it was only in the late summer, July 28, some eight weeks after Prof Jack Shaw's recommendation, that a representative of the SOED telephoned to inform the respective Chairs that while the merger had been approved the proposed name had not, and the SOED would be imminently issuing a press release to that effect. Further decisions on the merger, it appeared, would be taken by SOED without further reference to the Polytechnic or College. The Chairs and Principals were appalled, as well they might be: their conviction was that the way in which the Scottish Office was proceeding was contrary to the agreement with SOED that the merger and the name should be treated as separate issues and not referred to together in a press release, and that it was inappropriate to refer to the name as no formal application to the Privy Council had yet been made.

Sir Michael Hirst was both a Governor of Queen's College and the Chairman of the Scottish Conservative Party. Accordingly he was contacted and requested to telephone the Secretary of State in order to express the institutions' concerns, while an emergency meeting of the Queen's Governors was summoned for the following day to hear reports and deliberate. Sir Michael told them that the Secretary of State had been satisfied with Professor Shaw's recommendation but was very well aware that the royal appellation was not easily obtained and would be interested to know whether any consideration had been given to alternatives — to which Sir Michael had responded that as the Privy Council had not foreseen any difficulties with the preferred title, the question of alternatives had not been discussed at this stage.[6]

---

[6] Queen's College, Minute of the Governors' Extraordinary Meeting, July 29, 1992.

The Governors approved the Chair's actions and Sir Michael's on behalf of the College and expressed the view that SOED's lack of consultation had been 'insensitive and cavalier'. However they were concerned not to sacrifice the merger process at that stage. While they regarded the royal appellation to be very important they believed that the issue would be best pursued through communication with the Privy Council after the merger had been approved. It was resolved unanimously that the SOED be informed immediately

> of the great concern, dismay and anger of the Governing Body of Queen's College, Glasgow at the proposal to issue a press release coupling the approval of the merger with negative statements on the proposed title. This is entirely at odds with the situation the Governing Body believed to have been previously agreed, and is a position the Governing Body finds unacceptable.

They went on to request an early meeting with the Secretary of State in order to present the case for the proposed name. The representations were successful in the immediate term in that SOED withdrew its intended press release and a letter dated July 31, 1992 from the Secretary of State approved the merger of the two existing Colleges to form a new university.

The Disputes over Title

These events were however only the overture to further conflict over the name. At the beginning of September the two Chairs wrote to the Scottish Secretary enclosing documentation to support the proposed name. It emphasised that this name reflected elements of each founder institution in the title of the new university (a somewhat surprising claim) and that it had received uniform and widespread support from within both institutions as well as a range of prestigious external institutions. Moreover it would 'reflect the status and stability appropriate to an institution bearing a royal title'. The documentation contained statements of support from 40 Scottish institutions — including Strathclyde University.

Queen's University in Belfast informed the Governors of the nature of its objections.

> This University received its first charter in 1908 and, since that time, the title 'Queen's University', or the shortened form of 'Queen's' has been

understood throughout these islands, and in academic circles, to mean the Queen's University of Belfast. For this reason any use of the words 'Queen's University' in the title of another institution would lead to considerable confusion,and would cause major difficulties to employers and for our 45,000 graduates throughout the world who pride themselves on holding a 'Queen's degree'. This university would therefore object to your proposal.

Glasgow University was scarcely any less hostile, writing as early as January 1992 that the use of the words 'of Glasgow' might lead to confusion and that it was preparing to lodge objections with the Privy Council, and a little later concluded its communication with the remark, 'the *University* of *Glasgow* has been around for some time, and I think it is entitled to maintain the distinctiveness of its title.'

Hopes of a favourable outcome were finally extinguished in November when the two Chairs received a letter from Ian Lang, stating:

> I have given careful consideration to your proposal, but I regret to say that I am unable to make a favourable recommendation on it to Her Majesty. Her Majesty has been informed of your application and of my views.
>
> I know you will be greatly disappointed.... I would like to assure you that it in no way detracts from the importance I attach to the new university, or the valuable contribution I am sure it will make to the economic and academic future of Scotland. But demanding criteria must be satisfied before an application for a Royal Title ... can be given a positive recommendation and successful applications are necessarily rare.

Professor Wood replied on November 16, noting that the disappointment would be particularly felt in Queen's College, which must now lose its designation, and expressing concern over the time required to reach the decision, but nevertheless expressing appreciation too of the assistance received by the Polytechnic from the Scottish Office with recurrent and capital funding. He concluded by noting that the Polytechnic looked forward to welcoming the Secretary at the end of the month to open the newly-built Charles Oakley Laboratories.

That ceremonial occasion was disrupted by a student occupation of the new building and a near-riot. The students' indignation however had nothing to do with the naming but was directed against the Secretary of

State as the representative of a Government held to be responsible for slashing student financial support. Two members of staff, generally regarded as being of a radical disposition and therefore more likely to be listened to, were dispatched to try to persuade the students to lift their occupation so that Charles Oakley would not be slighted. Their exhortations however had no effect and the occupation continued, making it impossible to go through with the ceremony. At the sherry reception which went ahead anyway, a few demonstrators broke down the door of the room in which it was being held, but went no further — they may not in any case have belonged to the Polytechnic.

In assessing the authorities' rejection of the new university's wishes regarding its title, explanations need not be sought very far. The objections of the two senior universities inevitably put paid to it for they possessed far more clout in official circles than either the College or the Polytechnic could aspire to, regardless of the support that might be voiced by other institutions. Both appeared to feel that the proposed title would be damaging to their own interests. In the case of Belfast this might be understandable if a little stretched, but it is hard to see in logic why Glasgow University need have worried.

Finding a Name

The College and the Polytechnic were now in the anomalous position of being about to merge as a university (Paisley, Napier and RGIT had already assumed their university titles) but without a name for the new institution. Various proposals were canvassed. One which would have been favoured and regarded as satisfactory by staff and students in both institutions was 'City University of Glasgow', but the Scottish Office had made it clear in advance that it would reject that title, again on account of unhappiness on the part of Glasgow University. Strangely enough, despite its similar connotation, 'Metropolitan University of Glasgow' would have been acceptable and this was favoured by a number of Polytechnic staff, including Principal Mason, but others objected that it had too much of an English ring.

The suggestion was made that Glasgow should imitate Edinburgh and name the new institution after an individual — the Napier of Napier University was an eminent seventeenth century mathematician, the deviser of logarithms. The obvious choice in this respect, given the scientific and applied orientation of the two institutions, together with

Queen's proximity to the River Kelvin, would have been Kelvin University. But again Glasgow objected, feeling that it had a special connexion with Lord Kelvin and anyway already had a Kelvin Campus. A member of the Polytechnic Governors did suggest Adam Smith, but it was felt that in the context of the 1990s that would send out politically contentious signals.

The name which was eventually fixed on however proved to be even more contentious. On November 17 the two Principals circulated a memo to all staff and students which opened by stating that the merger process was going well and that it was vital to communicate the new corporate identity to 'our many external and internal audiences'. The memo went on to point out that

It was irritating to read the comments in a Sunday newspaper this weekend which speculated that our institution must now settle for a more 'prosaic' or 'mundane' title. The writer states that 'hot favourite at the moment is the somewhat mundane "The University of the West of Scotland" — words that will sound like music to the establishment's older rivals in Glasgow and across the water in Belfast'. Indeed the article quotes a spokesman for a local university who presumed that we did not have any idea what to call ourselves.

The title they announced was the 'Glasgow Merchants University', stating that it had gained strong support from the University Court designate, the University senior management group and had the endorsement of student and staff representatives. The claimed advantages were listed as being that the proposed name satisfied Privy Council criteria; was firmly rooted in Glasgow's history while being simultaneously outward-looking and international; and embodied values which were both enduring and representative of the new University — eg commerce and trade, exchange of ideas and learning, enterprise and endeavour, investment in engineering and construction, involvement in public health, establishing merchant banks and contributing to the development of mercantile law, creating wealth and sponsoring community projects. The memo ended with the sentence, 'It is with confidence and pleasure that we have today asked The Secretary of State for Scotland to approve the name: The Glasgow Merchants University as the title for our new University.' An advantage not mentioned but which was thought to be a consideration behind the choice is that it would help to forge and strengthen links with the Merchants' House of Glasgow.

The announcement provoked a storm. General opinion throughout both institutions found the proposed title unacceptable if not repugnant. Feeling was that it would make the new university sound like the training arm of a commercial enterprise rather than an academic establishment. Moreover, it was pointed out, the late eighteenth century merchants of Glasgow, the 'tobacco lords', who had first made the city into a major commercial centre (the proposed logo was the prow of an eighteenth century sailing ship), did not have an unblemished record. Although, unlike their Liverpool or Bristol counterparts, they were not directly implicated in the slave trade, their business had been founded on slave-cultivated tobacco in the North American colonies.

The President of the Polytechnic Students' Association, Steven Nicholson, told the press that,

> Although I am a smoker myself, the name smacks of the tobacco trade. It also has connotations of slavery and, to my mind, it describes a class which rose to privilege and prosperity on the backs of those who produced these things. It has very tenuous links with higher education.

The manner of the decision also aroused strong objections, having been taken by a small group without discussion or reference to either the Academic Boards or Governors' meetings of the respective institutions. The staff and student representatives disputed that they had indicated their approval, pointing out that when privily consulted they had urged the proposal to be put to representative bodies. Separate meetings of both staff, organised in a joint union committee, and students were held to denounce the intended title and the manner in which it had been advanced.

On November 19 the two Principals circulated a further memo acknowledging the unfavourable initial reactions of staff both to the name and the lack of consultation and expressing regret and apology for not having earlier involved staff at large. Nevertheless the memo went on to defend the name, which was described as 'distinctive, memorable and unique', and clearly reaffirmed the association of the city and the University.

It argued that surprise titles in other instances in England, such as Hallam, de Montfort, Brookes and John Moore's, had found acceptance. There being a severe disadvantage to students, staff and the new institution in the absence of an approved name, the Principals reaffirmed their intention to press on and looked to 'support in establishing the new name as a powerful and prestigious title', but a quickly organised ballot of the staff in the two institutions produced an 85 per cent majority for rejection.

On Wednesday November 25, Professor Mason and Professor Phillips addressed two general meetings of staff and students. The first was in the morning at Queen's College, where their support for the Merchants University title was reiterated, and in the afternoon at 3.00 in the largest lecture theatre of the Polytechnic, which was packed to capacity and overflowing. By the time it took place rumours were circulating that the decision was to be reversed and the initial statements of the two Principals, without being fully explicit, appeared to confirm this, neutralising the hostility which would otherwise have doubtless been manifest. A number of the students present made eloquent appeals. One of them greatly praised the quality of teaching in the Polytechnic compared with Glasgow University and urged that it should not be negated by foisting an absurd name on the new University. A disabled student appealed to the Principals not to add to her job-finding difficulties by obliging her to graduate from an establishment with such a name.

The following day the announcement appeared that the 'Merchants' name was to be withdrawn. The Finance and General Purposes Committee of Queen's College commented:

Following the disappointing rejection of the proposed title 'The Queen's University, Glasgow' by the Scottish Office, many staff and students at both institutions had jointly expressed opposition to the subsequent proposed name ...

The Principal and Glasgow Polytechnic's Principal, Professor Stan Mason, had acknowledged the real depth of feeling on this issue and informed the Scottish Office that they did not intend to seek approval for the proposed new name. Both Principals had sought and obtained consent to this course of action from their respective Chairs of Governors.

Members expressed their disappointment at the reaction of staff and students towards the proposed new name, particularly in view of the unanimously positive views expressed by external bodies consulted.

> The press would be advised that the name had been withdrawn. Further
> staff and student meetings would be held to make arrangements for the
> ballot process ... to select the name of the new University.[7]

The system now put in place for selecting the new name was, as compared
to the very centralised method used earlier, exceptionally open. A committee
of nine was established from elected Governors, together with union
representatives (non-academic as well as academic) and student presidents
to draw up a short list of three to four possible names. Meantime the
University Management Group and the lay Governors would be doing the
same. A joint meeting between the two collectives would then be held to
evolve a final short list which would be put to a vote of both staff and
students.

The four alternatives eventually put to the ballot, with transeferable
votes, were: Glasgow Metropolitan University; Glasgow Caledonian
University; Glasgow St Mungo University; and Glasgow Lomond University.
The result was announced on December 10, with Glasgow Caledonian
University the clear winner — though St Mungo had the largest number of
first preferences.

The Secretary of State established Glasgow Caledonian University by the
Glasgow Caledonian University (Establishment) (Scotland) Order 1993
and designated it as an institution eligible to receive support from funds
administered by the Scottish Higher Education Funding Council. The
Privy Council constituted the Governing Body of the University, the
University Court of Glasgow Caledonian University, by the Glasgow
Caledonian University (Scotland) Order of Council 1993. A closure order
closed Glasgow Polytechnic and the Queen's College, transferring property
rights and obligations to the University Court. The Association, which had
been the legal owner of Queen's College and its predecessor since 1908, and
whose final membership numbered 129, was now wound up.

Various statutory instruments were laid before Parliament to regularise the
University's position. The shadow bodies were able to immediately begin
operation according to their functions, transformed now into the actual
bodies of decision. The management of the University was reconstituted to
incorporate the personnel of both institutions, with Stan Mason taking over

---

[7]Queen's College, Minute of the Finance and General Purposes Committee, November
26, 1992.

Scottish celebrity JIMMY LOGAN, *FRSAMD* and MR BILL LAURIE, *BSc, MSc, Cphys, MinstP, MIOA* (present acting Principal of the University 1997/98) in 1994 when the University gave Jimmy the Honorary Degree of Doctor of Letters.

as Principal and Vice-Chancellor and John Phillips as Vice-Principal. The Governing Body was replaced with a University Court, of which Professor Wood became the first Chair. Glasgow Caledonian came into being on April 1, 1993 and was formally launched on April 28. Sir David Nickson KBE, the Head of the Clydesdale Bank, had agreed to serve as Chancellor and was installed at the formal inauguration on June 2, at which occasion Sir David, the racing driver Jackie Stewart and the Lord Provost of Glasgow, Robert Innes, became the University's first honorary graduates.

These events took place at a civic reception in the City Chambers, following a multi-faith service of dedication in Glasgow Cathedral, with readings from and prayers from representatives of the Catholic and Protestant churches, the Jewish and Muslim faiths. The University crest was combined from the arms of the College and the Polytechnic, and its logo was a white letter 'C' on a light blue square, a quite elegant design whose colours suggested overtones of the Scottish flag and was a considerable advance upon the rather clumsy and awkward logo which the Polytechnic had used. Professor Wood did not wish to remain Chair of the Court for an extended period. Upon giving up the office one of the main University buildings was named the Hamish Wood building in recognition of his outstanding services and he was awarded an honorary doctorate in 1994.

Establishing the University

The transition from the two founding institutions to the new University went smoothly on the whole although not entirely without hitches. When GCT had been transferred from local authority to central institution status in the mid-'80s its overall funding position had improved, but its salary structures and conditions for administrative staff remained those which had been inherited from the previous regime and were inferior to those prevailing at Queen's College, a central institution of long standing. Moves to harmonise the gradings between the two former establishments generated friction, for although the salaries and pension rights of the Queen's administrative staff were conserved, their holiday entitlements were threatened with being reduced and their promotion prospects affected adversely. The aggrieved staff threatened to make their point by boycotting the inauguration ceremony, but in the event an agreement was arrived at and the threat was not carried out.

The integration of teaching and departmental organisation proceeded relatively smoothly according to the plans prepared in advance. A three-faculty structure was established, respectively of Health, Business and Administration, and Science and Engineering, each under a permanent Dean. The new University found itself in possession of three campuses — the former Polytechnic, which was now named City Campus, the former Queen's College, now named Park Campus, and the buildings leased by Queen's adjacent to Jordanhill College, which being in the Southbrae area of Glasgow was termed Southbrae Campus.[8] It was initially hoped to develop the University as a single-site institution, with all parts of it moving to City Campus, but this was found to be impracticable. Nevertheless an ambitious building programme at City Campus was put in hand to greatly extend teaching, administrative and library space, and the student residences which up to the amalgamation the Polytechnic had always been unable to secure.

The integration of academic programmes on the whole proceeded smoothly as well — these were indeed generally complementary, as the pre-merger documentation had claimed, and a merger evaluation in October 1994 confirmed the success of the amalgamation. The University was anxious to develop its distinctive characteristics, prominent among which was its mission to broaden higher educational opportunities, especially among socio-economic groups for whom university entrance had not often appeared to be a realistic prospect. Mature students featured prominently in this regard.

Both of the founding institutions had been committed to the Credit Accumulation Transfer Scheme (usually referred to by its acronym CATS) aimed at allowing non-standard students to proceed in the manner that they found best fitted to their circumstances — at more than one institution and with broken periods of study if necessary. The Polytechnic had established a Continuing Education Department, and this was of course continued by the University. Its remit was to encourage the admission of non-standard students.

It was largely with the structure of CATS in mind that throughout the autumn of 1993 the University discussed going over to a system of modularising courses within a two-semester framework in place of the traditional three-term system. The idea was not universally popular, the objectors concentrating

---

[8]Which, since Jordanhill College was by then part of Strathclyde University, gave rise to what must have been the unique phenomenon of parts of two different universities on the same site.

on the difficulty of achieving a coherent and measured course of study within the time constraints of the 12-week modules, complaining that the CATS tail was wagging the University dog and referring irreverently to the scheme as 'S & M'. A further organisational problem was that the moveable date of Easter disrupted the second semester. Nonetheless the Senate agreed at the end of 1993 — not least on the argument that the majority of universities were going over to semesterisation — to introduce the new system at the beginning of the 1994–95 session for all courses except honours ones, which were delayed a further year. Not so controversial were the association agreements in pursuit of its broadening project entered into by the University at the end of 1993 with certain local further education colleges, such as Stow and the College of Building and Printing.

Also less controversial than the semesterisation/modularisation scheme were the university's endeavours to extend its work internationally, which had results in several dimensions. Agreements were arrived at with foreign governments for their nationals to follow courses within the University in areas regarded as being of particular national importance. The University also ran a long-standing exchange scheme with two universities in the USA. In addition, Caledonian campuses were established both in Oman and in Malaysia. Liberated South Africa became an area of special interest, not least because some members of the academic staff had had long-term connections with the Anti-Apartheid Movement. The University gave such advice and assistance as was within its power with the development of higher education in the new South African circumstances. In the summer of 1996 Caledonian was one of the eight universities which conferred an honorary degree on Nelson Mandela in a ceremony held at Buckingham Palace.

In the meantime building work (funded in partnership with private capital and with EU assistance) was continuing on a very extensive scale and this included a physical reconstruction designed to alter the entire appearance of the City Campus site. It involved a major extension to the library and the construction of a major new Health building, consequent on the agreement reached to concentrate nursing education in Scotland within the University — a bid which had been invited from all Scottish universities but in which Caledonian had succeeded. This contract was a testament to the reputation of the Nursing and Community Health Department and the staff which had built it up — it had certainly come a long way since para-medical courses had been an adjunct of the Humanities Department.

The Library, which had possessed for a time a more advanced electronic cataloguing system than either Glasgow or Strathclyde Universities, developed significantly in spite of severe budgetary constraints. Its physical extension has already been noted. In 1996 an archivist was appointed, one of the authors of this volume, and the acquisition of archival collections was developed. The institution's own archive naturally formed a base, but the University was fortunate in receiving offers of archival collections from outside bodies such as the Royal Scottish Society for the Prevention of Cruelty to Children. In 1997 Action for Southern Africa—ACTSA Scotland—transferred the Anti-Apartheid Movement in Scotland archive to the Library. Its principal concentration in this area however came to focus upon special collections and archives connected with the Scottish labour movement, and received a major impetus in 1995 when the former Glasgow councillor and MEP Janey Buchan transferred to the University several thousand books from the collection she had amassed with her late husband, Norman Buchan, renowned both as a Labour parliamentarian and expert on Scottish folk-song. Also in 1997 arrangements were made to bring into the University the former library of the Scottish Communist Party and the broader collection under the name of the William Gallacher Memorial Library, which had been housed in the building of the Scottish Trades Union Congress and was constantly in use as a major research source. In addition the STUC itself was on the point of transferring to other premises and it was agreed when it happened the STUC archive, in agreement with the National Library of Scotland, itself should also go to Caledonian's Library.

The 1997 Crisis and its Outcome

Background
It soon became clear that developments resulting from the 1991 White Paper and the creation of new universities in 1992–93 out of the polytechnic system did not mark a definitive settlement for British higher education. Demand continued to expand beyond the level the Government was prepared to fund at existing levels and unit resource continued to be squeezed throughout the system — though Caledonian, possibly because of its historic low funding, was comparatively fortunate in relation to other establishments. The Government attempted to try to square the circle by a variety of expedients. Student loans, which were far from covering basic needs, had been in existence

for some years and maintainance provision for students constantly shrank in real terms. For a student without generous parental support it became virtually impossible to avoid moonlighting — especially as access to benefit during holiday periods was also abolished — with consequent impact on academic performance.

The expedients applied to academic staff as well. Since the '80s the practice had become institutionalised throughout the system of trying to economise on academic salaries by cutting back on full-time contracts so far as possible and covering the difference by greater employment of either staff on short contracts or heavier use of postgraduate students as tutors. In the '90s came pressure to squeeze more out of established staff by audits of teaching, the Teaching Quality Assessments, and research, the Research Assessment Exercises — to which funding was linked by the Higher Education Funding Council (HEFC) and its Scottish counterpart, SHEFC — though what they mainly succeeded in squeezing out was a larger mass of paperwork. Invariably the old universities out-performed their new colleagues, demonstrating the importance of resources both human and material: within the tables of achievement of the latter, Caledonian attained respectable placings, as it did in the unofficial tables published in *The Times* and the *THES*. In one respect however, that of placement of its students in employment, it did better than respectably, coming out near the overall top.

Once it became evident that the national problem would not disappear of its own accord the Government appointed a Committee under Lord Dearing to do for the '90s what Robbins had done for the '60s and come forward with proposals for the comprehensive restructuring and funding of higher education into the first part of the 21st century. Rumours abounded that his Report, which was expected for the middle of 1997 and likely to be applied by whichever party won the May 1 General Election, would encourage mergers between universities wherever appropriate, and perhaps do more than merely encourage them. As the most recent foundation, least wealthy and smallest in a city with two-well established universities — though in terms of student numbers it was the fourth largest in Scotland — Caledonian had reason to feel nervous about its future under the forthcoming Dearing regime in spite of all that had been achieved since 1993.

The Crisis

These general considerations were not irrelevant to the crisis which struck the University in the late spring of 1997, although its local aspects were the ones which were publicised. In the course of 1996 the Principal floated a proposal for a far-reaching restructuring of the University's academic and administrative system. This suggested that the existing structure of three Faculties should be replaced by one of eight Schools, each headed by a Dean, and that these would form the University's administrative centres — responsible for admissions, course timetabling, research organisation and of course allocation of funds. In the original version of the proposal departments were to disappear altogether, to be replaced by informal discipline groups, but in an amended form they were retained to act as academic rather than administrative centres, with Heads of Department as academic leaders rather than administrators. Moreover, multi-disciplinary departments, it was proposed, would be broken up into their component parts and many new departments thereby created.

Opinion was divided on the academic merits of the proposal *per se*. Its proponents argued that it rationalised the discipline structure of the University (after all, what were Departments of Social Sciences, Psychology and Biology doing in a Faculty of Health?) and would allow for a more specific allocation of resources through smaller cost centres more immediately in touch with grassroots needs. Opponents concentrated their disagreement on two issues. In the first place, they argued, the scheme would reduce accountability and concentrate authority in the hands of top management, for the new Schools proposal did not include any element of democratic governance. The Senate was also proposed to be restructured, with non-Head of Department representation reduced. Secondly, it was claimed very strongly that no convincing academic justification had been advanced in support of the proposal and that no meaningful consultation had taken place with the mass of those about to be affected. Large meetings of the unions had been held, both severally and jointly, and had strongly criticised the proposed restructuring, but their representations had been ignored.

Other considerations raised were that coming on top of the merger, then the semesterisation/modularisation upheaval, the restructuring represented an additional and unnecessary disruption to academics and administrators trying to teach and organise students and conduct and organise research amid a process of constant and bewildering changes. At one of the meetings a participant commented that he thought the Principal must be a Trotskyist — for he appeared to be addicted to permanent revolution. Less central, though not insignificant, was the implication for existing Heads of Department who did not become School Deans, and who were about to find themselves in a position of having their status and responsibilities diminished even though they retained their salaries and their titles. Finally, and very importantly, the question was asked why it was necessary to embark upon such a far-reaching, disruptive and divisive project when the imminent Dearing Report was likely to alter the entire context in which the University was functioning and might well require drastic changes on its own account.

Under pressure from the trade unions, who now took their grievance to the University Court, Professor Mason agreed to a series of meetings with the staff at large to explain the rationale of the restructuring and to answer questions. The Chair of the Court also attended these meetings, though not as part of the platform. The meetings were inconclusive however, sometimes bad-tempered, and failed in general to satisfy the participants. The accumulation of resentments caused some unknown individual with knowledge of University affairs to write to SHEFC alleging financial and appointment irregularities in the conduct of its affairs. A subsequent SHEFC investigation, while it did not immediately arrive at firm conclusions, showed that there was indeed a case to answer. At the Court meeting in May a confidential letter from Professor John Sizer was considered. It indicated that the investigation had identified aspects which were possible sources of concern and required further examination. The same meeting had before it a request from the Principal that his duties should be immediately relinquished, and this was agreed to.

The crisis could not have come at a less propitious moment, with publication of the Dearing Report being imminent. The possibility of Caledonian being absorbed on invidious terms by its larger neighbour, or even worse, being dismembered, with Strathclyde seizing only the most attractive bits, looked like ominous possibilities. The Court appointed Mr Bill Laurie, one of the Senior Assistant Principals, as Acting Principal pending a search for a permanent Principal from outside, which was what the times were believed to require. Shortly afterwards, at the beginning of June, the Senate, following a fairly impassioned meeting with eloquent speeches on both sides, voted by a majority to reverse all the restructuring changes implemented so far and appoint a committee comprising both ex-officio and elected members to examine the overall situation in regard to the University's structures.

Conclusions

The Dearing Universe

The Dearing Report (the Committee of 17 members contained five business persons but no rank-and-file academics) emerged on July 23, 1997, its recommendations being largely in line with predictions that had been circulating in the media and the academic world. If the Robbins Report could be regarded as the founding charter for the dramatic expansion in higher education which occurred in Britain during the second half of the twentieth century, the Dearing Report might be said to serve as its tombstone. Of course matters were not presented in this light. The Report spoke of further numerical expansion, encouragement for higher education to reach hitherto under-represented sections of the population, enhanced standards in teaching quality, being at 'the leading edge of world practice in effective teaching and learning'. The recommendation which made the biggest public impact was the proposal, as a solution to the perceived funding crisis, to charge all students a flat-rate contribution of around 25 per cent of tuition costs. The Government, even before the Report had appeared, announced tuition fees of £1,000 per year with means-tested reductions for students of lower-income background. It marked the end of a half-century of free higher education in Britain. How the imposition of additional financial burdens was supposed to encourage higher participation rates was not very coherently explained. In any case it soon became clear that institutions would not see a penny of the fees — they were intended to be appropriated in their entirety by the Government for central administration costs. Some members of the Caledonian staff were heard to remark that all this did not seem to be at all in line with what they thought they had voted for in May.

The Report also gave specific attention to Scotland. It referred both to the distinctiveness of Scottish higher education and the strengths derived from being part of a wider UK system, and wished to acknowledge that for over 500 years Scottish higher education institutions had played 'a vital role in promoting and underpinning civil society and Scottish culture'. It was clear from the subtext of the document however that the existing system was felt to be antiquated and out of tune with the supposed demands of the twenty-first century. Nothing was said directly to such effect, but it was implied fairly unmistakably that the standard Scottish four-year honours degree was obsolescent, and that in this respect at least the Scottish system should be brought more in line with the envisaged UK standard — a three-year core degree accompanied by a range of connected qualifications with different exit points, ranging from diplomas and certificates to 'honours of an academic or vocational nature'. The educational experience for future students (and staff for that matter) would be grimmer, less congenial and more utilitarian — even by comparison with the contemporary realities of underfunding and constant moonlighting in ill-paid, part-time service employment.

The constant expansion of higher education in Britain since the '50s (and in some respects for nearly two centuries), having remorselessly stretched the bounds of the traditional frameworks which had contained it, finally burst them. It had been clear since the mid-'70s, when the deterioration of unit resource first became an ongoing reality, was confirmed by the cuts of the '80s, and underlined by the creation of the new universities in the '90s, that no government was going to fund the expanded system to the same proportionate extent that its smaller predecessor had enjoyed in the earlier two decades. Emphasis upon quality control, flexibility, transferable skills and so forth, whatever else it might be, was primarily rhetoric and a public relations exercise putting the best face upon contracting resources. A further orientation of the Report, which might well cause Caledonian University worry along with many others, is towards the concentration of research funding in the most prestigious university establishments, threatening to reintroduce an effective binary line into higher education. The Report might not necessarily be accepted by the Government in every particular but there cannot be any doubt that its recommendations point the general direction of higher education policy. It might also be remarked that the trend is a global one and by no means confined to Britain.

Yet in the long run it is likely that in Britain the universities, old and new, will surmount the present crisis as they have surmounted different and even more threatening ones in the past. Tertiary education expansion (for all the problems that it brings) and even academic drift, are basically healthy trends. Though they are sometimes influenced — especially the latter — by less than creditable motives, they nonetheless primarily reflect democratic aspirations — nothing less than the demand by growing numbers of the citizenry to share in the intellectual as well as the material benefits that society has on offer. In *that* light even the target of a 50 per cent participation rate appears modest.

Caledonian University

Amid all this, how does Caledonian University find itself placed — internationally, nationally and locally? The challenges are certainly formidable. Having had to cope with a continuous stream of far-reaching organisational changes, frequently in a turbulent and confrontational atmosphere, it now finds itself faced with implementing whatever aspects of the Dearing recommendations are ultimately required. These may have a considerable impact. Undeniably, the University's preparedness for such necessities has not been enhanced by the series of internal calamities and the adverse publicity which fell upon it during the summer months of 1997 — a great deal of energy has had to go into dealing with immediate emergency and crisis. Nevertheless GCU has resources to enable it to master the situation and go on to realise its real potential.

The first of these is the core of the historical tradition it carries with it, namely response to the aspirations of groups of people excluded from the traditional tertiary establishments and their established curricula to develop otherwise disregarded disciplines or capacities to advanced levels. Such a project was manifest in the original cookery schools and the domestic science college which succeeded them. Once existence was secured, expansion in numbers and broadening of curriculum, despite contingent setbacks usually arising from national emergencies, proved to be an irreversible and historic process. By the time of the amalgamation Queen's College was — certainly by the criteria then being propounded — virtually a university in miniature, and its contribution over the decades to the city's social welfare had been enormous.

Glasgow College of Technology was the product of another age and outlook, but for all the differences in its origins and history it too represented an answer to contemporary deficiencies in provision, in this case the unsatisfied demand for higher education — by no means all from school-leavers — generated by the society of consumer affluence and which existing provision in the west of Scotland was unable to meet. Teaching methods, the character of student intakes, attention to student welfare and the general atmosphere of the combined establishment, were all profoundly influenced by these traditions.

The second and third major advantages possessed by the University are related to this last point. Since the time of GCT (Queen's is for evident reasons not comparable in this respect) great attention has been given to encouraging non-standard entrants, particularly mature students. Special efforts have likewise always been exerted to attract ethnic minority applicants (specifically mentioned in Dearing). In this instance at any rate the University is certainly already in accord with the Dearing principles and their emphasis on broadening participation and creating a 'learning society' — though it has been pointed out that the Report appears to neglect part-time students,[9] upon which GCU and its predecessors have concentrated special efforts. These long-established practices in themselves should put the University in a strong position to attract additional funding under Recommendation 2 of the Report.

The third advantage relates to the heritage of carefully designed degrees and syllabuses originally inspired by the CNAA. These were and continue to be drawn up with flexibility and, so far as possible, interchangeability deliberately kept in mind. That too is an approach mightily approved in Dearing and its recommendation of a 'programme specification' with a variety of potential exit points. GCU ought to be able to very readily adapt its programmes in the direction indicated. Whether what the Report has in mind amounts to good educational practice is however another matter.

As noted above, the recommendations on research funding are unlikely to represent good news for a new and still struggling university like Caledonian. Nevertheless it has a fourth advantage, one which may counteract this, in the shape of committed and active researchers throughout all its departments, who, whether government funding remains available or not, will doubtless continue to research and produce high-quality results on the basis of whatever funding they can generate. Evidently the withdrawal of regular funding under the Research Assessment Exercises, if it should come to that, will constitute a severe disadvantage — but such disadvantages can be overcome.

Fifthly, there should be noted a material point which is of no small importance — the quality of the University's buildings and the attractiveness of its city-centre main campus. The buildings, none of which is older than the late '60s, stand in a variety of architectural styles, not all of them aesthetically attractive, but they have been very well maintained and observers frequently compare their interiors favourably with those of other new universities. In addition, a major programme of building works is currently proceeding to add an extension to the library which will nearly

[9]THES, August 8, 1997.

double its capacity and to create a major new block to accommodate expanded health studies. To be sure, the noise of the building work has for a time created severe disruption to teaching and other work, but once complete a most striking and highly visible campus and congenial environment for study and other forms of academic work ought to be in existence.

The authors would conclude that in spite of the pressure of circumstances Caledonian University's future (barring some improbable contingency such as a government-imposed amalgamation) is largely in its own hands. The development of its components has reflected Glasgow's own career, its pinnacle and decline as a major commercial and industrial metropolis, followed by the city's eventual re-creation as a service and cultural centre in which tertiary education fulfils a central role. When, three or four generations down the line, the University as such arrives at its centenary there is every reason to hope and believe that by then it will have made a major contribution to the Scottish democratic intellect of the twenty-first century, extended higher education among hitherto under-represented groups, played a leading role in stimulating and underpinning the productive and service economy of the region and the country, and in overall terms accomplished and perpetuated the diverse visions of its different founders.

Bibliography

B oth Queen's College, along with its predecessors, and the Glasgow College of Technology and its successors generated a considerable archive. However until the appointment of an archivist in recent years they were maintained in a haphazard manner and large gaps exist. Both have been used extensively in this history. The collection of press cuttings kept by the College of Domestic Science have proved particularly useful, though these too are patchy and not always clearly referenced. The Report of Educational Institute of Scotland Annual Congress 1925 contains interesting background material on the central institutions. Two other primary sources relevant to the Colleges and Caledonian University are the Robbins and Dearing Reports. Publications with a bearing on the subject of the institutions' development are as follows.

Glasgow Chamber Of Commerce Journal

Scottish Educational Journal

Times Education Supplement

Times Higher Education Supplement

John Butt	*John Anderson's Legacy: The University of Strathclyde and its Antecedents 1796–1996*, Tuckwell Press, East Linton, 1996
Jennifer Carter and Donald Withrington	*Scottish Universities: Distinctiveness and Diversity*, John Donald Ltd, Edinburgh, 1992
S G Checkland	*The Upas Tree: Glasgow 1875–1975*, University of Glasgow Press, 1976

W Hamish Fraser and   *Glasgow Vol II: 1830 to 1912*, Manchester
Irene Maver, eds   University Press, 1966

John Highet   *Taken from School: A Sociological Study of the
                         Fee Paying Schools of Scotland*, Blackie & Son,
                         Glasgow, 1969

David R Jones   *The Origins of the Civic Universities*, Routledge,
                         London, 1988

Ellice Miller   *Century of Change: The Queen's College,
                         Glasgow*, pamphlet published by Queen's
                         College, no date but c 1975

Index